Critical Digital Pedagogy in Higher Education

Issues in Distance Education
Series editor: George Veletsianos

Selected Titles in the Series

The Theory and Practice of Online Learning, Second Edition
Edited by Terry Anderson

Flexible Pedagogy, Flexible Practice: Notes from the Trenches of Distance
Education
Edited by Elizabeth Burge, Chère Campbell Gibson, and Terry Gibson

Teaching in Blended Learning Environments: Creating and Sustaining
Communities of Inquiry
Norman D. Vaughan, Martha Cleveland-Innes, and D. Randy Garrison

Online Distance Education: Towards a Research Agenda
Edited by Olaf Zawacki-Richter and Terry Anderson

Teaching Crowds: Learning and Social Media
Jon Dron and Terry Anderson

Learning in Virtual Worlds: Research and Applications
Edited by Sue Gregory, Mark J. W. Lee, Barney Dalgarno, and Belinda Tynan

Emergence and Innovation in Digital Learning: Foundations and Applications
Edited by George Veletsianos

An Online Doctorate for Researching Professionals
Swapna Kumar and Kara Dawson

Assessment Strategies for Online Learning: Engagement and Authenticity
Dianne Conrad and Jason Openo

25 Years of Ed Tech
Martin Weller

The Finest Blend: Graduate Education in Canada
Edited by Gale Parchoma, Michael Power, and Jennifer Lock

Metaphors of Ed Tech
Martin Weller

Critical Digital Pedagogy in Higher Education
Edited by Suzan Köseoğlu, George Veletsianos, and Chris Rowell

Critical Digital Pedagogy in Higher Education

Edited by Suzan Köseoğlu,
George Veletsianos, and Chris Rowell

AU PRESS

Copyright © 2023 Suzan Köseoğlu, George Veletsianos, Chris Rowell
Published by AU Press, Athabasca University
1 University Drive, Athabasca, AB T9S 3A3
https://doi.org/10.15215/aupress/9781778290015.01

Cover design by Sergiy Kozakov
Printed and bound in Canada

Library and Archives Canada Cataloguing in Publication

Title: Critical digital pedagogy in higher education / edited by Suzan
    Köseoğlu, George Veletsianos, and Chris Rowell.
Names: Köseoğlu, Suzan, editor. | Veletsianos, George, editor. | Rowell, Chris
    (Researcher in educational technology), editor.
Series: Issues in distance education series.
Description: Series statement: Issues in distance education series |
    Includes bibliographical references.
Identifiers: Canadiana (print) 20220455368 | Canadiana (ebook) 20220455414 |
    ISBN 9781778290015 (softcover) | ISBN 9781771993654 (EPUB) |
    ISBN 9781771993647 (PDF)
Subjects: LCSH: Critical pedagogy. | LCSH: Web-based instruction. |
    LCSH: Internet in higher education.
Classification: LCC LC196 .C73 2023 | DDC 370.11/5—dc23

We also acknowledge the financial assistance provided by the Government of
Alberta through the Alberta Media Fund.

Government

Contents

Introduction   *3*

PART I: SHARED LEARNING AND TRUST   *13*

1. Talking about Nothing to Talk about Something   *15*
   Lynley Schofield, Anna Johnstone, Dorcas Kayes, and Herbert Thomas

2. Critical Pedagogy and Care Ethics: Feedback as Care   *31*
   Heather Robinson, Maha Al-Freih, Thomas A. Kilgore, and Whitney Kilgore

3. The Panoptic Gaze and the Discourse of Academic Integrity   *47*
   Matthew M. Acevedo

4. "Too Many Man"? Using Digital Technology to Develop Critical Media Literacy and Foster Classroom Discourse on Gender and Sexuality · *63*
   Alex de Lacey

PART II: CRITICAL CONSCIOUSNESS   *77*

5. Hacking the Law: Social Justice Education through Lawtech   *79*
   Kim Silver

6. When Being Online Hinders the Act of Challenging Banking Model Pedagogy: Neo-Liberalism in Digital Higher Education   *93*
   Frederic Fovet

7. Digital Redlining, Minimal Computing, and Equity   *111*
   Lee Skallerup Bessette

PART III: CHANGE   *131*

8   Critical Digital Pedagogy and Indigenous Knowledges:
     Harnessing Technologies for Decoloniality in Higher
     Education Institutions of the Global South   *133*
         Jairos Gonye and Nathan Moyo

9   *La Clave*: Culturally Relevant Pedagogy in Digital Praxis   *151*
         Maria V. Luna-Thomas and Enilda Romero-Hall

10   Not Just a Hashtag: Using Black Twitter to Engage in Critical
     Visual Pedagogy   *173*
         Mia L. Knowles-Davis and Robert L. Moore

PART IV: HOPE   *187*

11   To Exist Is to Resist: A Reflective Account of Developing
     a Paradigm Shift in Palestinian Teaching and Learning
     Practice   *189*
         Howard Scott and Samah Jarrad

12   Critical Digital Pedagogy for the Anthropocene   *205*
         Jonathan Lynch

13   Critical Digital Pedagogy Across Learning Ecologies: Studios
     as Sites of Partnership for Strategic Change   *219*
         Amy Collier and Sarah Lohnes Watulak

Conclusion   *233*

Contributors   *241*

Critical Digital Pedagogy in Higher Education

Introduction

Shortly after we started working on this book, we witnessed a class discussion on Twitter which highlighted once again how education, as a formal system and process, is not always liberatory for our students. In this discussion, a student protested that, though she had many talents and aspirations, a rigid and predetermined educational system was constantly working against her, leaving her feeling hollow (Poyraz, 2020a). She argued that students should be given opportunities to cultivate their interests, to learn in critical and creative ways, alluding to the fact that an authoritarian model of education seldom provides such opportunities (Poyraz, 2020b). The analogy that this student was drawing was of contesting labour, or of contesting forces, in education: the labour of education—no matter how hard, deliberate, or thoughtful it can be—might be at odds with students' backgrounds, aspirations, talents, and life experiences.[1] Educational resources, activities, spaces, expectations, norms, regulations—the system as a whole and in part—can contradict what a student might find meaningful in the immediate context, in the future, for one's self, or for one's community.

Based upon our own experiences in higher education, we are convinced that the search for meaning is also true for higher education staff. In higher education contexts, we have experienced significant pressures with serious implications for professional practice: cuts in higher education funding are justified and perpetuated by neo-liberal agendas, which reinforce the notion of "education as a commodity" and "students as customers" in an ever-expanding market economy.[2] Although there is growing emphasis on "value for money" and performance and outcome measures that often benchmark individuals and entire institutions against imposed criteria, less attention is given to the well-being and professional outcomes of staff, especially those who find themselves in precarious positions. In this environment, many digital technologies are touted by providers and adopted by institutions for efficiency, progress tracking, and automation, yet the outcomes of educational technology adoption are often questionable and contested. Such pressures and tensions are global and, increasingly, emblematic of educational technology (Veletsianos & Moe, 2017).

The COVID-19 pandemic has amplified and aggravated such issues. The chapters in this collection were written between 2019 and 2020, shortly before and after the first wave of the pandemic, which meant that the book took shape among complex social, political, and economic crises, one of which was the sudden pivot to online education in many countries around the globe. In this unexpected shift to the "digital" for all aspects of teaching and learning, educational technology both served as "a frontline emergency service" and became a crisis in and of itself (Williamson et al., 2020, pp. 107–114). The speed and nature of the transition to *remote* teaching and learning meant that, in many instances, digital practices were adopted without a good understanding of the spatial, temporal, and social dimensions of *online* teaching and learning. In our work contexts, especially early in the pandemic, many colleagues wanted to learn more about how to teach better in online and blended contexts. They wanted to know more about how to protect their students' well-being, privacy, and dignity; how to build meaningful connections and communities; and how to create inclusive and accessible educational materials and spaces. Also, importantly, many wanted to be able to practise a pedagogy of care (see, e.g., Bozkurt et al., 2020; VanLeeuwen et al., 2021) in a culture in which education is increasingly viewed as an economic transaction.

We find it remarkable and hopeful that there is so much humane and critical teaching, and desire to do so, given the pressures that educators are under. This is one of the reasons that we decided to edit this volume. Considering the current context of higher education, the practice and study of critical digital pedagogy have much relevance for teachers as well as researchers, learning designers, academic/faculty developers, and administrators. Here, like Bradshaw (2017), we do not use criticality as "a simple negativity or opposition" (p. 9). Rather, in the spirit of critical pedagogy, we see criticality as a commitment to understand ourselves and the world better through connections with other people: this is a self-reflective and dialogic experience. These two qualities of critical pedagogy reveal why it is difficult, or perhaps undesirable, to provide or prescribe a specific method of going about critical pedagogical practice in digital contexts. We agree with Giroux (2020), who said that critical pedagogy is "not about *a priori* method that simply can be applied regardless of context. It is the outcome of particular struggles and is always related to the specifics of particular contexts, students, communities and available resources" (p. 2).

There are some assumptions and shared values, however, that characterize critical pedagogy, guided by canonical texts such as *Pedagogy of the Oppressed* by Paulo Freire (2017; originally published in 1968) and *Teaching to Transgress: Education as the Practice of Freedom* by bell hooks (1994). Critical pedagogy intersects with social theories of learning in the sense that learning starts with experience, and that experience is always social or socially organized: the problems, issues, and realities of the society, as well as personal struggles and aspirations, shape educational processes and outcomes.[3] In this socio-political context, meaning making in critical pedagogy is imagined as a shared, mutual process grounded in the life experiences of both students and educators. Co-construction in education is good pedagogy, of course, but there is an important political dimension of critical pedagogy often missing in other approaches: this is a reflexive and democratic process that sees the humanization of education both as a pedagogical aim and as a frame of reference for pedagogical praxis—the iterative cycle of "action and reflection upon the world in order to change it" (hooks, 1994, p. 14). In other words, a desired outcome of pedagogical praxis in critical pedagogy is "critically informed social action" (Brookfield & Preskill, 1999, p. 36). Teaching democratically means that we, as educators, "make an effort to create conditions under which all voices can speak and be heard (including our own), and in which educational processes are seen to be open to genuine negotiation" (Brookfield, 1995, p. 45). Thus, critical pedagogy, as an educational philosophy and practice, opposes and resists authoritarianism, both in a political and pedagogical sense.

Traditionally, critical pedagogy is concerned with a critique of oppressive educational systems and practices through the lens of *power*. For example, critical pedagogues might ask who or which system has power in a particular context, why, and how? What are the consequences? Critical social theories, "a range of theoretical [social justice] projects that self-define or might be classified as critical" (Hill Collins, 2019, p. 56) directly inform critical pedagogy. These projects (for example, feminist, postcolonial, or disability studies) address the intersectional struggles of race, ethnicity, gender, class, disability, while at the same time such struggles change and intersect in different ways depending on one's social location. In simple and broad terms, perhaps critical pedagogy could be viewed as opening up spaces in education for deeply humane connections, to make education "vital and relevant" (Seal and Smith, 2021, p. 2) and rewarding for our students and for ourselves.

Critical education scholarship in general provides a solid base from which to draw for critical digital pedagogy. As this collection demonstrates, critical digital pedagogy thrives in scholarly literature and debate in different forms within and across different disciplines. Contributors to the collection critically examine digital pedagogy drawing from cultural studies, digital humanities, environmental studies, ethnography, history, law, music, politics, sociology, and education (including educational technology), reflecting the rich diversity in disciplinary and cross-disciplinary knowledge and practice in critical digital pedagogy.

In educational technology, we have seen in the last decade prolific writing showing how higher education teaching can engage in "reflective, nuanced, and critical thinking" (Stommel, 2014) about digital technologies, largely in response to "significant [and persistent] inequalities of educational opportunity, alongside poor-quality teaching, curriculum and school organization" (Selwyn et al., 2020, p. 1). As Bradshaw (2017) argued, this type of critically reflective work invites both practitioners and scholars to recognize how "culture interacts with learning and technology" (p. 20), and the ethics of this interaction, which largely has been absent in academic training and professional practice in educational technology programs. Public scholarship, typically outside the peer-reviewed journals that one might consider as the contours of the discipline has also helped to demystify the scholarship on critical digital pedagogy and to extend the reach and impact of ethical pedagogical practices and theories in educational technology (see, for example, #LTH-Echat on Twitter, the journal *Hybrid Pedagogy*, etc). With this book, we aim to build upon and contribute to previous work in this area as well as to assist in making issues of concern to critical digital pedagogy more widely available.

There is another significant aspect of critical digital pedagogy that this collection demonstrates: reflexivity in critical digital pedagogy—the ongoing inquiry into our "attitudes, thought processes, values, assumptions, prejudices and habitual actions" (Bolton & Delderfield, 2018, p. 13)—calls for frameworks of thinking, the use of concepts and ideas, outside disciplinary boundaries. These include Indigenous knowledge systems and practices, narratives passed down in families and communities, non-academic literature and our everyday observations and experiences—in other words, the many ways in which we make sense of our world. Borrowing from Hall, viewing critical digital pedagogy as "the opening of a transdisciplinary field of inquiry" (Media Education Foundation, 2021, 01:15) might be helpful in that it represents a field that cannot be confined to the boundaries of a traditional academic discipline. Nor does it lie strictly at the intersection of multiple disciplines. As the pedagogical work is reflective, it is always under construction.

A central theme that characterizes critical digital pedagogy in this collection is the humanization of education (Freire, 2017): the affirmation of students and educators as whole persons with cultural backgrounds, life experiences, emotions, beliefs, and values. With humanizing education, we do not suggest a way of life and thinking that privileges human concerns, feelings, and affairs above everything else. Rather, our position is that humanization is a starting point for the nurturing of students as critical and compassionate human beings able and willing to imagine different and better possibilities for themselves and others, including the material world. There seems to be a need to define more clearly and perhaps rethink our relationship with the digital to widen such possibilities. This is particularly important in the current educational landscape, where digital educational practice is a crucial element of teaching in higher education through different modes of practice (open, online, and blended education) and a variety of digital platforms and tools, such as learning management systems/virtual learning environments, blogs, wikis, and social networking tools, and certain practices such as datafication, credentialing, learning analytics, upskilling and reskilling, and flexible learning. Although much has been written about these topics, and critical scholarship on them has existed for decades, critical examination of them at a larger scale has only gained traction recently (Macgilchrist, 2021). That is not to say that optimism about the digital and techno-solutionist approaches to education have disappeared. On the contrary, critical approaches to digital learning have arisen amid an expansive resurgence of local, national, and global efforts that centre technology in education that begin with the premise of solving education's problems, of solving the problem of education, via technology.

When Freire was writing *Pedagogy of the Oppressed* in exile in the late 1960s, he yearned for democratic education, the teaching and practice of democracy as a life skill, a way of thinking, which at the time did not have much room to flourish in his native country of Brazil under the auspices of an authoritarian military regime. Similarly, the chapters in this book reflect the political and societal concerns of our times, and the pedagogical work can be seen as a direct response to some critical issues, which include but are not limited to the rise of extremism and white supremacy, inequality laid bare by the COVID-19 pandemic, climate catastrophe, structural racism, and digital hegemony. We invite you to approach this book as a pedagogical project still in the making in response to such critical issues.

We group the chapters into four themes corresponding to key concepts in critical pedagogy: shared learning and trust, critical consciousness, change, and hope. Although the categories might seem to be distinct, the themes are interrelated and often occur concurrently in the chapters. We elaborate on these themes in the conclusion of this book.

The chapters in Part I: Shared Learning and Trust challenge hegemonic teacher-student relationships and practices in higher education. In Chapter 1, Schofield, Johnstone, Kayes, and Thomas demonstrate how they develop relational trust in their teaching by embracing Pacific Indigenous values and ways of knowing. Next, in Chapter 2, drawing from an ethics of care approach to online course design, Robinson, Al-Freih, Kilgore, and Kilgore note "active listening, dialogue, trust, and openness without judgment" as some core values in online teaching. Also, in Chapter 3, Acevedo argues that an academic culture of distrust and surveillance is incongruent with creating learning environments that promote "creativity, expression, synthesis, and dissent." Finally, in Chapter 4, de Lacey shows the careful pedagogical work required to "break down patterns of domination in the classroom," essential for students to develop their critical media literacy and "interrogate normative representations of gender, sexuality, and race."

In Part II: Critical Consciousness, the chapters call for critical awareness of specific topics. Silver describes in Chapter 5 an interdisciplinary law and technology module driven by the ideals of social justice. Through an iterative process of co-construction and reflection, students engage critically with lawtech as a discipline, their learning, and "their place within this world." In Chapter 6, Fovet argues that critical digital pedagogy must include a reflexive analysis of how learners perceive online learning within a neo-liberal context. Skallerup Bessette, in Chapter 7, critiques unequal access to technology and stresses the need to understand students' cultural and material contexts to inform institutional decisions about technology. Her compelling discussion sits at the intersection of digital redlining, minimal computing, and equity.

The chapters in Part III: Change are concerned with the liberating potential of education. In Chapter 8, Gonye and Moyo, drawing from African Indigenous knowledge systems, imagine and put into practice a liberatory pedagogy that disrupts digital hegemony in the Global South. Next, in Chapter 9, Thomas and Romero-Hall discuss the demographic attainment gaps in higher education and provide practical suggestions for educators to use culturally relevant pedagogy and corresponding emancipatory pedagogies to address this critical issue. In Chapter 10, Knowles-Davis and Moore use Black Twitter as a site *of* and *for* doing critical visual pedagogy. They call for the creation of ethical educational spaces that challenge "social stereotypes, hierarchies, and oppressive structures, especially those that affect marginalized communities."

Although the thematic groupings overlap, the themes of "Change" and "Hope" are the most closely connected. The chapters in Part IV: Hope are united by a desire for things to be different and better, a desire that becomes a possibility, an optimistic endeavour. Scott and Jarrad write in Chapter 11 that "critical pedagogy needs to have hope, idealism, and inspiration at its heart—the power of the possible." Through an international collaborative project, the authors discuss how they use project-based learning as a method to dignify and educate students in a troubled Palestinian context, while acknowledging that emancipation through education is not always viable in a politically oppressed society. In a very different context, Lynch uses a post-humanist lens in Chapter 12 to offer a critical yet hopeful account of how technology can be used to form and sustain "interconnectedness with the more-than-human" world. Finally, in Chapter 13, Collier and Lohnes Watulak describe how they led "curricular change from the margins and into a partnership model" and how, in the process, they became oriented toward hope to open up new academic spaces that challenge existing academic hierarchies and silos of knowledge.

There is much in the pages that follow that can spark alternative practices, propel research agendas, and foster future research. The contributors to this collection, as well as we, the editors, often commented during the project on how pedagogical reflection and praxis are always works in progress: we learn significantly from our reflections and from our interactions with others deeply and passionately interested in humanizing education, with or without digital technology. We hope that you will be part of this reflective process too as you pick up the threads in this book and find different and unique ways to explore critical digital pedagogy in your scholarly practice, whether that is research, teaching, service, or administration.

Notes

1   In her tweet, Poyraz draws an analogy with classic pipe and water tank problems in Math Education. For example, as one pipe fills a tank in 4 hours, a drainpipe empties it in 8 hours. With both pipes open, how long would it take the tank to be filled?
2   See, for example, proposed government cuts in art and design, music, dance, drama and performing arts, media studies, and archaeology in the United Kingdom (Arts Industry, 2021).

3   This reminds us of Mills (2000), who wrote; "neither the life of an individual nor the history of a society can be understood without understanding both" (p. 3).

References

Arts Industry. (2021, July 21). Cuts to higher education arts funding to go ahead. https://artsindustry.co.uk/news/2587-cuts-to-higher-education-arts-funding -to-go-ahead.

Bolton, G., & Delderfield, R. (2018). *Reflective practice: Writing and professional development* (5th ed). Sage Publications.

Bozkurt, A., Jung, I., Xiao, J., Vladimirschi, V., Schuwer, R., Egorov, G., Lambert, S. R., . . . & Paskevicius, M. (2020). A global outlook to the interruption of education due to COVID-19 Pandemic: Navigating in a time of uncertainty and crisis. *Asian Journal of Distance Education, 15*(1), 1–126.

Bradshaw, A. C. (2017). Critical pedagogy and educational technology. In A. D. Benson, R. Joseph, & J. L. Moore (Eds.), *Culture, learning, and technology: Research and practice* (pp. 8–27). Routledge.

Brookfield, S. D. (1995). *Becoming a critically reflective teacher*. Jossey-Bass.

Brookfield, S. D., & Preskill, S. (1999). *Discussion as a way of teaching: Tools and techniques for democratic classrooms*. Jossey-Bass.

Freire, P. (2017). *Pedagogy of the oppressed*. Penguin Books. (Original work published 1968)

Giroux, H. (2020). *On critical pedagogy* (2nd ed). Bloomsbury Academic.

hooks, b. (1994). *Teaching to transgress: Education as the practice of freedom*. Routledge.

Hill Collins, P. (2019). *Intersectionality as critical social theory*. Duke University Press.

Macgilchrist, F. (2021). What is "critical" in critical studies of edtech? Three responses. *Learning Media and Technology, 46*(3), 243–249.

Media Education Foundation. (2021, April 14). *Trans-disciplinary thought & intellectual activism—Stuart Hall: Through the prism* [Video]. YouTube. https:// youtu.be/VbgVIEIR1vc.

Mills, C. W. (2000). *Sociological imagination: Fortieth anniversary edition*. Oxford University Press.

Poyraz, G. [@poyraztgizem]. (2020a, October 28). *Hani havuz problemlerinde üstteki musluklar havuzu doldurmaya çalışırken alttakiler de boşaltır ya, işte ben kendimi o havuz gibi hissediyorum. Yeteneklerim . . .* [Tweet]. Twitter. https:// twitter.com/poyraztgizem/status/1321535977165389826.

Poyraz, G. [@poyraztgizem]. (2020b, October 28). + *dolayısıyla tüm öğrenenlerin beyin havuzlarının özgür bırakılıp, eleştirel ve yaratıcı öğrenme olanaklarının sunulduğu ortamlar çok kıymetlidir. Örneğin içerisinde bulunduğum bu . . .* [Tweet]. Twitter. https://twitter.com/poyraztgizem/status/1321537959112417283.

Seal, M., & Smith, A. (2021). *Enabling critical pedagogy in higher education.* Critical Publishing Ltd.

Selwyn, N., Hillman, T., Eynon, R., Ferreira, G., Knox, J., MacGilchrist, F., and Sancho-Gil, J. M. (2020). What's next for ed-tech? Critical hopes and concerns for the 2020s. *Learning, Media and Technology, 45*(1), 1–6. https://doi.org/10.1080/17439884.2020.1694945.

Stommel, J. (2014). Critical digital pedagogy: A definition. *Hybrid Pedagogy.* https://hybridpedagogy.org/critical-digital-pedagogy-definition/.

VanLeeuwen, C. A., Veletsianos, G., Johnson, N., & Belikov, O. (2021). Never-ending repetitiveness, sadness, loss, and "juggling with a blindfold on": Lived experiences of Canadian college and university faculty members during the COVID-19 pandemic. *British Journal of Educational Technology, 52*(4), 1306–1322. https://doi.org/10.1111/bjet.13065.

Veletsianos, G., & Moe, R. (2017, April 10). The rise of educational technology as a sociocultural and ideological phenomenon. *Educause Review.* http://er.educause.edu/articles/2017/4/the-rise-of-educational-technology-as-a-sociocultural-and-ideological-phenomenon.

Williamson, B., Eynon, R., & Potter, J. (2020). Pandemic politics, pedagogies and practices: Digital technologies and distance education during the coronavirus emergency. *Learning, Media and Technology, 45*(2), 107–114.

PART I
SHARED LEARNING AND TRUST

Education can only be liberatory when everyone claims knowledge as a field in which we all labour.

—bell hooks

Education must begin with the solution of the teacher-student contradiction, by reconciling the poles of the contradiction so that both are simultaneously teachers and *students*.

—Paulo Freire

Talking about Nothing to Talk about Something

Lynley Schofield, Anna Johnstone, Dorcas Kayes, and Herbert Thomas

He aha te mea nui o te ao. He tāngata, he tāngata, he tāngata.

What is the most important thing in the world? It is people, it is people, it is people.

—*Whakatauki* (Māori proverb)

The Master of Contemporary Education is a practice-based, learner-focused, and solutions-driven program designed to support the development of in-service teachers and educational leaders in a rapidly evolving educational environment. The program encourages and enables educators to challenge the status quo in education and culminates in the implementation of a practice-based change project. Two part-time cohorts and one full-time cohort are enrolled in the program annually. Interaction between cohorts is encouraged. The program follows a blended, or hybrid, model (incorporating both in-person and online elements) with a strong emphasis on collaborative and agile approaches, supported by online communities, using multiple platforms and practical workshops.

In this master's program, we incorporate the Pacific cultural model of talanoa since experience has taught us that it benefits both Pacific Island candidates and other candidates. Talanoa is a traditional approach used in many Pacific countries to engage in inclusive conversation that allows the building of relationships (Cram et al., 2014). The word *talanoa* means to talk or speak about nothing in order to speak about something (Vaioleti, 2006). *Tala* means to inform, tell, relate, and command; *noa* means of any kind, ordinary, or nothing in particular. Talanoa is informal small talk and therefore not traditionally viewed as significant—particularly within educational settings.

In this chapter, we show how attention to a key cultural model of interaction contributes to the development of relational trust, a deeper understanding of social presence online, and purposeful learner interaction. From the perspective of critical digital pedagogy, the approach enables candidates and facilitators to interact online in ways more commonly associated with in-person communication and collaboration. Talanoa focuses attention on the networked interaction of tightly knit communities rather than the more rigid structure of topic-focused threaded discussions in online forums. In *talking about nothing*, strong personal relationships of trust are established. This prepares students to engage in honest, robust, non-confrontational discussions related to the complexities of bicultural and multicultural education in Aotearoa New Zealand.

Background

Before looking forward, it is important to look back at what has come before. A well-respected *whakatauki* (Māori proverb), *ngā tapuwae o mua, mō muri,* cautions us to begin by understanding what happened in the past if we are to make a difference in the future (Macfarlane, 2015). New Zealand's founding document, the Treaty of Waitangi, established a partnership between the Indigenous Māori people and the colonial government (Glynn, 2015). Although the treaty was meant to create unity, it has been the cause of much dissent and disagreement in political, social, and educational contexts. Historically, educational policies in Aotearoa

New Zealand, like those in other colonized societies, have focused on processes of assimilation and integration. In essence, one system of education was offered to all regardless of cultural background or need. Treating all learners in the same way was considered the best way to achieve educational success. Awareness and acknowledgement of culture were mostly ignored, and this led to underachievement by minority groups (Alton-Lee, 2005; Glynn, 2015; Samu, 2006).

In 1984, a bicultural approach to education was adopted by the New Zealand government. This approach sought to redress the inequity faced by Māori people in the traditional colonial educational system. However, little indication of how to achieve this redress was provided. Mostly, the focus was on strengthening and affirming the identity of Māori as equals (Lourie, 2016, 2018). Pedagogy was not redesigned to incorporate the development of strong relationships between educator and learner and among learners themselves. Such relationships are paramount to addressing the imbalance of educational achievement in the colonial educational system (Bishop et al., 2014; Glynn, 2015; Samu, 2006). Māori and Pacific cultures especially value face-to-face interactions to build trusting relationships (Berryman et al., 2016).

The current educational system is characterized by a genuine desire to correct educational imbalances brought about by colonial education (on decolonizing higher education, see Chapters 8 and 9 of this volume). Furthermore, a number of frameworks have been proposed to address these imbalances, but the widespread implementation of one or more frameworks has yet to find expression in teacher practice. Critical digital pedagogy and talanoa provide a framework and a set of aligned practices that hold the promise of developing strong relationships of trust in order to address power imbalances.

Critical Digital Pedagogy

To engage with critical digital pedagogy, clarification of each of the three constituent terms is required. First, critical digital pedagogy is critical to the extent that it draws from a broad critical tradition often seen to have been influenced, initially, by Karl Marx's definition of social class as a product of access to (or lack of access to) the means of production and thus wealth. Marx's ideas were later critiqued and built upon by members of the Frankfurt School, notably Adorno, Horkheimer, and Marcuse (Giroux, 2017). This initial critique of the injustice and social inequality brought about by unequal access to wealth was later extended to include the study of a range of other ways in which the workings of power and influence in society have led to injustice and social inequality, noticeably in regard to the interplay among race, class, and gender. It is the latter sense in which critical digital pedagogy is most often considered to be critical.

Second, the workings of power and influence affect all aspects of society, particularly those institutions that serve to entrench the power and influence of the ruling class. The school, from the perspective of critical pedagogy, is a place where prospective workers are prepared to enter a market-dominated society in which their skills will oil the wheels of industry (Freire, 1970; Giroux, 2011). In this sense, pedagogy is both a vehicle for entrenching the neo-liberal agenda and inherently shaped by that agenda. Paradoxically, pedagogy also provides a space in which critical pedagogists can engage the neo-liberal agenda in ways that illuminate the workings of power and influence in the service of benefiting some in society at the expense of others (McLaren, 2017). Pedagogy becomes contested terrain.

Third, pedagogy cannot meaningfully be separated from digital networks, platforms, and ways of being in a digital world. However, just as pedagogy itself is not value free or neutral (Bernstein, 2000), so too digital artifacts and ways of being are not value free or neutral (van den Hoven, 2007; Winner, 1980). In fact, all too often, digital artifacts and ways of being are appropriated by education from other contexts. One example is the use of presentation software for instructional purposes even though presentations encourage "lecture-style" instruction, which runs counter to the dominant social constructivist spirit of the educational age. Critical digital pedagogists seek to illuminate how power and influence play out in the design of such digital artifacts and how these digital artifacts demand pedagogical and social arrangements that benefit some learners to the detriment of others. For the purposes of this discussion, our focus is on elements of learning design that enable and encourage a talanoa approach to the development of relationships across the hybrid program.

The Talanoa Framework

The concept of talanoa was used to develop a Pacific research methodology (Vaioleti, 2006). A model evolved that incorporated four important values: *ofa* (love), *mafana* (warmth), *malie* (humour), and *faka'apa'apa* (respect). We see these values as the foundation upon which strong learning communities can be built. Talanoa offers cultural values that improve the online learning experience, build relationships, and strengthen learning to meet better the needs of diverse learners—including those who traditionally prefer in-person relationships in order to participate in their learning. What would be considered seemingly trivial talk actually contributes to thinking, learning, and knowledge building on multiple levels (Vaioleti, 2006).

This aligns well with another familiar concept in Aotearoa New Zealand education, *ako- a te ao Māori*, in which teacher and learner learn from each other. This entails the importance of reciprocity in and collaborative approaches to learning, building productive relationships, and empowering learning (Keown et al., 2005). The talanoa approach embraces the concept of *ako*. In teaching sessions, candidates become confident to share their views. These shared learning experiences are used by the teaching team to develop further the design and delivery of content. This affects learning not only for these particular candidates but also for the candidates in other cohorts.

Farther afield, the Talanoa Dialogue is a process that has been adopted as part of the United Nations Framework Convention on Climate Change and is based upon similar principles of inclusion, participation, and transparency. The purpose is to share stories, develop understanding, and build empathy and trust among participants (United Nations, 2019). Another key feature of the talanoa concept is that all those involved believe that their contributions are valued and that they can participate equally in the conversation or learning.

Talanoa in the Master of Contemporary Education

The talanoa concept—and associated values—lay the foundation that underpins the building of relationships in the Master of Contemporary Education (MCE).

The talanoa MCE framework begins with the learner at the centre. Learners have the opportunity to share openly who they are and where they have come from. The talanoa values *ofa* (love), *malie* (humour), *faka'apa'apa* (respect), and *mafana* (warmth) provide the foundation upon which socio-cultural elements are developed and strengthened as learners make connections to people and places. Learners begin to have a strong sense of confidence, belonging, respect, and empathy for and from

Figure 1.1.
The Talanoa MCE Framework.

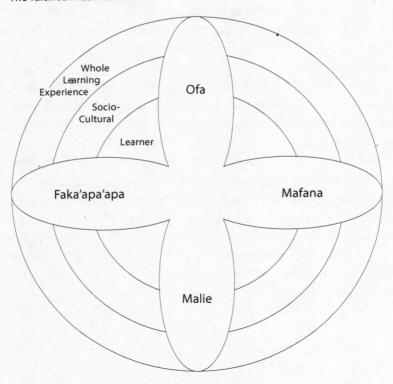

others—allowing full immersion in the opportunities and challenges of the whole learning experience.

In designing the program, careful thought was given to how we might best engage facilitators and participants against a backdrop of limited in-person connection. Since both facilitators and many participants are dispersed across the country, interaction and collaboration in the program take place largely online. Some of the questions that we asked were how could we best develop a learning community, and which tools could we use to create connections, foster critical discussions, and enable learning to push the participants to challenge their thinking and practice? Which tools could we use to help emulate the connections that normally would have been possible in a traditional, in-person program? How could the team enable participants to connect with each other and with the teaching team without the luxury of being together in a classroom? The relevant elements of program design presented below address these questions.

At the beginning of the program, candidates meet in-person during an orientation day. The day begins with a talanoa session, integrating the four values of talanoa: *ofa*, *mafana*, *malie*, and *faka'apa'apa*. Candidates are given the opportunity and freedom to talk about "nothing," to speak about themselves and reveal anything that they are comfortable sharing with the group. There is no direction from facilitators to answer specific questions, and they do not lead the discussion or determine who speaks when. Candidates have shared control of the experience. They determine what they say and when they say it. *Mana* (prestige, status, standing) is strengthened as candidates share; it is all about the speakers. The experience begins with the facilitators talking about themselves. This is crucial in modelling the process for following speakers. A culture of trust and respect begins to form. The space begins to close between the candidates and facilitators and among the candidates. This can take a long time, but it is time well spent. In establishing *mafana*, participants are encouraged to share who they are, where they are from, and who walks with them on this journey (for sample introductions, see below). This allows candidates and staff members to begin making connections with each other. It allows each cohort to create its own culture—a safe place to communicate—and creates the understanding that "we are all in this together." We all know who we are and who is joining us on this journey. Rather than traditional meet-and-greet icebreakers, in which one learns people's names or favourite colours, this talanoa approach takes longer and goes much deeper. The risk is greater because the spotlight is on each individual participant within the group. It can be intimidating, but the vulnerability creates the beginnings of *faka'apa'apa* and *ofa*. *Malie* is interwoven to help make people feel more comfortable.

> *Tēnā koutou katoa! Ko Ngāti Hāmoa tōku iwi.*
> Greetings, everyone! I am Samoan.

> *Ko Tuitu'i Pa'u Tuitasi tōku pāpā. No Malaeloa Tūtuila ia. Ko Elena Fanana Grey tōku māmā. No Vaitele ia.*
> My father is Tu'itu'i Pa'u Tuitasi, and his village is Malaeloa Tūtuila. My mother is Elena Fanana Grey, and her village is Vaitele.

> *Ko Paul Kayes tōku tane. Ko Dorcas Kayes ahau.*
> My husband is Paul Kayes. My name is Dorcas Kayes.

> *He kaitiaki ahau mō MCE.*
> I am a guardian of MCE.

> *Tēnā koutou katoa!*
> Greetings, everyone!

> *Ko Table Mountain te maunga. Ko Ātarānaki te moana.*
> My mountain is Table Mountain. My ocean is the Atlantic Ocean.

> *I te taha o tōku māmā, nō Huitene ōku tīpuna. I te taha o tōku pāpā, nō Wēra ōku tīpuna.*
> My mother's ancestors are from Sweden. My father's ancestors are from Wales.

I whānau mai ahau i Pretoria i Āwherika ki te Tonga. Ko Ōtautahi tōku kāinga ināianei.

My family lives in Pretoria in South Africa. I live in Christchurch.

He Pākehā ahau. Ko Herbert Thomas tōku ingoa. He kaitiaki ahau mō MCE.

I am Pakeha. My name is Herbert Thomas. I am a guardian of the MCE.

Nō reira, tēnā koutou, tēnā koutou, tēnā koutou katoa.

Therefore, greetings thrice over.

Program orientation is a critical time when connections begin, and people often verbalize their connections to people who have already introduced themselves. This is especially true for Māori and Pacific Island candidates, who become more confident as connections are made. *Malie* is frequently used to strengthen *mafana*.

As stories are shared and connections are made, *faka'apa'apa* occurs in the form of a sense of both respect (and pride) for oneself and respect for others. A strong sense of trust is established, as is an acceptance of everyone and the values that have been shared. There is the ability to build understanding of and empathy for who they are at this time, the pathways that led them there, and the values that they bring to this journey. As these values of talanoa develop, a strong sense of community is built, one in which students have each other's back. This sense of community is further supported by the development of smaller collaborative peer groups that provide support and opportunities for robust critique and discussion—not only about learning in the program but also about the application of that learning in classrooms and educational contexts in which participants work.

In addition to orientation day, in-person, on-campus study days are offered four times a year, and talanoa is reinforced on these days. Since we were unable to meet in-person in 2020 because of COVID-19, online opportunities had to be bolstered to ensure that candidates could still make real connections to each other. For the new cohort that started during this time, the talanoa values took longer to build. In online sessions, groups were smaller, and more time was given during each breakout (small online groups organized by the teacher) to ensure that the process of talanoa could occur. At the beginning of and during online sessions, time is set aside to allow candidates to talanoa, both as a class and in smaller groups, through the use of breakout rooms. It is important to ensure that time is set aside to allow this talanoa to happen so that candidates are more comfortable participating in robust discussions. This embeds the concept of talanoa, in which to be able to talk about something important one needs to be able to talk about nothing (Vaioleti, 2006). An illustration of this importance was when we forgot to allow time for candidates to talanoa in a cross-cohort session; the candidates themselves challenged us on the importance of allowing the talanoa process to happen to ensure that the academic discussion could occur.

In the online environment, opportunities for various types of communication connection are an important component of talanoa. Primarily, they occur via both asynchronous and synchronous online discussions. Evaluating previous programs—and how online spaces had been used—convinced the program team to provide more support in synchronous online discussions than had been provided in other programs. Asynchronous online discussions also needed to be bolstered effectively if candidates were to engage in rigorous and robust discussions.

Zoom, a video- and web-conferencing platform, is used as a synchronous online discussion platform for regular meetings. Full-time candidates have weekly Zoom sessions, whereas part-time candidates have fortnightly meetings. These meetings provide much more than the opportunity for synchronous discussion. They build relationships and understanding not only among fellow candidates but also, vitally, with the facilitation team. An integral aspect of these synchronous meetings is the opportunity to make real-time connections. Bridging the spaces between candidates and the facilitation team, and between the learning content and existing knowledge, is a key component of these sessions. In each session, candidates can make connections with each other via breakout rooms. These breakout sessions provide opportunities to build relationships and to critique, argue, and challenge the learning and the application of this learning to their own practice-based contexts. Rather than being lecture-type sessions or webinars, these sessions are meant to *teu le va*/close the gaps (Reynolds, 2019).

The use of asynchronous online discussion forums is provided through Slack, essentially an instant messaging tool. It allows users to communicate through closed and open channels and direct messaging, and it enables them to share content and files. Initially intended as a forum to be used for general connection and collaboration in the program, Slack soon played a much greater role. It enabled more robust online discussion and academic support of students. Furthermore, it became apparent that the platform could be used effectively to foster the development of a community of learning and a sense of connection, thus limiting feelings of isolation often experienced in online learning situations.

Each new cohort includes both full-time and part-time students. In Slack, a General Channel provides a space for interaction across all registered cohorts, regardless of where participants might be in their learning journeys. In addition, a Cohort Channel—and cohort full-time and part-time channels—provide cohort-specific spaces for interaction and collaboration. Furthermore, each cohort is divided into small (four to eight people) collaborative peer groups, and each of these groups is provided with a Slack channel. Finally, Slack also enables private messaging between participants. Candidates are thus able to use open, closed, and private forums to ask questions, provide answers, and make connections not only with the teaching staff but also with each other.

The immediacy and multi-channel nature of this interaction and collaboration enable participants to develop strong relationships of trust. These relationships are the bedrock upon which collaborative engagement with course content, assessments, topical issues, readings, and general work and life discussions are built (Stommel, 2020). The program teaching team provides additional Slack channels to support Māori and Pasifika candidates (ManaakiFono Channel) and candidates in need of additional academic support (Mahi Tahi Channel). Because of the ease of use and speed of instant messaging within Slack, communication often takes the form of natural conversation. Candidates also use Slack to alert staff members to challenges or technical problems that can be addressed before becoming more widespread or problematic (Vela, 2018). These channels provide the space for candidates to ask questions in smaller, more comfortable forums. Initially, these channels are used for discussion; however, as candidates become more comfortable in the ManaakiFono Zoom sessions, the channels are used more for housekeeping purposes. This is different from the general cohort channels, with the larger group dynamic that continues to use the Slack channels conversationally and for deeper academic discussion. The ManaakiFono group holds these academic discussions in an environment of *mafana* (warmth), *faka'apa'apa* (respect), and *ofa* (love).

The use of Slack surprised the facilitation team. It became a forum that provided more support and critical discussion than was first intended. This, we believe, is a result of several factors. First, the immediacy of the messaging enables questions to be answered and connections to be made regardless of the time of day. Spontaneous conversations between students often take place both during the day and late at night. Second, questions can be answered not only by the teaching team but also by fellow candidates. Third, because of the open channels available to everyone, candidates can respond from within or across different cohorts. And fourth, candidates can communicate in open or locked channels or via direct messages to either the teaching team or individual candidates.

Strengthening relationships, building connections, and providing spaces for conversation and collaboration are essential elements in bridging gaps in knowledge, relationship, and understanding that exist among people. From a talanoa perspective, *va* is seen as the space between relationships that operate across dimensions. Addressing these spaces through talanoa gives context and meaning to the learning. These spaces are integral to relationships, and rather than hinder such relationships they strengthen them. *Va* exists between facilitator and candidate and between candidate and candidate. It also exists between the digital tools that we use and the quality of relationships that we wish to develop. *Teu le va*, as we noted, is the closing of the space (Reynolds, 2019). It is through deliberate acts that these spaces are closed and relationships are built.

The approach adopted in the MCE program was somewhat vindicated during the COVID-19 lockdown in Aotearoa New Zealand. Candidates who had already established strong relationships of trust and were communicating online were able to focus on transferring the skills and knowledge that they had acquired in their learning to supporting others in moving abruptly to online study. In addition, candidates initiated connections using Slack as a means of support and encouragement. They created shared spaces in which they provided resources and ideas to help others address the challenges that the lockdown had created.

Conclusion

From the perspective of critical digital pedagogy, it is exactly these spaces in digital learning that represent interrupted relationships and allow the play of power and hegemony. Morris and Stommel (2020) argue that learning in online settings has to be allowed to evolve and grow and be situated in the real world, involving real-world experiences. Learning, they argue, should not take place behind closed doors, and academic rigour is enhanced by genuine engagement with the learning. Providing opportunities in online forums to talk about nothing is vital to developing meaningful interactions and building relationships. Once learners are comfortable in the online space and have built mutual feelings of trust and respect, deeper learning conversations can occur. The talanoa approach works with all cultures because in its essence it is about people and making authentic connections: *E hara taku toa i te toa takitahi engari he toa takitini* (I come not with my own strengths but bring with me the gifts, talents, and strengths of my family, tribe, and ancestors).

Key Takeaways

- The cultural framework of talanoa (talking about nothing to talk about something) is an effective model to develop relational trust in in-person and online spaces.
- *Teu le va* (closing the gap) ameliorates power relationships and allows active online discussions, creating the foundation for critical digital pedagogy.

- Building online relationships is more than an icebreaker activity and needs to be interwoven deliberately into the learning in an online space.
- Relationship building has to be designed across the program in different modes so that students hear each other, see each other, and connect with each other.

References

Alton-Lee, A. (2005). *Using best evidence synthesis to assist in making a bigger difference for diverse learners*. New Zealand Ministry of Education.

Bernstein, B. (2000). *Pedagogy, symbolic control and identity* (2nd ed.). Rowman & Littlefield.

Berryman, M., Eley, E., Ford, T., & Egan, M. (2016). Going beyond the personal will and professional skills to give life to Ka Hikitia. *Journal of Educational Leadership, Policy and Practice, 30*(2), 56–68.

Bishop, R., Ladwig, J., & Berryman, M. (2014). The centrality of relationships for pedagogy: The Whanaungatanga thesis. *American Educational Research Journal, 51*, 184–214. https://doi.org/10.3102/0002831213510019.

Cram, F., Sauni, P., Tuagalu, C., & Phillips, H. (2014). He mihi mutunga—Closing words. *Diversity in Higher Education, 15*, 315–322.

Freire, P. (1970). *Pedagogy of the oppressed*. Penguin Books.

Giroux, H. (2011). *On critical pedagogy*. Bloomsbury Academic.

Giroux, H. (2017). Critical theory and educational practice. In A. Darder, R. Torres, & M. Baltodano (Eds.), *The critical pedagogy reader* (3rd ed., pp. 31–55). Routledge.

Glynn, T. (2015). Bicultural challenges for educational professionals in Aotearoa. *Waikato Journal of Education*, Special 20th Anniversary Collection, *4*, 103–113. https://wje.org.nz/index.php/WJE/article/view/227.

Keown, P., Parker, L., & Tiakiwai, S. (2005). *Values in the New Zealand curriculum: A literature review on values in the curriculum*. New Zealand Ministry of Education.

Lourie, M. (2016). Māori language education policy: Different outcomes for different groups? *New Zealand Journal of Educational Studies, 51*(1), 19–31.

Lourie, M. (2018). Biculturalism: What could it mean in education in Aotearoa New Zealand? *Teachers' Work, 15*(1), 24–27.

Macfarlane, A. (2015). Restlessness, resoluteness and reason: Looking back at 50 years of Māori education. *New Zealand Journal of Educational Studies, 50*(2), 177–193.

McLaren, P. (2017). Critical pedagogy: A look at the major concepts. In
A. Darder, R. Torres, & M. Baltodano (Eds.), *The critical pedagogy reader*
(3rd ed., pp. 56–78). Routledge.

Morris, S., & Stommel, J. (2020). *An urgency of teachers: The work of critical
digital pedagogy*. Hybrid Pedagogy.

Reynolds, M. (2019). Walking the Palagi/Pasifika edge: The va of mediated
dialogic research. *Waikato Journal of Education, 24*(1), 33–42.

Samu, T. W. (2006). The "Pasifika Umbrella" and quality teaching: Understanding
and responding to the diverse realities within. *Waikato Journal of Education, 12*,
35–50.

Stommel, J. (2020). How to build an ethical online course. In S. Morris & J. Stommel
(Eds.), *An urgency of teachers: The work of critical digital pedagogy* (pp. 65–72).
Hybrid Pedagogy.

United Nations. (2019). *Talanoa Dialogue—Everything you need to know*. UN
Climate Change Conference, COP 23, Fiji. https://cop23.com.fj/talanoa
-dialogue/.

Vaioleti, T. M. (2006). Talanoa research methodology: A developing position on
Pacific research. *Waikato Journal of Education, 12*, 21–34.

van den Hoven, J. (2007). ICT and value sensitive design. In P. Goujon,
S. Lavelle, P. Duquenoy, K. Kimppa, & V. Laurent (Eds.), *The information
society: Innovations, legitimacy, ethics and democracy* (pp. 67–72). Springer.

Vela, K. (2018). Using Slack to communicate with medical students. *Journal of the
Medical Library Association, 106*(4), 504–507. https://doi.org/10.5195/jmla.2018.482.

Winner, L. (1980). Do artifacts have politics? *Daedalus, 109*(1), 121–136.

Critical Pedagogy and Care Ethics
Feedback as Care

Heather Robinson, Maha Al-Freih, Thomas A.
Kilgore, and Whitney Kilgore

In this chapter, we describe how a care ethics approach to online course design and delivery is necessary in laying the foundation for critical pedagogy. A primary goal of critical pedagogy is to help students develop as critical thinkers and thus to empower them to bring forth constructive changes for themselves and their communities (Freire, 1971). This is fostered through a process-oriented approach to education that redefines classroom practices and relationships among learners, instructors, and the learning process. Critical digital pedagogy—as pedagogy of affect—can be an overwhelming and emotional experience for both learners and instructors, requiring the sharing of power in the instructor-student relationship and the reinvention of their roles (Zembylas, 2013). A climate of care in an online learning space—with its focus on community building, relationships, and the learners' expressed needs (versus assumed needs of the instructor, school, or educational system) through active and mutual listening, dialogue, trust, and openness without judgment (Noddings, 2012)—can support the development of safe and inclusive spaces that enhance the potential for critical pedagogical practices and aims to emerge and grow. Furthermore, an ethics of care approach to education, with its emphasis on caring *relations*, as opposed to a single moral agent, places both instructors and students in caregiver and cared-for positions interchangeably (Noddings, 2012), enhancing the potential for both parties to embrace the complexity and "mutual vulnerability" that arise from enacting critical digital pedagogy, whether in-person or online (Zembylas, 2013).

The call for a critical pedagogical approach to learning has been voiced by a number of scholars in response to the dominant educational practices that tend to reinforce hegemonic power structures and social norms. Critical pedagogy questions these classroom norms by immersing students in a transformed learning community in which the voices of each student are acknowledged, heard, and explored (hooks, 2014). This requires explicit attention to the emotional ramifications of engaging learners in difficult, complex, and challenging experiences (Zembylas, 2013). A great example of this shift to more critical pedagogies in a digitally connected age is the Equity Unbound course founded by Maha Bali, Catherine Cronin, and Mia Zamora. They describe this course as "an emergent, collaborative curriculum which aims to create equity-focused, open, connected, intercultural learning experiences across classes, countries and contexts" (Equity Unbound, n.d.). The course explores digital literacies through the lens of equitable and intercultural learning, and it is open to all interested learners and educators around the world. A call for "ungrading," voiced by many scholars, researchers, and practitioners in the field of education (Flaherty, 2019), is another example and gives students more control and agency over their own learning and reframes assessment in terms of student continuous learning and growth rather than "ranking" or "judging" (Blum & Kohn, 2020; Buck, 2020; Sackstein, 2015) (for more on ungrading, see Chapter 3 of this volume).

Progress has been made in terms of scale and access, but a better understanding of critical digital pedagogies and care-centred practices is needed to shift the focus from the affordances of digital technology to address the systemic forces of disempowerment that shape experiences of individual students and their needs. In this chapter, we first explore a care ethics approach to feedback in supporting a communal place where the learner is accepted as a *whole person*, acknowledging the learner's voice and perspective (hooks, 2003, 2014). We then focus on one element of the online learning experience: namely, student feedback. Finally, we provide some examples and pedagogical strategies from our research that demonstrate, from a student perspective, the important role that feedback plays in creating a climate of care in an online learning space in ways that empower learners and support the enactment of critical pedagogy in practice.

Care-Centred Education

According to Noddings (1984), teaching from a care perspective consists of

- *modelling,* instructors' genuine demonstration of caring behaviour that they expect of their students (e.g., honesty and promptness);
- *dialogue,* a back-and-forth conversation with learners with no prejudgment in an attempt to build relationships, develop norms, reach shared understandings, and invite deeper conversations;
- *practice,* opportunities for students to practise the act of caring with an explicit focus on the act of helping and supporting peers (e.g., collaborative and cooperative learning activities); and
- *confirmation,* the act of supporting the development of a better self by encouraging and affirming the best in others.

Central to the care-centred model of education is the relational and cyclical nature of care, in which the caring relationship between an instructor and students is complete only when the cared-for (the student) signals that the caring has been received, requiring continuous dialogue and extended interaction. From this view, students' intellectual and personal growth is nurtured when students are engaged in critical dialogue and reflection about their learning and empowered to *co-create* meaning and understanding with their instructors, peers, and community. For care ethicists such as Noddings, maintaining open and genuine relationships with the cared-for does not require responding to needs that the carer deems immoral or mistaken; however, it does necessitate that the carer remains open to dialogue and listens so as to maintain caring relations. When engaging in such relationships in the classroom, the roles of instructors and students shift; rather than instructors holding all of the answers and students simply following with little or no critical or deep reflection and thinking, instructors and students are on a shared journey built upon trust in each other, respect for diversity, and hope for a better future. "By keeping open the avenues of communication, we may find a way to ameliorate the hate, distrust or rage we've detected and, thus, be in a better position to protect others in the web of care" (Noddings, 1984, p. 206).

Emotion and Feedback in the Digital Space

Research at the intersection of feedback and emotion in digital spaces continues to emerge. Although understanding of the relationship between feedback and emotion is still growing, available research points to the strong emotional responses that students attach to feedback (Ryan & Henderson, 2018; Shields, 2015). Studies have recently highlighted the possible negative reactions that students experience to feedback from instructors and pointed out the importance of tailoring feedback to the respective needs of students. For instance, a study at two Australian universities found that students are more likely to experience negative emotions, such as feeling discouraged or upset, after receiving critical feedback from instructors, which can affect their motivation and willingness to act on the feedback to improve their performance (Ryan & Henderson, 2018). Not only that, but also feedback has been shown to affect learners beyond their courses in ways that shape their identities as learners and boost—or hinder—their self-esteem and confidence in their abilities (Shields, 2015). We discuss two types of feedback, passive transmission and dialogic, and provide examples with additional reflection on the importance of dialogic feedback to providing a higher level of care in online courses.

Feedback as Passive Transmission

The passive transmission of feedback from instructor to student is one perspective widely studied in education (Ajjawi & Boud, 2017; Beaumont et al., 2011). This method of feedback places the student in a passive role in which information is received from the teacher or expert (Evans, 2013), and it is rooted in what Freire (2005) calls the "banking" concept of education, in which teachers, or the "narrating subjects," deposit information into students' heads, and the role of students is limited to receiving, memorizing, and regurgitating that information. Missing in this approach to feedback is the opportunity for instructors and students to engage in conversation about the meaning of this feedback and how it relates to the personal realities of students.

Dialogic Feedback

Dialogic feedback is a process of discovering and building knowledge through dialogue rather than a knowledge transmission event. Feedback can be "viewed as a conversation which provides students with opportunities to engage in continuing dialogues about their learning" (Carless, 2017, p. 12) as opposed to the more common method of one-way delivery (from instructors to students). Dialogic feedback methods challenge standardized and impersonal approaches to giving feedback. Pekrun et al. (2014), for example, found that the type of feedback anticipated by students had a direct impact on their emotions and learning goals, and the researchers recommend that instructors provide students with self-referential feedback (or feedback referring to learners and their work) and try to limit the amount of standardized feedback. In our experience as educators and researchers, this is valuable for vulnerable students—such as first-generation college students and students coming from disadvantaged or marginalized backgrounds—who can benefit from the added support or guidance.

Based upon our experience as instructors, we have noticed that, even when detailed and personalized feedback is provided, not all students know how to engage with it beyond its role in improving their grades. In courses taught in Saudi Arabia (by one author), we have struggled to get some students to engage with the detailed and personalized feedback provided to them, and in some instances it took the initiative of requesting meetings with students to discuss their work with the goal of modelling to them what it looks like to reflect on this feedback, empowering them to challenge us as instructors, and helping them to understand feedback as a continuation of the learning process rather than an end to it. In such instances, we can clearly see the intersection of care ethics and critical pedagogy at play. Our dialogues with students were not limited to the specifics of the feedback provided to them but also aimed at encouraging students to take a more active role in their own learning and empowering them to share their opinions, perspectives, and experiences in a safe and trusting environment. This is precisely why we believe that explicit attention to ethical caring practices in a learning space, whether online or face to face, offers some valuable insights that can inform and support that enactment and implementation of critical pedagogies. It places the student at the centre of the teaching and learning process by creating a safe space in which instructors get to know their students and tailor their pedagogical practices to meet their collective and individual needs. Feedback as dialogue, centred on interaction and attention to emotional and relational support, renders growth and learning (Steen-Utheim & Wittek, 2017). In our own research, we found that online instructors can demonstrate a higher level of care through dialogue and feedback (Robinson et al., 2020).

Understanding the Student Experience from a Care Perspective

We are all educators and active researchers in the field of instructional design and learning technologies. To understand better the relationship among faculty online pedagogical practices, care, and the student experience, we sought to shed light on the lived experiences of students through qualitative inquiry. We gathered information through online interviews with 14 participants who had taken at least one online class at a public university in the United States. Eight participants identified as female and two as male, and four chose not to identify a gender. All but one participant had a college degree and ranged in age from 25 to over 55. In our narrative analysis, we used the four elements of the framework of Noddings: modelling, dialogue, practice, and confirmation. Our online meetings and discussions provided us with the opportunity to clarify our individual perspectives and try to understand better how each of us—the research team—interpreted the information garnered from the interviews conducted with students. Our method was deeply reflective, and we kept written entries to develop a thick description of findings (Lincoln, 1985). These reflections are woven into our discussion on student feedback for this chapter as we explore and interpret the good and poor examples encountered in our research from a care perspective.

What Do Students Say about Feedback When Learning Online?

When we interviewed online students to find out what was most important to them in their educational experiences, they reported feedback (in terms of responsiveness, quality, scaffolding learning, and demonstrating caring) as critical to their learning processes. The responsiveness of instructors means much more than simply the timely provision of feedback; it also includes being responsive to questions, discussion posts, emails, and other communications that students send. We found that, during the first and last semester of 2020 (in the beginning and middle of the COVID-19 pandemic), students used emails more frequently than in previous semesters to inquire about assessment deadlines and to discuss health-related issues. The timeliness of responses, flexibility with deadlines, and understanding were appreciated. Indeed, research shows that such communications demonstrate to students that they and their opinions and positions are cared for, supported, and valued in the teaching and learning experience.

Also, though feedback is critical to the process of teaching and learning, there are both positive and negative effects of such feedback in regard to influencing emotions. For instance, timely feedback that is simply a number grade is less effective than a detailed summary of how students can improve their work or feedback specific to a student's assignment or task. Feedback can and should provide thoughtful scaffolding so that students feel supported and cared for in their learning journeys. Personalized and thoughtful feedback on their work evokes *hope*, whereas the anticipation of standard feedback instigates feelings of anxiety (Pekrun et al., 2014).

Feedback and Supporting Students

Some of the negative issues related to feedback arise when there is a lack of responsiveness from the instructor. When faculty do not offer proper feedback, students can be left feeling that they are not properly supported. One student shared the experience of wanting to drop a class because of the lack of instructor feedback and support, but doing so would have meant graduating a semester later, the only reason that the student chose to remain in the class. Unclear communication can also lead to frustration in a student. As one student stated, "I had one course where the instructor almost never responded to inquiries in a timely manner. This was especially difficult when assignments were close to deadline. When responses were received, they tended to be unhelpful and required multiple back-and-forth emails to get usable information."

It is important as an instructor to be consistent with the quality and timeliness of feedback. If something has changed that will delay one's ability to respond, then it should be communicated effectively to students. In our interviews, students indicated that getting proper and adequate feedback quickly was extremely important to them. Delays in feedback typically affect students' ability to reflect on their learning, especially if they are working in isolation. One student shared that "the most challenging thing I think for me is when we're doing an online course, and it goes a long time without any feedback from submitted assignments. So you're submitting assignments over and over again over several weeks and not getting any feedback." Another student lamented that "there were a few times that feedback on assignments was not provided in time to make improvements."

Such situations lead to frustration among students and diminish the feelings of trust and care that might have been established early in the learning experience. If a student emailed the instructor privately to get clarity about an assignment or feedback, then the response might be helpful for other students to know. The information could be shared in an announcement or discussion forum so that all students in the course could benefit from it.

Clarity and Unclarity

When students are asked to complete complex assignments that require them to spend many hours preparing the deliverable (project, paper, etc.), they have an expectation that it will be read, viewed, reviewed, and critiqued thoughtfully. One student shared this experience: "I had one course where . . . all of a sudden, one day, all these assignments were graded at the same time, and I'm thinking where was the care and the effort put into really reading what I submitted, or did I just spend all that time for very little?"

Personalized feedback supports the student-teacher relationship. Instructors should make it obvious to students that assignments are being reviewed and provide them with feedback that is detailed, scaffolded, and specific to support their learning. This practice demonstrates care, as evident in this comment: "In one of my courses, I was required to blog weekly. A particular instructor I had always took the time to leave a specific response to my blog posting. I felt this instructor cared so much for students that they were willing to take the time to read each individual posting. This to me was admirable as many posts were long."

Clear feedback—specific and actionable—is also valued by students. Descriptive and qualitative feedback that presents modelling of the expected outcome is more valued than simply a score. The back-and-forth discourse generated by thoughtful comments from the instructor is perceived as caring about students. As one of the students interviewed said, "I think it makes a big difference when an instructor actually puts a comment in, they actually read it versus just a grade, and so to me it seems like I don't feel quite as cared for or there isn't quite as much care [when just a grade is given]."

This type of discourse by the instructor can also take the forms of voice and video, and they were mentioned in our interviews as ways that educators can provide quality feedback. Students not only associated video feedback with a quality response but also deemed it a demonstration that the instructor cared about them. One student shared that "the use of video feedback from a few teachers has proven that some teachers care about the well-being of their students in an online course."

Care for Students

Our research demonstrates that educators should not underestimate the complexity of students' emotional investment in learning. Dialogue with students is one way, Noddings (1984) suggests, that educators demonstrate *caring for*. One can demonstrate such care for students by taking a personal interest in them and how they are doing in addition to their work. Investing time in dialogue with students to check on them on a personal level via email, text, audio, or video formats is valued by learners since it shows a level of care for them beyond the course. Scaffolding support for students with such dialogue manifested itself in our interviews in statements such as "being told that a project had real potential for future development," which gives learners confirmation that they are moving forward in the right direction and making progress. One learner said that "I was very confused with a topic and emailed my professor for clarification on an issue. They not only responded with great detail but asked follow-up questions to make absolutely sure I understood."

It is this dialogue with faculty that supports learning and empowers students to push forward in their learning. Feedback is one of many ways that instructors demonstrate that they care for students and can greatly affect outcomes through meaningful discourse. As we have highlighted in this section, students value timely feedback, quality interactions with instructors, and a sense that faculty *truly care* for them. Consistency in the timing and quality of feedback, as well as the clarity of messages received, can have very positive influences on the student's journey. When feedback is detailed and personalized, and shows that instructors care for students and their success, it is valued and makes a difference in how students perceive being cared for through their learning.

Implications

We would like to expand our findings presented to the broader discussion on critical pedagogy and the ethics of care, connecting what our participants said to our experiences as instructors in terms of criticality in education. Critical theory and pedagogy seek to promote learning experiences that are transformative and empowering for both students and teachers. Some of the criticism of critical pedagogy concerns its over-emphasis on abstract notions and that "the discourse of critical pedagogy constructs and sustains its own disciplinary affects . . . which may well be repressive" (Zembylas, 2013, p. 177). As educators, we must be cognizant of the complexity of emotions triggered by the enactment of critical pedagogy and practices and support learners individually and collectively in ways that empower them to think critically about their own realities to effect change not only for themselves but also for the world around them. From the perspectives of Freire (1971) and hooks (2003, 2014), learning communities centred on caring relationships with students who are valued as whole people—taking socio-cultural, -economic, or -political contexts into consideration—can facilitate learning and growth. Combining the principles of ethics of care and critical digital pedagogy theory has the potential to overcome some of these barriers to implementing critical digital pedagogy.

We posit that digital technologies can be used to support critical pedagogy, specifically when it comes to feedback and care, in a variety of ways, as evident in the statements by students in the research presented in this chapter. Some of the key issues addressed in our analysis relate to students' needs in receiving responses to questions, seeing instructors' participation on discussion boards, email responses, announcements, and other communications in a timely fashion. Timeliness was important, but so was the quality and clarity of feedback. All of these aspects can be supported and facilitated using digital technologies with students to lay the foundation for critical pedagogical efforts to succeed and thrive.

We acknowledge the difficulties that many instructors face when attempting to enact more open and flexible pedagogies that address students' needs on both collective and individual levels while conforming to institutional and academic pressures stemming from accreditation requirements and increasing students' achievement on standardized tests (Noddings, 2012). Although this requires a complete re-evaluation of the aims and purposes of education, beyond the control of instructors, there are some pedagogical practices and online design considerations that individual instructors can implement in their classrooms. We are currently rethinking our pedagogical efforts because of what students have experienced and their expressed needs in the semesters taught during the COVID-19 pandemic. Allowing flexibility in due dates, encouraging group efforts for projects (if chosen), and establishing peer help forums are several approaches that we have used.

A pedagogical approach that we have used recently is to remove the standard requirement of one initial post and two responses in a forum activity. A discussion is launched by the instructor with a research article and prompt or case, but students have the choice to reply or build upon the ideas of an existing post. We hope to have students connect on a higher level by crafting thoughtful replies through feedback or referring peers to different ideas and sources, using video responses too if they are comfortable doing so. The goals are to build upon an idea or discussion and to analyze different angles as opposed to presenting a new idea with each thread. We want to build community and encourage dialogic peer-to-peer feedback with this small change to the traditional use of a discussion forum.

We have reflected on the importance of dialogic feedback in creating a climate of care, inclusion, and equity, and our methods are evolving with the fruition of our research and understanding. An online course requires additional time and effort for both instructor and student to engage in meaningful communication that focuses on learning because there is often one-way communication (instructor to students). However, both teachers and students learn and benefit from two-way feedback and communication. For students, this type of relationship with the instructor enhances their sense of ownership of and agency over their learning, and in turn it empowers them to think critically and independently about the world around them. For instructors, this ongoing dialogic relationship with their students allows them to know their students at a deeper level, which enables them to provide genuine and relevant feedback. The dialogic method can help teachers to work toward the ideal of social justice in a course and equity in the online space. If we use feedback and other communication with students as a diagnostic tool for overall course improvement, then we might be able to reduce implicit bias by considering all voices. This is a continuous improvement cycle that can develop a communicable place of learning based upon a healthy feedback loop. The involvement can empower students and prompt constructive change.

How students feel about their learning can matter even more for vulnerable and marginalized students. Many of our students are working parents and community college students living in remote rural areas and juggling life with added COVID-19 pandemic concerns. They are trying their best to complete each semester and the goals that they set. Students contact us about physical and mental health concerns, lack of access to software because of campus closures, and personal struggles that they are facing during the pandemic. They have heightened emotions, and timely and appropriate communication might be the nudge that helps them to continue pursuing their school work and goals. Active listening, dialogue, trust, and openness without judgment (Noddings, 2012) have been the core of our online courses, but those in the semesters during the pandemic have intensified the importance and reconsideration of the methods used.

Equality and empowering students in the online learning space are important considerations in the discussion of digital technologies and the practice of critical pedagogy and care ethics. Future research would be beneficial in identifying modes of feedback and how different modes affect students in digital spaces. In particular, feedback as dialogue allows students to have equitable roles (Carless, 2017; Steen-Utheim & Wittek, 2017) when applied to digital classrooms. We believe that the principles underlying a care ethics approach to learning and education can overcome the challenges facing educators in the enactment of critical theory and pedagogy in a virtual space and enable the creation of a safe environment in which critical education can emerge and take shape.

Key Takeaways

- Feedback received from instructors can significantly influence and shape the student learning experience at an emotional/affective level.
- Dialogic feedback plays an important role in creating a climate of care in an online learning space and supports the enactment of critical pedagogical practice.

- Both teachers and students can benefit from dialogic feedback.
- Digital technologies play a vital role in the provision of feedback from a care ethics perspective.

References

Ajjawi, R., & Boud, D. (2017). Researching feedback dialogue: An interactional analysis approach. *Assessment & Evaluation in Higher Education, 42*(2), 252–265.

Beaumont, C., O'Doherty, M., & Shannon, L. (2011). Reconceptualising assessment feedback: A key to improving student learning? *Studies in Higher Education, 36*(6), 671–687.

Blum, S. D., & Kohn, A. (2020). *Ungrading: Why rating students undermines learning (and what to do instead)*. West Virginia University Press.

Buck, D. (2020). *Crowdsourcing ungrading*. Pressbooks. https://pressbooks .howardcc.edu/ungrading/.

Carless, D. (2017). *Scaling up assessment for learning: Progress and prospects*. In D. Carless, S. M. Bridges, C. Ka Yuk Chan, & R. Glofcheski (Eds.), *Scaling Up Assessment for Learning in Higher Education* (pp. 3–17). Springer.

Equity Unbound. (n.d.). About. http://unboundeq.creativitycourse.org/about.

Evans, C. (2013). Making sense of assessment feedback in higher education. *Review of Educational Research, 83*(1), 70–120.

Flaherty, C. (2019, April 2). When grading less is more. *Inside Higher Ed.* https:// www.insidehighered.com/news/2019/04/02/professors-reflections-their -experiences-ungrading-spark-renewed-interest-student.

Freire, P. (1971). *Pedagogy of the oppressed* (M. Bergman Ramos, Trans.). Continuum.

Freire, P. (2005). The "banking" concept of education. In D. Bartholomae & A. Petrosky (Eds.), *Ways of reading* (8th ed., pp. 256–270). Bedford-St. Martin's.

hooks, b. (2003). *Teaching community: A pedagogy of hope*. Routledge.

hooks, b. (2014). *Teaching to transgress: Education as the practice of freedom*. Routledge.

Lincoln, Y. S. (1985). *Naturalistic inquiry* (Vol. 75). E. G. Guba (Ed.). SAGE.

Noddings, N. (1984). *Caring: A feminine approach to ethics and moral education*. University of California Press.

Noddings, N. (2012). The caring relation in teaching. *Oxford Review of Education, 38*(6), 771–781. https://doi.org/10.1080/03054985.2012.745047.

Pekrun, R., Cusack, A., Murayama, K., Elliot, A. J., & Thomas, K. (2014). The power of anticipated feedback: Effects on students' achievement goals and achievement emotions. *Learning and Instruction, 29,* 115–124.

Robinson, H., Al-Freih, M., & Kilgore, W. (2020). Designing with care: Towards a care-centered model for online learning design. *International Journal of Information and Learning Technology, 37*(3), 99–108.

Ryan, T., & Henderson, M. (2018). Feeling feedback: Students' emotional responses to educator feedback. *Assessment & Evaluation in Higher Education, 43*(6), 880–892.

Shields, S. (2015). "My work is bleeding": Exploring students' emotional responses to first-year assignment feedback. *Teaching in Higher Education, 20*(6), 614–624.

Steen-Utheim, A., & Wittek, A. L. (2017). Dialogic feedback and potentialities for student learning. *Learning, Culture and Social Interaction, 15,* 18–30.

Sackstein, S. (2015). *Hacking assessment: Ten ways to go gradeless in a traditional grades school.* Times 10 Publications.

Zembylas, M. (2013). Critical pedagogy and emotion: Working through "troubled knowledge" in posttraumatic contexts. *Critical Studies in Education, 54*(2), 176–189.

The Panoptic Gaze and the Discourse of Academic Integrity

Matthew M. Acevedo

In this chapter, I critique the discourse of "academic integrity" as popularly used by institutions and individuals in higher education, arguing that the digital technologies used in service of this discourse create antagonistic environments in which students operate constantly in a context of surveillance. As an entry point for analysis, a detailed look at virtual proctoring technologies is useful. Virtual proctoring, in which students are observed by a proctor through a webcam while taking an examination via the internet, is a method of mitigating cheating and "promoting academic integrity" during high-stakes assessments that is steadily growing in popularity in distance education courses, hybrid courses, and traditional in-person courses alike. These online proctoring platforms are offered by a number of corporations, each of which offers a variation on the theme. Typically, in a virtual proctoring setup, the student logs in to the proctoring service's environment, verifies that his or her microphone and webcam are working properly, shows to a live proctor the test-taking environment through the webcam to ensure that no prohibited materials are nearby, authenticates his or her identity through a series of challenge questions pulled from the student's credit background, allows the proctor to take control of his or her computer remotely to close any prohibited programs, and finally begins the exam. Often the student pays a fee directly to the corporation for the privilege of taking the exam under the surveillance of the proctor. During the exam, the proctor monitors a dozen or more test takers at once; the test taker does not know how many students the proctor is watching simultaneously or whether the proctor is watching him or her in particular at any given moment to note a breach of academic integrity. The test taker is compelled, at all times, to act as though the proctor is watching.

This perceived need to watch students while taking tests is invariably tied to the idea of high-stakes assessments of learning: that is, the stakes of a test are so high that students' identities must be verified, and students must be watched to ensure that they do not consult prohibited materials or other people. Students must abide by the expectation of a specific performance privileging memorization, not resourcefulness.

Virtual proctoring, in a literal fashion, recreates the idea of the panopticon, an architectural design for a prison in which cells are arranged on the edges of a circular or semi-circular structure, facing inward toward a central guard tower. From that tower, the overseer can watch any particular cell at any given moment, but an inmate is unable to discern whether the overseer is watching him or her at any given moment to note a breach in the rules of the prison. The inmate is compelled, at all times, to act as though the overseer is watching.

The panopticon was proposed by philosopher Jeremy Bentham in the 18th century as a system of perfect control over prisoners. In *Discipline and Punish: The Birth of the Prison*, Foucault (1977) notes that the major effect of the panopticon is

> to induce in the inmate a state of conscious and permanent visibility that assures the automatic functioning of power. So to arrange things that the surveillance is permanent in its effects, even if it is discontinuous in its action that the perfection of power should tend to render its actual exercise unnecessary; that this architectural apparatus should be a machine for creating and sustaining a power relation independent of the person who exercises it; in short, that the inmates should be caught up in a power situation of which they are themselves the bearers. To achieve this, it is at once too much

and too little that the prisoner should be constantly observed by an inspector: too little, for what matters is that he knows himself to be observed; too much, because he has no need in fact of being so. In view of this, Bentham laid down the principle that power should be visible and unverifiable. Visible: the inmate will constantly have before his eyes the tall outline of the central tower from which he is spied upon. Unverifiable: the inmate must never know whether he is being looked at any one moment; but he must be sure that he may always be so. (p. 201)

In a virtual proctoring environment, the technologies employed are different from the penal version of the panopticon (the webcam and microphone versus the architectural arrangement of the prison), but the relations of disciplinary power are the same. The behaviour of students is controlled and manipulated, via their own webcams, in a type of panoptic gaze.

Foucault (1977) extended the logic of the panopticon to the power relations in contemporary society, suggesting that the panopticon

must be understood as a generalizable model of functioning; a way of defining power relations in terms of the everyday life of men. No doubt Bentham presents it as a particular institution, closed in upon itself. . . . [T]he Panopticon presents a cruel, ingenious cage. The fact that it should have given rise, even in our own time, to so many variations, projected or realized, is evidence of the imaginary intensity that it has possessed for almost two hundred years. But the Panopticon must not be understood as a dream building: it is the diagram of a mechanism of power reduced to its ideal form; its functioning, abstracted from any obstacle, resistance or friction, must be represented as a pure architectural and optical system: it is in fact a figure of political technology that may and must be detached from any specific use. (p. 205)

Foucault's (1977) extrapolation of the panopticon to represent power relations in society writ large applies similarly to the social relations between teachers and students. The literal panopticon of virtual proctoring is only one of *many* examples of the panoptic gaze enabled by digital technologies used in the service of "academic integrity"; plagiarism detection platforms, attention tracking in video-conferencing software, learning analytics, and even learning management systems themselves all facilitate the pervasive surveillance of students in learning contexts.

An approach grounded in critical digital pedagogy offers a perspective different from that of academic integrity. My understanding and usage herein of critical digital pedagogy are influenced by the work of Giroux (2011), who framed critical pedagogy not as a distinct set of teaching strategies but as a way "to examine the various ways in which classrooms too often function as modes of social, political, and cultural reproduction, particularly when the goals of education are defined through the promise of economic growth, job training, and mathematical utility," and, importantly, "how teacher authority might be mobilized against dominant pedagogical practices as part of the practice of freedom" (p. 5). In the context of learning experiences that use digital environments, platforms, and spaces, critical digital pedagogy prompts us to confront, interrogate, and dismantle problematic educational practices, such as the panoptic gaze enabled by surveillance technologies under the guise of integrity.

In this chapter, I examine the discourse of "academic integrity," suggest a new framing of the term, and present practical examples of this tenet based upon my own teaching practice and informed by the emerging tradition of critical digital pedagogy. I must acknowledge that my own perspectives and practices discussed herein are informed by my own experiences teaching in an American higher education context, in which I am relatively fortunate to have some degree of autonomy in my classrooms, whether in-person or online. I understand that others in different regions and teaching contexts might not have the same flexibility to enact certain pedagogies or resist certain institutional policies. I hope that this chapter retains some value for those teachers and serves as a call to action for institutions to offer more support to students and instructors in ways that curtail the use of surveillance technologies while promoting authenticity, creativity, and discovery. Ultimately, in this chapter, I seek to address this question: rather than using digital technologies to reproduce panoptic social relations with our students, how can we, as critical educators, enact a reimagining of academic integrity that responsibilizes us to foster meaningful learning experiences premised on trust and student agency?

The Discourse of Academic Integrity

The ideas of "mitigating cheating" and "preventing academic misconduct" exist within the framework of what is commonly referred to as "academic integrity," used as a shorthand for responsibilizing students to act in ways expected by the institution—to exhibit obedience to authority, particularly in the assessment of learning. Cheating and plagiarism are the two main rallying cries of academic integrity, which signals the officially sanctioned role of students under these headings. The role of faculty members and institutions in the discourse of academic integrity is superficial; they are expected to "promote a culture" of academic integrity at their institutions or "foster environments" in which students can behave correctly.

An exploration of how higher education institutions frame their institutional approaches to academic integrity is informative, and I will draw examples from two institutions that I consider home: the University of Miami (UM), an ostensibly elite private institution where I lead a team of instructional designers and faculty developers, and Florida International University (FIU), the large, Hispanic-serving state school a few miles down the road from UM, where I teach as an adjunct in the Honors College and the Department of Educational Policy Studies.

The University of Miami (2020) has published an eight-page honour code that articulates precise definitions of cheating, plagiarism, collusion, and academic dishonesty and outlines a complex process of investigations, charges, hearings, and sanctions. The purpose of the honour code is couched in the neo-liberal language of competition and presents no responsibility for the instructor other than to indicate requirements:

> These Codes are established for the student body to protect the
> academic integrity of the University of Miami, to encourage con-
> sistent ethical behavior among students, and to foster a climate
> of fair competition. While a student's commitment to honesty
> and personal integrity is assumed and expected, these Codes are

intended to provide an added measure of assurance that, in ful-
filling the University's requirements, the student will never engage
in falsification, plagiarism, or other deception regarding the materials he/she presents. Each student is responsible for completing the
academic requirements of each course in the manner indicated by
the faculty. (para. 6)

FIU takes a different tack. Its academic integrity page features a flashy,
interactive, branching story video with high production values (Florida
International University, 2020). The viewer takes the first-person role of
a student named Jim confronted with three scenarios: the possibility to
reuse a friend's old essay, the chance to use a test answer key found on
the internet, and the opportunity to pay a mysterious, anonymous figure
to take the course. In the video, for each scenario, the viewer can click to
select one of two paths (e.g., reusing the friend's essay or working hard
to do one's own work). The "wrong" path invariably leads to a bad outcome (getting caught through plagiarism detection with the threat of
misconduct proceedings), and the "right" path leads to a favourable
outcome (praise from the teacher and an offer of a recommendation
letter). The ultimate lesson—and the title of the video—are *Learn It to
Earn It*.

The common denominator in these two approaches—and likely those
of the vast majority of institutions—is that the responsibility for maintaining academic integrity invariably falls on students. Meanwhile,
instructors are meant to employ technologies and strategies to mitigate
and catch cheaters—by using invasive proctoring, plagiarism detection
tools, and so on—not to examine their own pedagogical practice. Faculty
members, academicians by trade, have only reactive and superficial roles
within academic integrity.

The scholarly literature on academic integrity and academic misconduct has focused similarly on and responsibilizes only students, commonly
using language that problematically hyperbolizes the issue of cheating.
Singhal (1982, p. 775) suggested that "cheating has become one of the
major problems in education today." Haines et al. (1986, p. 342) referred
to cheating in college as an "epidemic" and, based upon survey research,

found that the underlying factors that prompt cheating include student immaturity, a lack of student commitment to academics, and a "neutralizing attitude" that justifies their immoral actions to themselves and others. Manly et al. (2015, p. 579) suggested that "college faculty members face a continual battle to maintain integrity in their classrooms," employing the language of violence and war in relation to their interactions with students. Some of the more recent literature has increased in nuance, with discipline- and region-specific research studies on cheating or the relationships with more complex variables such as religiosity, but these studies remain similarly problematic, almost inevitably positioning academic integrity in relation and opposition to students' moral failings (Manly et al., 2015; Nelson et al., 2017). Furthermore, the increasing prevalence of online courses and communication technologies in recent decades has certainly exacerbated concerns about cheating (Corrigan-Gibbs et al., 2015; Malesky et al., 2016).

In the institutional and scholarly frames, students are the moral equivalent of criminals. Returning to Foucault (1977), though the panopticon is ostensibly designed to punish criminals and prevent crime, the prison, as he explains, serves to *create* criminals by forcing inmates into meaningless work, subjecting them to the "arbitrary power of administration" (p. 266), creating conditions amenable to the formation of criminal organizations, and releasing them under conditions that leave them unable to find legitimate employment (pp. 264–268). The invasive disciplinary technologies of virtual proctoring and other surveillance technologies in the context of high-stakes assessments do not mitigate cheating as much as they *create* cheaters by shaping environments that bring them into being. In other words, high-stakes assessments—and the pervasiveness of technologies to ensure their "integrity"—cause the circumstances in which students "cheat" by virtue of their implementation. Why would any student cheat if it weren't for the artificially high stakes enacted by the teacher?

One can hardly blame students for cheating in some circumstances. Systems of higher education serve to reproduce social inequalities (Boliver, 2017; Marginson, 2016), and many students enter learning environments at significant structural disadvantages in relation to their peers. When a low-income student who is employed full time to take care of her family and relies on the maintenance of a certain grade point average to keep her scholarship is faced with a high-stakes exam worth the majority of her grade in a class with a faculty member who has no pedagogical preparation, why shouldn't she "cheat" if her future and the well-being of her family depend on her ensuring her grade? We owe it to this hypothetical student—and to all students—to do better.

To clarify, my goal in raising these issues of high-stakes assessments and cheating is not to blame or vilify individual teachers but to problematize certain pedagogical practices related to popular understandings of academic integrity as well as to foreground other practices that might exist beyond the boundaries of some teachers' pedagogical paradigms. In the next section, I suggest an alternative conceptualization of academic integrity, one that transfers the responsibilization for abiding by academic integrity to instructors and frames students not as the perpetrators of crime but as the casualties of high-stakes environments.

Reimagining Academic Integrity

An approach to working with students grounded in critical digital pedagogy necessitates an alternative to the problematic discourse of academic integrity. In keeping with the basic idea of "integrity" as a term meaning "doing the right thing," this alternative framing of academic integrity transfers the responsibilization for its creation and maintenance from students to teachers. Teaching faculty, as the primary conduits of power and the bearers of authority in academic environments, should imagine how *they* might uphold academic integrity—should *do the right thing* in academic contexts—by designing learning environments that do not cause the creation of cheaters.

The panoptic gaze imbued in the traditional discourse of academic integrity is typically realized through high-stakes testing (which can be proctored and surveilled) or closed-ended written assignment prompts (which can be processed through a corporate database of the products of other students' unpaid labour for quantitative machine comparison). A reimagined conceptualization of academic integrity incorporates forms of teaching that privilege authentic creation and critical thinking rather than high-stakes testing. Furthermore, the traditional understanding of academic integrity creates false binaries: a given student is labelled honest or dishonest, a scholar, or a cheater. In contrast, this reconceptualization of academic integrity, upheld by teachers, is not a binary but an ideal. We must strive—continually—to foster learning environments of integrity for our students.

In the sections that follow, I outline four possibilities—by no means an exhaustive list—that college teachers might consider in the pursuit of academic integrity: *privileging learning over grades, honouring a plurality of experiences, embracing open-endedness,* and *enabling students as creators.* These are not intended to be specific strategies as much as they are philosophical considerations, though their translation to lessons, activities, and general classroom approaches is possible across subjects and disciplines. However, to better illustrate the practical potential of these considerations, I relate my own efforts in striving for this new conceptualization of academic integrity, drawing from my own experiences as an educator and professional faculty developer. I make no claim of being an exemplar and render myself open to critique and improvement, but I hope that a discussion of the ideas in the previous section is actualized in a real-life university class.

At the FIU Honors College, I teach a fully online seminar course entitled "Urban Inequality and HBO's *The Wire,*" which uses the television program widely lauded for its gritty and realistic portrayal of urban crime and policing as well as its commentary on institutional dysfunction. Also using academic journal articles and other resources, students in this class explore issues related to race, class, policing, poverty and economic inequality, and neo-liberalism; it is from this particular class that I will share specific examples of my own teaching approach.

Privileging Learning over Grades

As discussed, the high-stakes context of assessments is one reason that some students feel compelled to "cheat." The goal of these students is presumably to obtain good marks, which will enhance their overall course grades, their transcripts, and their grade point averages (and then career prospects and so on). In these environments, the process of teaching and learning is purely transactional. As Bowles and Gintis (1977) suggested, a correspondence exists between the school environment and the social relations of capitalism: teachers are akin to the bosses of a company, and students are the workers, trading their labour for currency—in this case, that of grades.

The system of grading and grades, now seemingly unassailable in contemporary higher education, shifts the purpose of the classroom (whether in-person or online) from learning to the achievement of grades, which are not necessarily equivalent. Grades and high-stakes assessments are also drivers of student anxiety, which has a self-defeating effect on academic performance (Barrows et al., 2013; Numan, 2017). But what would our classes look like without grades, in which the goal is learning, discovery, or even occasional epiphany?

Ungrading is an increasingly popular (but still relatively uncommon) approach to teaching and assessment in which traditional letter grades are abandoned in lieu of detailed, individualized, narrative feedback (Blum, 2017; Stommel, 2017). This strategy acknowledges the problematic nature of grades, including their poor fit in providing feedback and their role in causing anxiety. Productive alternatives to assigning a letter grade include providing input and constructive critique, asking follow-up questions, sharing one's own experiences and perspectives, and starting a conversation.

An ungrading approach works well with a revise and resubmit protocol. Ultimately, learning is a process, not a product. Why should anything be perfect the first time, especially from non-experts and neophytes? Students are better than we might think at receiving input and improving projects, and surely this approach leads to a more meaningful and productive learning experience than high-stakes assessments.

I practise ungrading in my class, providing detailed and personalized feedback on every student submission. Logistically, in Canvas, FIU's course management system, I achieve this through the comments feature on assignments. In addition to narrative feedback and despite ungrading, I do use Canvas's grading options of "complete" and "incomplete."

Complete is shorthand to indicate my sense that a student's submission addresses all of the prompts and is suitably well thought out and justified. Incomplete is an invitation to the student to revise and resubmit the assignment based on feedback. Students are encouraged to incorporate their own opinions, perspectives, and experiences as they relate to any given assignment as well as to indicate to me what was confusing or where they struggled. Since I am required to submit a final grade to the institution for each student, I ask my students at the end of each semester what grade they think I should enter on their behalf with a brief reflection on their engagement with the class. Many students report an initial uneasiness with this approach, but most indicate, by the end of the term, a feeling of having a pressure removed and a newfound freedom to express their perspectives and their processes of struggling with difficult material without fear of penalty or judgment.

Honouring a Plurality of Experience

Both the preparation for and the auditing of teaching with digital platforms (e.g., Quality Matters) emphasize the display to students of measurable behavioural learning objectives (Acevedo, 2019a, 2019b): that is, what they should "be able to do" as a result of instruction. Although our students come to us from all walks of life and different sorts of backgrounds with different goals, expectations, fears, and hopes, these standardized learning objectives assume that all of our students represent a singular form and funnel them into a generic educational experience. The panoptic technologies used in the pursuit of "maintaining academic integrity" perpetuate and reproduce this genericism.

Honouring a plurality of experience means acknowledging and embracing the fact that each student will engage in her or his own experience. Different aspects of any given course or lesson will resonate differently with students. Individual students will struggle with particular aspects. Four or five years after their time with you, students will remember something unique that stood out to them. Critical digital pedagogy offers us the ability to embrace the plurality of experience; students can and should be afforded the space to learn in different ways, times, and places and to express their understanding of the material in ways that resonate with them.

My class on *The Wire* culminates with a project in which I ask my students to synthesize themes from the class. In the guidelines that I provide to the students, I try to create a balance between providing helpful guidance and allowing space for creativity, expression, synthesis, and dissent. As with the other assignments in the class, I do not "grade" these projects or use rubrics; I position myself not as an evaluator of their work but as a supporter of their journey by elevating guidance over critique.

For this project, I attempt to honour a plurality of experience by creating space for students who prefer to engage creatively (multimedia production, fiction writing) and those who prefer to engage through more traditional academic ways (book reviews, position papers). Some students choose the "negotiated project," in which *they* tell *me* how they want to demonstrate their engagement with the issues that we tackle in class. There is no particular way that I expect the topics and themes that we cover to resonate with my students, so there is no single way that I expect them to demonstrate their engagement with these ideas.

Embracing Open-Endedness

In high-stakes assessments such as examinations, closed-ended prompts are the norm. Tests often employ multiple choice or short answer questions; even essay prompts commonly result in nearly identical responses with changes only in wording, prose, or organization. Similarly, rubrics for papers or projects, often praised for their utility in setting clear expectations and providing a veneer of objectivity to a purely subjective form, foreclose opportunities for what students can and should produce by setting more boundaries than guidelines.

The world that we want to prepare our students for is much less clearcut. If we expect them to leave us with the ability to think critically and solve complex problems, then we should create the opportunities for them to learn these skills. Part of this is embracing the open-mindedness of the world by incorporating open-mindedness in our teaching. Our assignment prompts, guiding questions, conversation starters, and even feedback methods should encourage our students to think in divergent, critical ways and respond with different—and differently correct—answers (for more on types of feedback, see Chapter 2 of this volume). These opportunities could prompt students to reflect on their own lives and experiences as they relate to the material, to interrogate their own biases and assumptions, to make judgments and provide critiques, to seek different viewpoints, and to engage in their communities. Privileging open-mindedness is more than just "moving up," Bloom's overused and often misunderstood taxonomy of learning; it is a matter of unpacking what we value and our expectations of our students as democratic citizens.

In my class on *The Wire*, many of the activities involve reflective writing that synthesizes journal articles with what students have watched in the show. For example, one of the major themes in the show is the War on Drugs. I assign an article entitled "Race, Crime and the Pool of Surplus Criminality: Or Why the War on Drugs Was a War on Blacks" (Nunn, 2002), which extends Marx's theory of surplus labour to argue that black Americans have been disproportionately targeted in the War on Drugs. In a reflective writing prompt, I ask students to evaluate this argument, using references to the show and to real life. This sort of evaluative thinking in relation to potentially divisive and controversial topics is a notable example of embracing open-endedness.

Enabling Students as Creators

Rather than *verify* students' learning through high-stakes assessments, we should give students the opportunity to *express* their learning through acts of creation. As designers of learning environments in which we strive for academic integrity, it is our responsibility to activate students' potential as creators by providing them with opportunities for expression. These are also valuable points at which students can relate topics from the class to their own experiences, lives, and perspectives. With a grounding in critical digital pedagogy, there are seemingly innumerable ways that digital technologies can facilitate creation: podcast-style audio projects, documentary or narrative videos, interactive presentations, websites, and digital documents. Creative opportunities are also collaborative opportunities. Collaborative assignments can lead to greater academic achievement and more positive attitudes toward learning (Springer et al., 1999; Terenzini et al., 2001). Students can work together, leveraging each individual's unique skills and talents, toward the generation of creative products that express analysis, synthesis, and evaluation of topics and issues related to their learning experiences.

In the final project for my class on *The Wire*, the many different engagement options are intended to elevate students' position as creators. Some options involve the use of multimedia and digital tools, whereas others are more traditionally "scholarly" in the form of written work. This flexibility in giving students agency over their creations has led to an amazing array of projects, from original empirical survey research on peers' perspectives on various social issues, to compelling and entertaining podcast-style audio productions, to an original video documentary by an international student who spent time with a police squad in Brazil. Every time I teach I am astounded at the calibre of these projects as well as their creativity, maturity, and nuance. As a teacher, there is no more rewarding result than to learn from my students, and this happens often as I engage with their work.

Conclusion

Critical digital pedagogy challenges us to consider "how teacher authority might be mobilized against dominant pedagogical practices as part of the practice of freedom" (Giroux, 2011, p. 5), and as critical educators we have an opportunity to imagine new possibilities for creating environments that promote discovery, divergent thinking, skepticism, resourcefulness, and creativity. This entails rejecting the traditional discourse of academic integrity that activates technologies that create and reproduce a panoptic gaze premised on distrust and surveillance. Possible avenues for reimagining academic integrity include privileging learning over grades, honouring various experiences, embracing open-endedness, and enabling students as creators by leveraging creative technologies. Although I believe that these strategies transcend geographic location, cultural setting, and particular subject matter, critical educators should consider their own conceptualization of what striving for academic integrity, or "doing the right thing," means for their own contexts and goals.

Key Takeaways

- Digital technologies used in the service of "promoting" academic integrity create and reproduce a panoptic gaze premised on distrust and surveillance.
- The discourse of academic integrity unfairly responsibilizes students for maintaining academic integrity in high-stakes contexts that promote lower-order thinking over resourcefulness and authenticity.
- Academic integrity can and should be reimagined to responsibilize teachers to create learning environments that promote creativity, expression, synthesis, and dissent.
- An approach grounded in critical digital pedagogy provides a space for this reimagining by privileging learning over grades, honouring a plurality of experience, embracing open-endedness, and enabling students as creators.

References

Acevedo, M. M. (2019a). The autopsy of quality in online higher education. *Philosophy and Theory in Higher Education, 1*(2), 75–93.

Acevedo, M. M. (2019b). *Auditing quality: A critical exploration of faculty members' experiences with Quality Matters* [Doctoral dissertation, Florida International University].

Barrows, J., Dunn, S., & Lloyd, C. A. (2013). Anxiety, self-efficacy, and college exam grades. *Universal Journal of Educational Research, 1*(3), 204–208.

Blum, S. D. (2017, November 14). The significant learning benefits of getting rid of grades. *Inside Higher Ed*. https://www.insidehighered.com/advice/2017/11/14/significant-learning-benefits-getting-rid-grades-essay.

Boliver, V. (2017). Misplaced optimism: How higher education reproduces rather than reduces social inequality. *British Journal of Sociology of Education, 38*(3), 423–432.

Bowles, S., & Gintis, H. (1977). *Schooling in capitalist America: Educational reform and the contradictions of economic life*. Basic Books.

Corrigan-Gibbs, H., Gupta, N., Northcutt, C., Cutrell, E., & Thies, W. (2015). Deterring cheating in online environments. *ACM Transactions on Computer-Human Interaction (TOCHI), 22*(6), 1–23.

Foucault, M. (1977). *Discipline and punish: The birth of the prison.* Vintage.

Giroux, H. A. (2011). *On critical pedagogy.* Continuum.

Haines, V. J., Diekhoff, G. M., LaBeff, E. E., & Clark, R. E. (1986). College cheating: Immaturity, lack of commitment, and the neutralizing attitude. *Research in Higher Education, 25*(4), 342–354.

Malesky, L. A., Baley, J., & Crow, R. (2016). Academic dishonesty: Assessing the threat of cheating companies to online education. *College Teaching, 64*(4), 178–183.

Manly, T. S., Leonard, L. N., & Riemenschneider, C. K. (2015). Academic integrity in the information age: Virtues of respect and responsibility. *Journal of Business Ethics, 127*(3), 579–590.

Marginson, S. (2016). The worldwide trend to high participation higher education: Dynamics of social stratification in inclusive systems. *Higher Education, 72*(4), 413–434.

Nelson, M. F., James, M. S., Miles, A., Morrell, D. L., & Sledge, S. (2017). Academic integrity of millennials: The impact of religion and spirituality. *Ethics & Behavior, 27*(5), 385–400.

Numan, A. (2017). Test-anxiety-provoking stimuli among undergraduate students. *Journal of behavioural sciences, 27*(1), 1–20.

Nunn, K. B. (2002). Race, crime and the pool of surplus criminality: Or why the war on drugs was a war on blacks. *Journal of Gender, Race & Justice, 6*, 381–445.

Singhal, A. C. (1982). Factors in students' dishonesty. *Psychological Reports, 51*(3), 775–780.

Springer, L., Stanne, M. E., & Donovan, S. S. (1999). Effects of small-group learning on undergraduates in science, mathematics, engineering, and technology: A meta-analysis. *Review of Educational Research, 69*(1), 21–51.

Stommel, J. (2017, October 26). Why I don't grade. https://www.jessestommel.com/why-i-dont-grade/.

Terenzini, P. T., Cabrera, A. F., Colbeck, C. L., Parente, J. M., & Bjorklund, S. A. (2001). Collaborative learning vs. lecture/discussion: Students' reported learning gains. *Journal of Engineering Education, 90*(1), 123–130.

University of Miami. (2020, February 19). Honor Code. https://doso.studentaffairs.miami.edu/honor-council/honor-code/index.html.

"Too Many Man"?

Using Digital Technology to Develop Critical Media Literacy and Foster Classroom Discourse on Gender and Sexuality

Alex de Lacey

In 2007, James Alexander, then the president of the National Union of Students in the United Kingdom, addressed a delegation in Scotland. Alexander was strident about the need for undergraduate involvement with syllabus construction, stating that "we must engage with students in a richer, more deliberate way at the course level that acknowledges their right . . . to participate in the development and design of their own curriculum." This statement, whether Alexander was aware of it or not, signalled a policy alignment for the National Union of Students with an already fervent school of thought, credited to Paulo Freire (1972) and calcified as critical pedagogy. Critical pedagogy's political incentive highlights the importance of world making through learning, with a view toward addressing issues of systemic racism, sexism, and ableism that pervade both society and the classroom, through empowering student contributions.

I teach popular music, and in my discipline critical pedagogy has become prized in recent years, with many citing music's transformative potential when addressing social issues owing to its embeddedness within everyday cultural practice (Abrahams, 2005; Karvelis, 2018). Notably, there has been an attentiveness to the enabling power of hip-hop (Abramo, 2011; Keyes, 2002).

Within the British setting, I have been trying to find ways to teach curriculums that are receptive to both my student base at Goldsmiths College and the locale in which I teach. Studies of local hip-hop practice can be useful, and students can resonate with artists' lived experiences. For Muñoz-Laboy et al. (2007), ethnographic research on New York's club scene helped them to understand *gender minority script* within hip-hop, and Tobias (2014, p. 52) noted the "importance of local context in the ways young people engage with, interpret, and make meaning of Hip Hop music."

Goldsmiths is located in New Cross, part of the London Borough of Lewisham. According to recent projections, its population will be majority BAME (black, Asian, and minority ethnic) by 2036 (GLA Intelligence, 2015) (on closing the BAME attainment gap, see Chapter 9 of this volume). Although the popular music syllabus at Goldsmiths is wide ranging, coverage of local practice among its black population is under-represented, and this is true for many popular music programs across the United Kingdom. Furthermore, gender equity is lacking in the archive, on both sides of the Atlantic, particularly with respect to the documentation of black female practice: Farmer (2018), for example, notes how black women feel "out of place in the [US] archive," and Bryan et al.'s (2018) *The Heart of the Race: Black Women's Lives in Britain* acts as a "powerful corrective" contra their erasure from British history (Akpan, 2019).

As a DJ of grime music (a black British performance form originating in London at the turn of the millennium), I saw an opportunity to create a curriculum that brokered complex issues of authenticity, race, and gender in popular music, using grime as a critical lens and an "enabling text" (Tatum, 2009, p. 2). By using a form familiar to my student base, and more reflective of the locale in which I taught, my aim was to cover advanced theoretical material, through aligning familiar aspects of quotidian music making, and co-created content, with challenging concepts as a means to break down the impasse between theory and practice. Using grime music as a lens for these discussions, I hoped to develop students' critical media literacy skills[1] through addressing reductive readings of gender and essentialized representations of black creative practice.

It is important to stress that, though the activity that I describe in this chapter was a small part of my wider pedagogical practice, it shows how co-creation of material—through technological means or otherwise—can not only develop participants' skill sets but also foster a more equitable classroom environment. Critical pedagogy undergirds my decision making, and commitment to the student voice is at the forefront of my approach. With the caveat that this intervention is a modest one, there are three key outcomes that I will endeavour to show in this chapter.

First, I will demonstrate how a synthesis of an accessible digital interface that offers anonymous contributions helps to facilitate and encourage student engagement and break down archetypal patterns of domination. Although technologies are far from perfect, they can be used productively as part of a multi-modal approach to critical pedagogy. Second, I will show how the incorporation of student examples into class sessions enables the co-construction of syllabus material and facilitates the collective interrogation of media sources. During my period of investigation, this approach brought forth fervent classroom discourse, instances of reciprocal peer learning, and means to critique reductive representations of black creative endeavour. And third, I will present the implications of the study, both for the student body and for future critical pedagogical practice that utilizes the digital as part of a larger commitment to equitable teaching within higher education.

A Life of Grime: Critical Digital Pedagogy in Popular Music

Advanced Popular Music Studies (APMS) is a third-year elective undergraduate module that I coordinated. This module was designed to fit with the specialism of the lecturer who taught it each year, affording relative freedom with respect to the syllabus as long as content was constructively aligned with the course's core learning outcomes. I therefore saw this as an opportunity to interface more concertedly with the student cohort. As long as their work was rigorous and demonstrated an understanding of wider issues of contemporary popular practice, the subject matter—and examples utilized—could converge more readily with students' interests and social justice themes.

Grime music is well suited for such discussions. The commercial resurgence of grime in the 2010s prompted much popular critical commentary as well as a growing amount of academic work. Grime has been positioned in these discourses in a manner similar to much writing on popular music: it has been tied to a particular place and set of social circumstances (East London and black British working-class men), associated with a few leading figures (Dizzee Rascal, Skepta, Stormzy), and ascribed an increasingly fixed kind of social significance. An engagement with grime, then, might enable students both to explore and to critique these issues, consequently developing their critical media literacy skills. Hall (2017, p. 344) has noted how "hip-hop-based curricular interventions are driven by a desire to teach critical media literacy and foster critical consciousness, especially as they intersect around racial identity politics." This is also true for grime.

The genre is subject to racialized popular writing and censorship through regressive social policy (see Riley, 2017). Media publications often resort to somatic readings of grime performance, rendering it as a priori primitive. In 2004, for example, a journalist writing for a prominent newspaper in the United Kingdom compared grime performance to "relentless assault and battery" (Campion). For journalist Simon Reynolds, East London MC Crazy Titch "hoarsely holler[ed]" down the microphone (2007, p. 377). These ascriptions are both complicit with prior racialized writing on Afrodiasporic practice such as reggae and hip-hop and demonstrate an enduring racism within writing that needs to be addressed (see Gilroy, 2002). Therefore, through brokering these tensions and issues, students hopefully would develop a more nuanced approach to black musical practice and refine their critical media literacy skills.

This module that I taught was intended to interrogate representations of gender and sexuality within popular music. Grime music—and hip-hop more broadly—have problematic relationships with the representation of women. By working with audiovisual examples throughout the course, I intended to address hypermasculinity within the form, question how a "politics of respectability" is imposed on black musical styles (in ways that other forms are not subjected to), and foreground female and LGBTQIA+ practice[2] within the form (Brooks-Higginbotham, 1993).

Adopting an equitable agenda that exhibits a focus on female and LGBTQIA+ practice can be an act of world making by dislodging a hegemonic masculine understanding of hip-hop and grime practice. Issues of hypermasculine posturing are covered in Jeffrey Boakye's *Hold Tight: Black Masculinity, Millennials and the Meaning of Grime* but made manifest in creative practice. Boakye (2017, p. 103) examines fifty tracks from grime's emergent canon, noting how a large majority of work "endors[es] misogyny as a by-product of asserting their masculinity [through] objectifying women to be won like a trophy or fixed like a problem." Furthermore, North London grime collective Boy Better Know's single "Too Many Man" (2014) mockingly addresses gender disparity in the club at grime events. The track's sardonic hook "we need some more girls in here, there's too many man," does not call for greater representation. Rather, it rearticulates the male gaze, presenting women as sex objects.

This module, through both addressing aspects of grime that engage with misogynoir and hypermasculinity and celebrating the work of female and LGBTQIA+ artists in grime, employed grime as a critical lens to deliver a full appraisal and engage students with complex discussions on gender and sexuality in popular music.

Matrices of Domination: Foregrounding the Student Voice Using Digital Technology

In addition to using grime as a critical lens and an "enabling text" for these sorts of discussions, I wanted to foreground the student voice as part of a critical digital pedagogical framework. Grime music's commercial resurgence meant that the form was common parlance for my cohort, and there was real scope for students' contributions to influence course content as the module progressed.

Incorporating technology as part of teaching should not be seen as arbitrary or an afterthought. My key concern was to locate how students could collaborate and contribute without rearticulating patterns of dominant behaviour. This is where the digital becomes valuable. In her work on *radical musicking* and the rise of critical pedagogy within a music set-ting, Juliet Hess (2017) highlights tensions in the classroom that can arise from adopting a critical pedagogical framework. With the fundamental aim to democratize the classroom, there is a danger that—by asking for students' contributions—the same, often white male, voices are heard again and again (p. 178).

For Patricia Hill Collins (2000), there exists a *matrix of domination* in the classroom: certain students have privilege over others because of factors such as race, gender, and class. Recognizing this and dismantling, rather than reinscribing, the dominant is a crucial consideration. One way that I addressed this in my teaching is through anonymous digital contributions, which to some extent absolved positionality. And though I continue to use a wide array of digital technology in teaching, issues of anonymity were assuaged in this instance through the employment of a collaborative post-it tool, or an online sandpit, named Padlet.

Padlet and similar tools are now used in a number of educational circumstances, including music (Dunbar, 2017, p. 27; Sundararajan & Maquivar, 2017). In my case, Padlet acted as a supplement to the univer-sity's virtual learning environment. Prior to the commencement of the 10-week APMS course, I set up Padlet with columns for each week of the teaching session and a brief selection of resources. From that point onward, I gradually introduced ideas and encouraged contributions (see Figure 4.1). Rather than students putting up their hands, being chosen on the spot in class, or reinscribing patterns of domination, students could present their ideas without fear of judgment from peers or the "profes-sorial gaze." I aimed to move outside the institutional glare and empower all students to guide progression of the class and its content.

Addressing Misogynoir and Developing Critical Media Literacy

After a number of weeks working informally with Padlet in the class-room, I set my first instructional task using it. This task formed part of week 6's session on gender and sexuality. There were a couple of reasons that I chose this session to ask students to use Padlet actively (rather than rely on informal suggestions). First, grime's problematic relationship

Figure 4.1.

Screenshot from the Padlet used in Advanced Popular Music Studies.

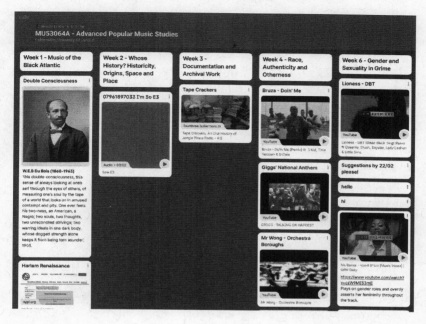

with hypermasculinity (addressed above) offered grounds to interrogate these issues head on. Second, I wanted to give students space in which to become acclimatized to Padlet. Imposing a new system too quickly can be construed as unwelcoming. Rather, I hoped that Padlet would be a collaborative, student-led space. By week 6, students had become free flowing with suggestions, and I thought that we were in a position of trust that meant there would be a number of really interesting contributions.

Before the session, I asked students to suggest ideas on Padlet, from any form of grime practice that broadly related to articulations of gender and/or sexuality. I deliberately left this open so that there would be scope to critique hypermasculine assertions alongside the practice of female, non-binary, and LGBTQIA+ grime MCs. Nearly half of the students put forward suggestions on Padlet, and the class had its highest attendance (92%) since the introductory lecture of the module. This was perhaps because students had a vested interest in the material on show (a factor facilitated by the anonymous posting through Padlet).

The in-person session started with a lecture that provided theoretical grounding, followed by a seminar-style discussion of three musical examples, the latter two selected by students: *Dead Black Ting* by Lioness, *Hood B*tch* by South London rapper Ms Banks, and *Hoe Diaries* by gay femme MC Karnage Kills. Critical to this discussion was the nature of the analysis undertaken as a group. For Karvelis (2018, p. 47), music videos offer an "unparalleled glimpse into realities." Here I diverged from this unexacting approach and encouraged students to look at the deliberated meaning making at work in the performance and its visual representation. Part of engaging with the digital extends to having a firm pedagogical framework that augments the cohort's critical media literacy. In doing so, I encouraged the cohort to move into a complex discussion of the expectations and taxonomies imposed on non-male hip-hop practice and how artists have counteracted these representations, referring to Missy Elliot as a disrupter of expectations of how women should "perform correctly" in hip-hop (Lane, 2011, p. 775; White, 2013). Here, then, we were not only analyzing songs as a group but also critiquing artists' performativity, visual practice, and normative gender expectations.

The first student example discussed was *Hood B*tch* by Ms Banks (GRM Daily 2019), which repurposes hypermasculine tropes within her context as a rapper. Aside from the song's producers, Splurgeboys, the only men who feature in the video occupy a subservient role: either raining plaudits on Banks as she walks down a makeshift catwalk or handing over money to Banks at gunpoint in a foiled drug deal. These aspects are furthered by the sexual autonomy asserted in her lyrical content: in the first verse, men are always on "her dick"; later she raps that she doesn't "need dick I have my own toy" before the sound of a vibrator cuts through the mix. This toying with male subjectivity recalls Perry's (1995, p. 526) work, which notes how female MCs "enter the male body, generally as a metaphor for their strength and power, but also to expand self-definition." Furthermore, Banks embraces derogatory terminology, such as "b*tch," subverting its meaning as an act of reclamation, much like its usage by Juice Crew's Roxxane Shanté and MC Lyte (Keyes, 2002, p. 200). In addressing the inversion of gender stereotypes by Banks, students were able to engage fully in critical media literacy (as per the definition of Tobias, 2014), observing Banks's confounding of normative expectations and hegemonic power relationships.

In the subsequent class discussion, we continued to speak about visual representation, lyrical content, and performativity. One student brought up Banks's use of "ratchet"—a term derived from Louisianan creole for "wretched"—as an empowering term, and the significance of her gold "grille" of teeth, with reference to St. Louis rapper Nelly's 2005 hit "Grillz." We then spent a substantial portion of the discussion going through these themes as a group.

One moment in particular was challenging yet led to a beneficial outcome. A male student, typically outspoken in class, voiced a regressive opinion challenged by nearly all other members of the cohort. This moment, which had the potential to be fractious, actually saw the class collaborate, enter into fervent discourse (without my interjection as lecturer), and challenge this student's position. In this instance, the tools were at hand for the students through both theoretical grounding and practical application. Its success was crucially augmented by empowering students to speak. Their suggestions through Padlet were legitimised by being used as part of course material, and the class felt confident enough to challenge a base-level reading of femininity and move productively toward a resolution.

This was evident in feedback from students at the end of the course. One student stated that "I enjoyed the group discussion that came from this. It also challenged me to do my own research, so I could share something on the Padlet." Another student commented that "it was nice to have input into the lecture, . . . made it a more interactive session." A third student was disappointed about not contributing: "I didn't end up posting anything, and I wish that I had done after seeing how people's posts were discussed in class." These reflections and the outcome in the session indicate both the substantial engagement of all students and the enlivening classroom discourse that arose from examining these examples, with peers questioning another student's reductive readings of femininity.

The track *Hoe Diaries* by Karnage Kills, the second student-chosen example used in the session, was also of particular interest. The track spoke evocatively to Kills's positionality as a gay femme MC in the grime scene while celebrating his sexuality. The following discussion helped to consolidate the set reading from Rinaldo Walcott (2013) on heteronormativity and how hip-hop performance—and hip-hop pedagogy—can challenge and overcome stereotypes. Later that week a student anonymously posted an interview with Kills that went into greater depth about his approach as an artist, and another student based the final assessment on LGBTQIA+ practice.

Pedagogical Praxis: Implications and Moving Forward

The activity that I have described here carries wider implications for critical pedagogy not only in music but also in other fields seeking to employ digital technologies. First, it has shown how the combination of digital tools and a critical pedagogical frame enabled me to create a collaborative space that fostered student contributions and remedied patterns of domination and fear of the professorial gaze that pervade the typical classroom environment. Students' contributions made me realize their wealth of knowledge. Their suggestions were provocative, relevant, and unfamiliar to me.

Second, I found value in teaching curriculums receptive to the student base in the locale where I teach. Although grime is predominantly popular in the United Kingdom, a similar approach could be employed in other locations: for example, *gqom* in Durban, *drill* in Chicago, or *bongo flava* in Dar Es Salaam. With a local genre as a critical lens through which to teach complex issues, students were able to interrogate normative representations of gender, sexuality, and race because of their familiarity with the content on show. Developing critical media literacy skills with examples from an abstracted social milieu can be challenging. A move toward localized and student-led content offers a "way in" to critique and comment on wider issues of power, race, and hegemonic constructions of gender.

Third, there exists a longer-term, transformative need for critical digital pedagogy to be fully realized within an educational setting that employs relatable material from local contexts as teaching tools. As Bali (2014, p. 4) notes, "each [student] has valuable experience from their own context to bring to the classroom," and we must continue to take steps toward realizing the value of students' ideas and experiences through digital means or otherwise. If we are to move from word to world making, in a shift from theorizing to implementing practical changes, then a more concerted effort needs to be made to ensure student engagement and involvement with syllabus construction across the board rather than in isolated sessions as part of elective modules.

Fourth, issues of positionality must be considered. As Hess (2017) pointed out, there is a danger that an educator's own privilege—for example, my privilege as a white male teaching within a critical digital pedagogical framework—can affect the learning process. Although my initial use of Padlet in the classroom was part of a continued commitment to the student voice, and the recognition of black creative practice in what are still majority white spaces, limitations still exist. Dominant patterns can still be rearticulated in the classroom itself, and a white scholar's presence at the front of the class—irrespective of the potentialities of technology—can perpetuate inequity. Academic institutions must challenge "dominant paradigms" and build toward a more representative environment in which to learn and flourish. Although I have shown in this chapter how critical pedagogy in a hybrid context can foster enlivening classroom discourse and develop critical media literacy, further steps must be taken. Digital technologies should therefore be used *in conjunction with* equitable hiring, teaching, and learning practices to substantiate real and considered change.

Key Takeaways

- There is a need for critical digital pedagogy to be fully realized within an educational setting that employs relatable material. Using local musical forms as a critical lens encourages participation and allows students to develop their critical media literacy skills.
- Co-creation of content brings forth fervent classroom discourse and instances of reciprocal peer learning.

- Anonymous contributions help to facilitate and encourage student engagement with challenging theoretical issues and break down patterns of domination in the classroom.
- Digital technologies should be used in conjunction with equitable practices to substantiate real and considered change in higher education.

Notes

1   In this chapter, I use "critical media literacy" as Evan Tobias (2014, p. 67) employs the term in his work on hip-hop, in which it "helps students unpack taken for granted assumptions and critique normative representations of human experience . . . taking into account issues of power, ideology, representation and voice."
2   LGBTQIA+ is an inclusive acronym for people who identify as lesbian, gay, bisexual, transgender, queer, intersex, or asexual. The + accounts for others who are gender non-conforming and might not align fully with any of these terms.

References

Abrahams, F. (2005). The application of critical pedagogy to music teaching and learning: A literature review. *Update: Applications of Research in Music Education, 23*(2), 12–22. https://doi.org/10.1177/87551233050230020103.

Abramo, J. M. (2011). Queering informal pedagogy: Sexuality and popular music in school. *Music Education Research, 13*(4), 465–477. https://doi.org/10.1080/14613808.2011.632084.

Akpan, P. (2019). How the stories of black women in the UK are being reclaimed. *Refinery29*. https://www.refinery29.com/en-gb/black-women-history-uk.

Alexander, J. (2007). Keynote address, Engaging Students in Higher Education Conference, Harrogate, Yorkshire, UK.

Bali, M. (2014, September 9). Critical pedagogy: Intentions and realities. *Hybrid Pedagogy*. http://hybridpedagogy.org/critical-pedagogy-intentions-realities/.

BBC Radio 1 Xtra. (2014). Boy Better Know—*Too Many Man* at 1 Xtra Live 2014 [Video]. *YouTube*. https://www.youtube.com/watch?v=Cs5ztSClRPw.

Hall, H. B. (2017). Deeper than rap: Expanding conceptions of hip-hop culture and pedagogy in the English language arts classroom. *Research in the Teaching of English, 51*(2), 341–50.

Boakye, J. (2017). *Hold tight: Black masculinity, millennials and the meaning of grime*. Influx Press.

Bryan, B., Dadzie, S., & Scafe, S. (2018). *The heart of the race: Black women's lives in Britain*. Verso.

Campion, C. (2004, May 23). Inside grime. *The Guardian*. https://www .theguardian.com/arts/features/story/0,,1223537,00.html.

Collins, P. H. (2000). *Black feminist thought: Knowledge, consciousness, and the politics of empowerment*. Routledge.

Dunbar, L. (2017). Using Padlet to increase student interaction with music concepts. *General Music Today, 30*(3), 26–29. https://doi.org/10.1177/ 1048371316687076.

Farmer, A. (2018). In search of the black women's history archive. *Modern American History*, 1(2), 289–293. https://doi.org/10.1017/mah.2018.4.

Freire, P. (1972). *Pedagogy of the oppressed*. Penguin.

Gilroy, P. (2002). *There ain't no black in the Union Jack*. Routledge.

GLA Intelligence. (2015, November). *2014 round ethnic group population projections*. https://londondatastore-upload.s3.amazonaws.com/Demography/ document_archive/update_2014rnd_ethnic_group_results.pdf.

GRM Daily. (2018, May 6). Lioness—*DBT (Dead Black Ting) Remix ft Queenie, Stush, Shystie, Lady Leshurr & Little Simz* [Video]. *YouTube*. https://www .youtube.com/watch?v=O6hXSS01pYY.

GRM Daily. (2019, January 24). Ms Banks—*Hood B*tch* [Video]. *YouTube*. https:// www.youtube.com/watch?v=czW9ME53mlI.

Hess, J. (2017). Critiquing the critical: The casualties and paradoxes of critical pedagogy in music education. *Philosophy of Music Education Review, 25*(2), 171–191. https://doi.org/10.2979/philmusieducrevi.25.2.05.

Higginbotham, E. B. (1993). *Righteous discontent: The women's movement in the black Baptist Church, 1880–1920*. Harvard University Press. https://gold.idm .oclc.org/login?url=http://hdl.handle.net/2027/heb.00476.

Karnage Kills. (2017, June 11). Karnage—*Hoe Diaries* [Video]. *YouTube*. https:// www.youtube.com/watch?v=RISUgZOXPqU.

Karvelis, N. (2018). Race, class, gender, and rhymes: Hip-hop as critical pedagogy. *Music Educators Journal, 105*(1). 46–50. https://doi.org/10.1177/ 0027432118788138.

Keyes, C. L. (2002). *Rap music and street consciousness*. University of Illinois Press.

Lane, N. (2011). Black women queering the mic: Missy Elliott disturbing the boundaries of racialized sexuality and gender. *Journal of Homosexuality, 58*(6–7), 775–792. https://doi.org/10.1080/00918369.2011.581921.

Muñoz-Laboy, M., Weinstein, H., & Parker, R. (2007). The hip-hop club scene: Gender, grinding and sex. *Culture, Health & Sexuality, 9*(6), 615–628. https://doi.org/10.1080/13691050701528590.

Perry, I. (1995). It's my thang and I'll swing it the way I feel! Sexuality and black women rappers. In G. Dines & J. M. Humez (Eds.), *Gender, race, and class in media: A text-reader* (pp. 524–530). SAGE.

Reynolds, S. (2007). *Bring the noise: 20 years of writing about hip rock and hip hop.* Faber.

Riley, M. (2017). State of play: The grime report is the first ever study focusing on public attitudes toward grime music. https://discover.ticketmaster.co.uk/stateofplay/grime.pdf.

Sundararajan, N., & Maquivar, M. G. (2017). 731 How to increase student participation and engagement using Padlet: A case study of collaborative discussion in an animal sciences course. *Journal of Animal Science, 95*(4), 356. https://doi.org/10.2527/asasann.2017.731.

Tatum, A.W. (2009). Enabling texts: Texts that matter. *Edge.* National Geographic School Publishing/Hampton Brown. 1–4.

Tobias, E. (2014). Flipping the misogynist script: Gender, agency, hip hop, and music education. *Action, Criticism, and Theory for Music Education, 13*(2), 48–83.

Walcott, R. (2013). Boyfriends with clits and girlfriends with dicks: Hip hop's queer future. *Palimpsest: A Journal on Women, Gender, and the Black International, 2*(2), 168–173. https://doi.org/10.1353/pal.2013.0024.

White, T. R. (2013). Missy "Misdemeanor" Elliott and Nicki Minaj: Fashionistin' black female sexuality in hip-hop culture—Girl power or overpowered? *Journal of Black Studies, 44*(6), 607–626. https://doi.org/10.1177/0021934713497365.

PART II
CRITICAL CONSCIOUSNESS

The goal of the educational process is to create human beings who have human concerns, human beings who know and understand themselves and are able to pass human judgments on what's going on around them. Education should not mould the mind according to a prefabricated architectural plan; it should rather liberate the mind.

—Angela Davis

Hacking the Law
Social Justice Education through Lawtech

Kim Silver

In this chapter, I describe how an interdisciplinary team of academics from law and computer science devised and delivered an innovative law and technology module that made productive use of digital technology to achieve social justice.[1] In the module, final-year students from law and computer science work side by side to create digital solutions to authentic, real-world problems. Although our experience can be applied to other disciplines, the module was grounded in our own disciplinary and professional practice, so some specific background is necessary. I will first explain the educational setting and briefly describe the recent developments in "lawtech" (the application of technology to legal services) that led us to develop the law and technology module. I will then describe the module and the pedagogical process, illustrated by case studies, before concluding with reflections on the pedagogy.

The Setting

The Law Division at London South Bank University is a community law school with a strong mission to widen participation. It serves a highly diverse student body in Inner London. Non-traditional students[2] in British universities face many different barriers, and we have to work hard to ensure that our students will succeed and find worthwhile employment after graduation. The ethos of the Law Division is social justice. This permeates our teaching, with an emphasis on human rights throughout or courses. We see our role as that of preparing and empowering our students to enter the legal sector as well as other types of graduate employment. However, we also hope that our graduates will serve their communities and recognize the real issues of social justice locally, nationally, and internationally. To put human rights and social justice into practice, we aim to equip our students with an appreciation of the importance of ethics and the ability to think critically about difficult issues.

Our practice is underpinned by a strong belief in experiential learning, in learning by doing. Second-year law students are required to take an employability module to introduce them to the skills required for the legal sector, which includes a work placement in local law firms, advice settings, and local government.

Legal Advice Clinic

We also offer an extracurricular Legal Advice Clinic, which provides some of these work placements. The clinic uses an innovative drop-in model in which students provide initial social welfare law advice (including housing, family, employment, welfare rights, and consumer law) to clients under the supervision of legally qualified staff, signposting where necessary to other advice agencies (Russell, 2013). The impetus for the clinic was, and remains, social justice.

There is significant unmet legal need in the United Kingdom, including London (Hogan Lovells & Southwark Law Centre, 2018), particularly since the restriction of civil legal aid in 2013, and the clinic cannot see all those who present themselves, contributing to the problem of referral fatigue (Russell, 2016).[3] The clinic has been supplemented by court help desks, offering immediate information to litigants in person on a similar model of supervision. Clinical legal education is intimately connected to critical pedagogy since it offers significant opportunities for students to experience "greater agency, autonomy and . . . justice" (SpearIt & Ledesma, 2014, p. 251) in a real-life context. Clinic staff have been active on the law and technology module, seeking meaningful and ethical use of digital tools and resources to address unmet legal need.

Law and Technology: The Explosion

The legal world that our students will enter is changing rapidly. They are not alone. All professions, from journalism to education, are facing "fundamental and irreversible change" in which "increasingly capable [digital] systems will bring transformations to professional work that will resemble the impact of industrialization on traditional craftsmanship" (Susskind & Susskind, 2015, pp. 1, 2). In the context of law, even before COVID-19, the use of digital technologies to undertake different aspects of legal work (i.e., lawtech) was rising exponentially. Susskind (2017) argues that the employment market for law graduates will be affected adversely but that new jobs will emerge bridging the gap between technologists and lawyers—this can also be seen in other fields, such as education. Large firms are recognizing the need for such roles and setting up lawtech training schemes. At the least, new lawyers will need an understanding of how digital tools such as chatbots and document preparation systems work. Over the past few years, we have sought to prepare our students to step into that space, both practically and with a critical understanding of the social and ethical implications of changes to the law and legal practice that will ensue.

However, today's students, of all disciplines, will not just be working in the new world. They will also be living in it and, at the same time, shaping it. The COVID-19 pandemic has shown us some of the surprising shifts in patterns of living and working that we can expect and demonstrated how technology, more easily accessed by the wealthy and educated, can exacerbate existing inequalities. Morris and Stommel (2018) argue that "computers manifest human politics and human politics are made manifest in our technologies." We are keen to develop students' critical consciousness—a Freirean concept that hooks (1994, p. 14) defines as "critical engagement and awareness"—in this area (for more on critical consciousness, see Chapters 6 and 13 of this volume). This means that students should be able to evaluate the law, the technologies available, and the effects of both on users and wider society and therefore implement change.

Law and Technology Module

As both lawyers and educators, we began to ask whether, through a critical analysis of technology, we could develop some solutions to the problems of access to justice faced by clients of our clinic and other advice agencies here and abroad. Fortunately, colleagues in computer sciences were eager to collaborate with us. They were looking for external "clients" for student projects. Initially, we brought students together for an extracurricular hackathon, and law staff went into computer science classes as clients. Hush (2019) describes one of the first projects to emerge, automating a client questionnaire to provide a document suitable for use by unrepresented parties in child custody proceedings. It was clear that there was space for a joint module in which computer science and law students could work together to explore critically and address legal problems.

The law and technology module is currently offered as a compulsory practical project for final-year computer science students and an option for final-year law students. There are about five computer science students to every law student in the class. Students analyze the impact of lawtech on law and the delivery of legal services and work in mixed teams to develop a piece of legal technology software to design or prototype stage.

Assessment is in two parts. Students work together as an interdisciplinary team to create inclusive access to justice resources (70% of the module mark). Each team is given a "client," a member of the law staff from outside the module team, legal practitioners, and charities, which offer a brief based upon a real-world problem for the team to solve. The group develops a prototype solution using software of its own choice. In theory, the law student researches the law, and the computer science students build the prototype, though in practice the roles become slightly more blurred. The other 30% of assessment consists of a reflection on an aspect of law and technology and how the students are going to apply their learning from the module in their future career aspirations.

Pedagogical Design

The module involves an iterative process, co-construction, and reflection. Freire (1970, p. 72) wrote that "knowledge emerges only through invention and re-invention [iteration], through the restless, impatient, continuing, hopeful inquiry human beings pursue [reflection], in the world with the world, and with each other [co-construction]." Above all, this is a module in which students work with each other, with teachers, and with clients on projects that, by nature, are iterative and collaborative.

Each group works on a brief toward a prototype. Usually, a client works with two or three groups in any one semester, using the same brief. Responses to the brief vary, potentially enriching the eventual project. The brief can be used profitably in succeeding years because every group approaches the problem with different design priorities, often deploying different technologies and bringing different experiences to bear.

While in progress, teams meet the client weekly in the presence of one of the module tutors. Crucially, the tutor intervenes as little as possible. The students negotiate and construct the solution among themselves. Although the client is an expert in a particular legal field, the expertise offered by the computer science students means that the client cannot dominate the relationship. Students make sense of the lawtech world, and of their own learning, through a process of activity—participating in the group project—and reflection. The assessment requires them to reflect on what they have learned and, by extension, their place within this world.

The interdisciplinary approach in the module must seem very unusual to the students. They work with others whom they have never met before in small teams and rely on them for a final-year grade, are assessed partly on an unfamiliar subject (digital products for law students and law for computer science students), and are learning about a subject (lawtech) changing rapidly as they study it. However, students are supported to think about their learning from new perspectives. For example, there is discussion about why group work is important and how to make it work. Students participate in a team roles exercise to help them find out their "best fit" and get the most from the experience.

Legal Design

We also placed significant emphasis on legal design, based upon design thinking, "a problem-solving approach with a unique set of qualities: it is human centred, possibility driven, option focused, and iterative," and it is used in a wide variety of organizations (Liedtka et al., 2017). Legal design aims to focus the design of law and legal services on the user, for example turning complex consumer or employment contracts into easily understood and accessible visual resources (Hagan, n.d.). Learning about legal design underlines the fact that all resources produced must be sensitive to issues of inclusion and diversity. Is the language used appropriate, and is there an easy way of translating it? Do names and pictures or videos represent a wide range of users? Are resources easily accessible to all users, whatever their abilities? The first (formative) task that the student teams work on is a legal design project in which they are asked to produce an accessible contract for a social media platform aimed at adolescents. Students have produced cartoons, animations, and videos with imagination and enthusiasm. As well as considering the needs of their target audience, they have thought critically about social media platforms that they might use and the hidden legal implications of their terms and conditions. Two case studies presented below further illustrate how the projects worked.

Student Projects

In one brief, my colleague Robert Hush, a family lawyer, asked the students to produce a fully automated chatbot to triage queries from potential clients routed through our local law society. The students considered the problem and explained that it was too complex for the time and resources available, which helped Robert to realize that the scope could be narrowed down to enquiries about domestic violence, a significant social issue. In further discussion, the students rejected the chatbot option as overly complex and proposed a dashboard on a website instead. By answering a series of questions, the potential client would produce a summary of the case, which could be accessed by solicitors to decide whether they were equipped to take the case. Victims of domestic abuse would have a smooth and secure path to getting advice that would enable them to take steps to escape from their situations.

The law students led on working out a protocol between the website and the solicitors involved and drafted a notice for the public to understand the process and the use of the information collected. Although the computer science students worked on the underlying technology, Robert noted that they were very interested in the legal issues and the problems of domestic violence. Some of these issues and problems had to be reflected in the design of the website, enabling clients to hide open windows quickly and avoid leaving search histories. This project was undertaken by two groups, one of which took it through to a working prototype. The other group reached the design stage. The project could be a candidate for funding from one of the growing number of bodies seeking to encourage access to justice lawtech. It could also be adopted in other practice areas and geographical locations.

Another colleague, Alan Russell, a housing lawyer, regularly appears as a duty solicitor in court representing homeowners facing repossession proceedings.[4] Alan sought a three-stage solution for these vulnerable people. First, the digital platform should assess their eligibility for legal aid and, if eligible, direct them to specialist lawyers. If they are not eligible, then the app or website should collate the necessary information to present to the duty solicitor at court on the day of the hearing or to enable them to present the best case possible under the circumstances to the judge if unrepresented. Users could also employ the app to prepare information for an appointment with a lawyer at an earlier stage if they have funding to instruct one.

The students came up with creative solutions, including a home page explaining the purpose of the site and how it worked to make the platform more inclusive and accessible. To humanize the help materials, they recorded a video of Alan talking to users and explaining what they needed to do using a mobile phone. The students also thought that the app should prompt the user to answer questions to brief the solicitor, providing an easy way to generate a document in the most suitable format for the purpose. Again, this app could be repurposed for different practice areas and locations. Alan, one of the Legal Advice Clinic's founders, also saw it as potentially useful for clients who could not be seen by the clinic because of the limited number of appointments available each week.

Groups worked on a variety of projects in the module covering real-world legal problems brought to them by the clients:

- a child custody questionnaire developed during an extracurricular hackathon with computer science and law students (Hush, 2019) presented to two further groups;
- an app for human rights volunteers who act as international trial observers assessing whether trials meet international fair trial standards, allowing them to store and send their trial notes securely and to record trial data for statistical purposes;
- an app for reporting racist incidents to a racism-monitoring organization, with out-of-hours advice and signposts to further advice and assistance;
- an employment law resource providing information to potential clients and a triage process for a local law firm.

Pedagogical Praxis

The word *critical* can have several meanings (Rorabaugh, 2020), but for lawyers it means questioning the law on behalf of clients and exposing students to situations in which they too will question it. Social justice is at the heart of the student projects. Students from both disciplines confront the structural inequalities of the world of clinic clients, in which accessing the digital world can be an almost insurmountable hurdle for some and basic legal rights are routinely denied by rogue landlords, violent partners, or employers to others. At the same time, following Giroux's (2013, p. 7) prescription, "critical pedagogy becomes a project that stresses the need for teachers and students to actively transform knowledge rather than simply consume it." Students take that next step by working on a project to take action on these inequalities. In doing so, they not only develop academic skills and knowledge but also learn how to become responsible citizens and active participants in their communities. Law students are exposed to discussions about human rights and inequality from their first year, but for some computer science students this is completely new territory, and the clients note their immediate engagement and interest. This fulfills McLaren's (2019, p. 178) demand that "critical pedagogy is about the creation of critical citizenship" rather than "consumer citizenship."

Technology cannot be welcomed uncritically either. COVID-19 has accelerated the existing debate about whether access to justice is best achieved through technological solutions and how the digital divide can be bridged. In an ideal world, all potential clients would be able to access in-person legal advice directly, but technology can at least help to bridge the gap for some. It is crucial that those building and using the technology understand both its power and its potential perils. Our innovation in this module is in asking students to learn, use, and develop or shape technology in a direct attempt to further social justice. As Papert (1981, p. 4) wrote, computers are "carriers of powerful ideas and of the seeds of cultural change. . . . [T]hey can help people form new relationships with knowledge that cut across traditional lines." Students are actively involved in creating digital applications that could transform the information and advice available to users of the Legal Advice Clinic and similar organizations. We see this as a "pedagogy of hacking" (Morris & Stommel, 2018).[5]

This is a powerful model for teaching because, first, instead of being passive consumers of technology through the virtual learning environment or social media, the students are *building something with it.* This is revolutionary for both law and computer science students in different ways. Studying law consists of using words in written or, to a lesser extent, spoken form. Outputs tend to be transient even where they are grounded in real experience, such as advice given to a clinic client. The computer scientists in this module are not expected to develop solutions from scratch but instead to make appropriate use of existing technologies, familiar to them if not to the rest of us. However, our computer science colleague notes that "it is normal for computer science students to be building systems using technology, but it is very different to be building a system to address a real problem that supports social justice. It provides great motivation for students, which they cannot get by working on made up set tasks or case studies" (L. Otoyo, personal communication, August 12, 2020).

Second, the involvement of the computer scientists and the following collaborative work *demystify the tech* (for a similar discussion, see Chapter 7 of this volume) for the lawyers, law students, legal academics, and visiting experts, making it potentially more accessible. There is a long-standing argument in the lawtech community over whether lawyers need to be able to code. Watching our students at work together indicates that this is unnecessary, but nevertheless familiarity with the tech, its possibilities and limitations, can empower the user.

Third, the students make deliberate choices about the use of technologies; they *have agency* in the process. While recognizing that technology cannot be neutral, we are open to different choices. Technologies are evaluated based upon their suitability for the purpose and the extent to which they satisfy the values underpinning the module. Students consider the ethical implications of what they are building and how they are building it, including issues of accessibility and inclusion. Often the students have direct personal experience of the issues involved or know people who do. They are aware of the human dimension of the legal problem, and studying the module helps to bring this home to them. This is an additional layer of expertise that benefits the project since the students concerned can identify the key issues and problems that projects must address. Suggestions from students help us to see the projects in a new light, and we learn from them, underlining the importance of co-construction.

Fourth, the *reflective process aimed at social justice* requires that all of the students understand the needs, circumstances, and living situations of users. These aspects are then taken into account through the processes of legal design. This can be seen from the domestic violence project described above, in which clumsy implementation could make the user's situation even worse. This reminds us that, as Dewey and Dewey (1915, p. 246) noted, "unless the mass of workers are to be blind cogs and pinions in the apparatus they employ, they must have some understanding of the physical and social facts behind and ahead of the material and appliances with which they are dealing."

We have started the journey of encouraging the "agency and ultimate empowerment of learners" (Rorabaugh, 2020), but this can and should grow. Students' active involvement in the projects that underlie the module can have a transformative effect. At present, projects are proposed by lecturers and outside experts, but students work in the clinic, and in other advice settings, and experience legal problems themselves. We could open up the proposal system to allow the wider student body to suggest projects.

The module, and the products designed in it, are first steps toward social justice transformation. They are still at the prototype stage, but we are sharing our practice with other universities and advice agencies in the United Kingdom and farther afield and working on selected prototypes in order to put them into action. Note that interdisciplinarity need not stop with computer science—there is the potential to include colleagues in education, psychology, housing studies, criminology, and other disciplines within the basic model. We believe that, though we have started with a relatively small and limited module, this co-constructed, reflective, iterative, and critical approach has far-reaching potential.

Conclusion

The experience from our project is easily transferable to other law schools in the United Kingdom, and we are happy to discuss that experience in more detail. Is it transferable to other disciplines and other countries? We would argue that it is. For example, education and computer science students could work with learners in their community to develop digital learning or support resources.

Digital technology is not simply a mode of delivery—it is the subject of the learning itself, a revolutionary development for law students. In our context, students from law and computer science are taken outside their comfort zones, and we ask them to think about how they are being taught and what they are learning. The reflective aspect of the assessment reinforces this. Above all, the module encourages real-world engagement with profound social problems, and we recognize that students from both disciplines bring their own lived experiences—whether as tenants, benefit claimants, employees, or victims of human rights abuses—to the design and development of the products; in the process, students show us how they can be the agents of change in the world.

Key Takeaways

- We have developed an interdisciplinary law and technology module driven by social justice and student agency.
- The module enables a critical approach to the inequalities of access in the current legal system and the potential of technology to solve them.
- The principles of legal design, based upon design thinking, help students to construct accessible, inclusive, and user-centred resources.
- Learning in the module is iterative and reflective and comes from the process of co-construction.
- Students in this module not only develop academic skills and knowledge but also learn how to become responsible citizens and active participants in their communities.

Acknowledgements

With thanks to the law and technology team for their contributions. Andy Unger, head of the Law Division, and Lucia Otoyo, deputy head of the Division of Computer Science and Informatics, devised the module. Robert Hush and Alan Russell, senior lecturers in the Law Division, were in the team of internal and external expert clients.

Notes

1. In UK terms, a "module" is a unit of study. Students study six 20-credit modules per year, making 360 credits over a 3-year degree.
2. Traditionally, UK undergraduates have been white and middle-class, and they have entered university right after graduating from high school.
3. This can occur if clients are passed from one potential source of advice to the next repeatedly, with the result that they can see no prospect of success and give up.
4. Duty solicitors appear on a rota at courts dealing with eviction proceedings. They represent clients with no other source of legal representation, meeting them for the first time on the day of the hearing.

5   The term "hacking" is used here in the sense of a clever solution to a problem rather than illicit access to a computer system.

References

Dewey, J., & Dewey, E. (1915). *The schools of tomorrow*. E. P. Dutton.

Freire, M. (1970). *Pedagogy of the oppressed*. Continuum.

Giroux, H. A. (2013). *On critical pedagogy*. Continuum.

Hagan, M. (n.d.). *Law by design*. http://www.lawbydesign.co/en/home/.

Hogan Lovells & Southwark Law Centre. (2018). *The unmet legal need in Lewisham* [Report]. https://www.hoganlovells.com/~/media/hogan-lovells/pdf/news/2018/the-unmet-legal-need-in-lewisham.pdf?la=en.

hooks, b. (1994). *Teaching to transgress: Education as the practice of freedom*. Routledge.

Hush, R. (2019). Supporting litigants in person in the family court. *Family Law, 49*(3), 304–309.

Liedtka, J., Salzman, R., & Azer, D. (2017). *Design thinking for the greater good: Innovation in the social sector*. Columbia Business School Publishing.

McLaren, P. (2019). Teaching against the grain. *Griffith Journal of Law & Human Dignity, 7*(1), 173–202.

Morris, M., & Stommel, J. (2018). *An urgency of teachers*. https://urgencyofteachers.com/.

Papert, S. (1981). *Mindstorms: Children, computers and powerful ideas*. Basic Books.

Rorabaugh, P. (2020). Occupy the digital. In J. Stommel, C. Friend, & S. Morris (Eds.), *Critical digital pedagogy: A collection*. Hybrid Pedagogy.

Russell, A. (2016). University based drop-in legal advice services in the UK: Widening access to justice and tackling poverty. In C. S. Duarte, A. Giannattasio, F. Bastos Pereira, G. Rodrigues, L. Pereira, & M. Gomes Da Crus (Eds.), *Academic stand against poverty ASAP Brazil conference* (pp. 83–97). https://openresearch.lsbu.ac.uk/item/872q7.

Russell, J. (2013). *LSBU drop-in clinic manual*. https://www.lsbu.ac.uk/__data/assets/pdf_file/0020/17291/lsbu-drop-in-clinic-manual.pdf.

SpearIt & Ledesma, S. (2014). Experiential education as critical pedagogy: Enhancing the law school experience. *Nova Law Review, 38*, 249–276. https://ssrn.com/abstract=2498782.

Susskind, R. (2017). *Tomorrow's lawyers* (2nd ed). Oxford University Press.

Susskind, R., & Susskind, D. (2015). *The future of the professions*. Oxford University Press.

When Being Online Hinders the Act of Challenging Banking Model Pedagogy

Neo-Liberalism in Digital Higher Education

Frederic Fovet

In this chapter, I examine my phenomenological journey as an instructor in shifting a master's-level course on critical pedagogy (CP) from in-person delivery to a fully online design. I explore the resistance that I have experienced in shifting a course designed with CP tenets in mind—such as curriculum co-creation, critical examination of classroom power dynamics, oppressive structures in higher education and the inequities that they perpetuate, and so on—to a fully online format. This course was delivered in-person seven times before it was offered three times online. I assumed that, beyond simple matters of redesign for online delivery, the content would function in the same way and trigger similar discussions and reflections on the nature and essence of CP. For three semesters, however, I experienced a substantial degree of resistance from students when encouraging them to challenge traditional formats of delivery, conventional classroom dynamics, and *banking model pedagogy* (Freire, 2017). The banking model describes, in a Freirean context, a pedagogy that perceives knowledge as a commodity passively transferred from instructor to student.

I assert that the current branding of online teaching in higher education, in a neo-liberal landscape, predisposes many learners to resist an explicit challenge to the banking model and therefore makes it arduous to teach critical pedagogy online. I explore here my attempt at meaning making while I interpret how online design of a course on CP—far from freeing participants to challenge, contest, and rethink traditional pedagogy—seemed to lead them to seek overly traditional relationships, roles, and pedagogical experiences. In the final section of the chapter, I open a wider discussion on some of the challenges that arise from the tension identified within the very concept of critical pedagogy in online spaces: the ambivalent perception of being both freed and hindered in challenging traditional classroom practices.

Critical Pedagogy

Critical pedagogy can be difficult to define with precision since it is interpreted and implemented in widely differing contexts; it is perceived at times very differently because it merges critical theory and postmodern thought (McLaren, 2020) and, as such, reconciles what are frequently radically different theoretical perspectives. Critical theorists, for example, place much emphasis on minority identity, on the discourse of oppression, and on the sense of affiliation shared by marginalized individuals in the use of common language to describe identity. Postmodern thinkers, conversely, shift progressively toward a distinct view of oppression and end up rejecting language (e.g., "racialized" or "LGBTQ2S+") that defines marginalized identities as categories because they believe that this language can perpetuate marginalization.[1] This can cause significant tension within CP circles, and, though most scholars have similar aims when it comes to challenging power dynamics in education, they can have opposite ideas about how to challenge hegemonic power dynamics.

There are, however, key features always present in the formulation of critical pedagogy (Villanueva & O'Sullivan, 2019). As mentioned in the previous section, CP rejects the banking model, seen as traditional teaching approaches that focus on the passivity of the learner and on the mistaken perception of knowledge as a commodity transferred by the teacher in an almost mechanical way. CP argues that the role of the educator is to awaken learners out of this torpor by making them conscious of how traditional education is oppressing them. CP then focuses on supporting learners' search for voice and their eventual efforts at emancipation from oppressive practices (Blanchard & Nix, 2019; Giroux, 2011). In practice, this might, for example, encourage racialized students to challenge the hegemonic whiteness of academia (Vidal-Ortiz, 2017), Global South and Indigenous students to seek the decolonization of the curriculum and assessment practices (Malik, 2017), or LGBTQ2S+ students to query the heteronormativity of disciplines (Boustani & Taylor, 2020).

Online Learning and Critical Pedagogy

Perhaps because of its emphasis on the learner voice, dialogic learning, and justice, CP has had an ambivalent relationship with online teaching and technology more generally (Boyd, 2016). During the emergence of the internet, many critical pedagogues were predictably and vehemently opposed to the web, seeing in its emergence a plethora of ways that it might end up accentuating social inequities. It is in this context that the concept of the *digital divide* was created and developed (AlSadrani et al., 2020). It took over a decade before critical scholars started rethinking this opposition and acknowledging the potential of the web to serve as an affordance in the process of emancipation of oppressed and marginalized individuals (Mapotse, 2014). Since then, a large body of literature has focused on the numerous ways that technology, virtual platforms, software, and social media have all played key roles in developing CP online. There have been CP initiatives developed online with LGBTQ2S+ students, homeless youth, racialized learners, Indigenous students, and students with disabilities (Alvarez, 2019). Digital literacy as a field, in particular, has been an exceptionally dynamic locus where CP and technology have been blended and integrated with great success.

The pendulum swing has not been smooth or complete. The CP field now has a huge potential for transformative action via the internet but remains suspicious of the virtual world, like any space, in which polarization and discrimination occur, particularly as a result of organized and concerted action by political entities (Mizan & Ishtiaque Ahmed, 2018). This dichotomous positioning has become crystallized in the creation of an entirely new field of scholarship: critical digital pedagogy (CDP). This body of literature emphasizes the dual nature of the internet as a place of simultaneous emancipation and oppression (Young, 2019). It calls for extreme scrutiny from users and practitioners and a focus on power dynamics when integrating online technology in teaching and learning (Williamson et al., 2020), when developing open practices (McKenzie, 2020), when supporting minority voices in these spaces (Kumi-Yeboah et al., 2019), and when navigating the hyper-commercialization of higher education online practices (Nichols & Stahl, 2019).

The very existence of a scholarship on CDP supported my original assumption that shifting my course on CP online would be conducive to rich engagement and dialogue. The course in its in-person format supported the participants in challenging traditional banking model practices and seeking authentic dialogical practices. It explicitly discussed CP and its objectives. Moving the course to an online format should therefore have widened the opportunities for rich, genuine discussion of CDP; the online design that I produced indeed seemed to provide more systematic opportunities for the amplification of learners' voices, for a shift in the instructor's role as facilitator rather than lecturer, and for a fluid renegotiation of traditional learner habits within an innovative medium. This is not how it eventually unfolded, however, as I explain below. The exploration of this transition in design is addressed from my subjective experience through the process and driven by a stance that aligns with phenomenology.

Methodological Reflection:
Phenomenology in Educational Research

Phenomenology is increasingly used as a perspective in research on higher education, particularly in regard to teaching and learning (Webb & Welsh, 2019). This paradigm is focused on examining the lived experiences of individuals in order to analyze the "meaning making" that they carry out as they interact with specific phenomena in their everyday existence (Neubauer et al., 2019). It is a powerful perspective in research because it acknowledges the fact that subjective, individually crafted realities are important and worthy of analytical, empirical, and scientific investigation. These subjective constructions of realities are indeed often the key variables necessary to understand complex human interactions within the social sciences (Sandi-Urena, 2018). Phenomenology is focused on examining meaning making as a process worthy of analysis in its own right.

Phenomenology is particularly well aligned with a reflection on the teaching of CP online. CP indeed pushes instructors, perhaps more than any approach to teaching and learning, to reflect deeply and personally on how their identity, being, lived experience, and affiliation or lack of affiliation with hegemonic or minority groups shapes their teaching. Teaching CP with authenticity becomes a systematic and experiential process of self-reflection and unpacking of self (Tien, 2019). Phenomenology is uniquely positioned as a theoretical lens to frame and support this deeply personal professional experience.

Reflections: Working toward Dialogic Teaching and Learning

I examine here my experience as a faculty member responsible for the delivery of a course on CP at the Master of Education (MEd) level. From the start of 2016 to the end of 2018, I was employed as an assistant professor within a Faculty of Education on a Canadian campus. In this role, I was allocated a course on CP that I developed and taught each semester to in-person cohorts. Since 2018, I have continued to teach on this campus as a sessional instructor, and I was asked on three occasions to offer the same course to online cohorts. I present and analyze here my experiences as an instructor offering the same course, and the same opportunities to challenge the banking model, in two different formats. The course was radically redesigned for online delivery, but the objectives remained the same, though the assignments were adapted to the new medium. The opportunities for key discussions among participants were retained but triggered in different ways. I carried out, throughout the delivery of the course online, a deep reflection on its design but did not identify any specific issue with the design itself. In short, though the designs differed, both the online course and the in-person course dealt with CP in significant ways and modelled its key tenets in the delivery and assessment format.

I offered the same master's-level course on CP seven times in an in-person format with some online elements over a period of two and a half years. I was extremely invested in this course from the start and determined not solely to construct an engaging course but also to model the concepts taught to the greatest extent possible. I therefore included elements of dialogic education from the first class, with a renegotiation of the classroom space and of the power dynamics symbolized by the traditional class layout: screen and instructor desk at the front of the class, instructor in control of the projector screen, students in rows, et cetera. The course also modelled elements of curriculum co-creation. It challenged banking model practices by rejecting the notion of a course reading list dictated by the instructor and replacing it with a flexible, personalized, student-centred approach to the selection of class readings, within which students were encouraged to select specific examples of CP in a real-world context and readings associated with their examples.

Each unit kicked off with an open discussion of media features meant to offer the opportunity for personal and reflective debates on current issues in social justice arising from the learners' everyday concerns and positions within society. The course also integrated elements of active learning in the sense that learners spent a large amount of classroom time investigating and critically evaluating real-world examples of CP implementation in classrooms. This process inevitably led on each occasion to an examination of how the course itself stood up compared to these case studies and illustrations. The course also included an active and dialogic exploration of films that deal with CP or its key themes. A detailed analysis of the complex relationship between popular culture, particularly motion pictures, and CP was central to course development. This section created much enthusiasm and engagement among students. Some of the films explored and integrated into the course were *Entre les Murs* (2008), *Half-Nelson* (2006), *La Haine* (1995), *Dear White People* (2014), *Girl* (2018), *Rabbit Proof Fence* (2002), *CRAZY* (2005), *Polytechnique* (2009), and *Get Out* (2017).

Importantly, when the course explored indigenization and decolonization, participants were actively invited to debate how the course could be improved, become more authentic in this respect, and succeed in integrating yet more Global South and Indigenous perspectives and voices into the syllabus. Course evaluations through these seven iterations were high, and I was consistently surprised by the exceptional degree of engagement among participants, their authentic reflection on self as a learner, and their desire to challenge almost every aspect of traditional pedagogy remaining in the format.

Friction and Resistance in Online Spaces

Delivery of the same course in an online format, despite the careful redesign, did not go according to plan. The opportunities for dialogic interactions with the learners were retained—and even extended—in the redesign for online delivery. In each unit, spaces were created to discuss readings, class concerns, and a large number of media pieces extracted from the news. Since this is a course with a dialogic format and flavour, students' reactions were evident from the beginning. Areas of friction and resistance are indicated below.

- Students who engaged online felt intimidated by the curriculum co-creation components; they repeatedly expressed their preference for predetermined course content.
- Students were resistant to engaging in the dialogic dimensions of the course, perceiving them from the start as overly time consuming; they compared the workload with that of other online courses that they had taken in which the format was what they described as "read and post," requiring no challenge to the teaching and learning format.
- There was a general reluctance among the participants to embrace elements of choice incorporated throughout the course even though learner identity, voice, and emancipation were central and explicit concerns of the course. A frequent comment was that participants were content to read about it but not insistent on

experiencing it first-hand. Self-determination in regard to possible readings was outright rejected, students suggesting that the reading list should be narrowed down and made compulsory.

- There was little enthusiasm for the exploration of popular culture and CP; nor was any genuine engagement demonstrated in regard to the films introduced. Once again the argument about time was used, and this activity was seen as overly time consuming for a three-credit course. The message was clear on three occasions that this course was offered online: make it less organically and democratically free flowing; anchor it down with teacher-led decisions; discuss CP but do not attempt to model it since it is too resource intensive for the participants.

Although the experiences described above summarize the majority views on the course on the three instances that it was offered online, some students did engage in a wider reflection beyond the time frame for completion. Some participants remained in contact with me and carried out their own reflections on some of the resistance that they had experienced, identifying the tensions between their initial reactions and the explicit course objectives and questioning the causes of the phenomena that they had experienced. This was a deep and rather painful exercise in self-reflection for some of these learners, but it occurred after the 12-week course.

On the third occasion that this course was offered online, some students specifically placed their resistance in the wider context of the marketing of the online version of the MEd program, the branding of the courses in the faculty catalogue, and the business-like approach that the campus adopted in relation to students' time commitment and ability to complete courses while working.

There can be many reasons that a student engages differently in an online versus an in-person environment, including mental health considerations (Patterson Lorenzetti, 2015), disabilities (Perera Rodríguez & Moriña, 2019), family commitments, employment workload (Farrell & Brunton, 2020), or simply inexperience with virtual spaces (Mishra et al., 2020). An instructor's lack of comfort in online spaces is also a frequent factor in student disengagement online (Kebritchi et al., 2017), and my phenomenological analysis included this process of self-reflection on design and online pedagogy. Although I have engaged in deep reflection about the specific design needs of learners, for the rest of the chapter and for an ongoing exploration of the above arguments, I will focus on neo-liberalism as an underexplored dimension affecting learners' perceptions of engagement in an online course of this type.

Through my phenomenological analysis, I observed how the wider and endemic phenomenon of master's degree students' perceptions of online instruction—its goals, potential, and limitations—often seemed to be the rather unidimensional product of a societal construction of online instruction and of a historical branding of online learning after a decade of a particularly powerful neo-liberal branding of mere convenience (Kentnor, 2015; Manhaus, 2012). The perception of the higher education student as a consumer is now omnipresent (Silverio et al., 2021). In such a landscape, convenience, speed, ability to navigate employment while completing graduate degrees, and ability to take courses in multiple formats (in terms of both length and type) have become key values (Andrade, 2018; Harrison & Risler, 2015; Lederman, 2018). I argue here that this positioning as consumers affects learners' expectations of deep engagement and personal investment in the curriculum itself and as a result can hinder genuine dialogic opportunities when teaching CP in online formats.

The observations in this chapter should not be interpreted as an inherent and insurmountable hurdle when it comes to teaching critical pedagogy online. Conceptually, there is nothing that might make it challenging to teach CP in an online format. In fact, the key features of CP make it particularly adaptable to the virtual environment: it is a teaching approach, after all, that encourages students to challenge conventional pedagogical practices and take on non-traditional roles; it might even be tempting at first to assume that students can find it easier to do this in the virtual environment since it is innovative and fluid (Green & Chewning, 2020). CP seeks to challenge the banking model, and in principle the online space remains a privileged locus for this reflection to happen (Bradshaw, 2017; Chun, 2018; Pandit & Rahaman, 2019).

The Impact of Neo-Liberalism on Learners' Perceptions of Online Teaching

From my experiences with the online version of this course, the potential of online delivery to support CP is less in question than the perception of online teaching among many students (Fidalgo et al., 2020). Online education—indeed education in every modality—must be examined within a wider neo-liberal context within which it has been reshaped and portrayed over the past two decades: it has indeed been branded in terms of convenience, cost effectiveness, time efficiency, and lower engagement that is easy to integrate into busy lives (Broucker et al., 2020; Toufaily et al., 2018). In this particular faculty, the course on CP is now offered not just online over 12 weeks but also online over 6 weeks and even as a face-to-face intensive course over 10 days. Often these alternative formats have little to do with a realistic exploration of pedagogical outcome or content (Ball, 2016) and become marketing exercises that seek to fit course objectives into student expectations and life commitments—whatever they might be. Higher education institutions are highly aware of the competitive landscape in which they operate, and delivery formats become primarily marketing and branding strategies (Van Vught & Huisman, 2013).

Neo-liberalism is a theory from the field of economics that unexpectedly has become prominent in the field of education since the 1980s (Tight, 2019). It is a lens that magnifies market forces as key in social structures and shows that the markets need to be free to achieve optimal outcomes for the majority of stakeholders (Azevedo et al., 2019). It has led to the adoption of a business model approach that currently frames most dimensions of the postsecondary sector. As a result, students are often perceived as customers, and courses marketed as commodities, with value for money, convenience, time efficiency, and ease in achieving outcomes seen as key desirable and commercially competitive features (Olivares & Wetzel, 2014; Pizarro Milian, 2017; Pizarro Milian & Quirke, 2017; Toma, 2012; Tomlinson, 2017).

The neo-liberal packaging of online learning often positions students to expect more superficial engagement, less interaction, and faster progression through topics (Brown & Carasso, 2013). The current image of online learning necessarily leads learners to expect fewer radical challenges to the banking model and less authentic, deep, rich experimentation with student-led learning (Munro, 2018). In my experience, this particular branding might have led some students within this specific course to think that they could retain fairly traditional roles, akin to the banking model, and avoid deep interaction with the process required within CP. Interestingly, having been confronted repeatedly now with students' reluctance in this course to engage deeply online with processes that could lead to conscientization, I have created more spaces for open discussions about these feelings. In these interactive spaces, students have offered narratives on the time element, minimal interactive nature, and directive feel that they considered the features that attracted them to the online courses.

The key outcome, and call for action, suggest that the aims of CP could be achieved online but that any course of this nature delivered virtually would have to create a process of conscientization first (for more on conscientization, or critical consciousness, see Chapter 13 of this volume) among learners regarding the impacts of neo-liberalism on their perceptions of online course objectives and format of engagement. This has been my key practical takeaway as an instructor and the main recommendation that I offer colleagues. Instead of delivering a course on CP online despite this resistance and pushback, we can integrate the experiences of students proactively, leading to a wider reflection on how critical pedagogy and critical digital pedagogy need to be positioned within a neo-liberal landscape of higher education in order to be palatable and meaningful to learners. In my current offering of the course at this stage, the need to address these spontaneous concerns, disruptions, and discussions has become a course activity of its own that tends to occur organically and can almost be planned for.

This does mean in practice not only that such a course on CP would have to be designed differently for online delivery but also that a significant portion of the course would need to focus on the process of conscientization on the impact of neo-liberalism on learners' expectations described above. A conceptual takeaway emerges here: critical digital pedagogy in higher education cannot hope simply to transfer critical pedagogy to a virtual medium; rather, it must include a deep and challenging reflection on the ways that learners perceive online learning.

Neo-Liberalism in the Context of COVID-19

This discussion is particularly relevant in the current COVID-19 crisis. The world has observed since March 2020 a rapid pivot to emergency online delivery (Witze, 2020). This contingency online teaching is tainted with the same ambivalent image of expediency, superficiality, and limited authentic engagement (Herman, 2020; Moore et al., 2021). It is not online learning per se, however, that is described in the numerous but less than flattering features that have popped up worldwide about the COVID-19 pivot (Wong, 2020); it is instead a poor alternative, equivalent simply to a unidimensional shift from on-campus design to an alternative platform or medium (Lederman, 2018). Beyond that even, the disillusioned discourse observed about the online pivot echoes a rhetoric that existed before the COVID-19 crisis: except on rare occasions and exceptionally invested campuses, online teaching was then already much viewed as a "less than" alternative (Fain, 2019; Muthuprasad et al., 2021). This perception was the result of over a decade of neo-liberal marketing that implicitly associated it with few genuine pedagogical values and instead with connotations of convenience and ease (Munro, 2018).

The COVID-19 crisis, though it has dramatically highlighted public deficit perceptions of online teaching and learning, might offer a silver lining. The health crisis indeed has triggered significant debate and reflection on the true essence and nature of online learning, and a positive narrative is emerging, filled with hope about pedagogy in virtual space (Dhawan, 2020). This narrative seeks to deconstruct and reframe perceptions and embrace new ambitions and dreams for online teaching since it is now here to stay (Zhu & Liu, 2020). It is hoped that in the decade to come the field might see more students genuinely willing and able to engage authentically in online courses with concepts such as CP. This might represent an eventual shattering of the rather wobbly and counterproductive neo-liberal image of online pedagogy (Troiani & Dutson, 2021).

Conclusion

Although this chapter builds its reflection upon a feeling of unease—the perception of being proven fundamentally wrong about one's assumptions in regard to the offering of a course on CP online—it quickly shifts to a radically different perspective. This reflection unearths an opportunity to reshape our collective views and perceptions of online teaching, a reflection that could not have come at a more opportune time in the context of the pivot required by COVID-19 and the numerous questions that it leaves unanswered.

As I have asserted in this chapter, there are numerous misunderstandings of the notion of online teaching, and some of these misconceptions are the result of the commercial branding that online teaching and learning have been given for over a decade within the increasing omnipresence of neo-liberalism in the landscape of higher education. The illustration offered in this chapter of the friction that occurs when instructors attempt to teach profoundly dialogic courses online indicates the momentous work that must take place to reframe online learning in the eyes of students. I argue that CP in particular, as course content, can serve as a key cathartic tool to help reshape radically the potential, format, and ambition of online pedagogy in the eyes of students of higher education. Courses on critical pedagogy offered online might therefore become a primary battle ground for this reflection to occur.

Key Takeaways

- The unexpected tension that can arise when shifting courses in critical pedagogy to online delivery should be explored.
- This tension should be analyzed in a way that avoids reductionist interpretations that might portray critical pedagogy as incompatible with online modes of teaching.
- The subtext of this perceived tension and how neo-liberalism shapes the branding of online teaching and in turn learners' attitudes toward learning should be examined.

- This reflection should be situated within the context of COVID-19, in which online delivery has become a requirement rather than a choice.

Note

1 Lesbian, gay, bisexual, trans, queer or questioning, two-spirited, and other sexual and gender minorities.

References

AlSadrani, B., Alzyoudi, M., Alsheikh, N., & Elshazly, E. (2020). The digital divide in inclusive classrooms. *International Journal of Learning, Teaching and Educational Research, 19*(3), 69–85.

Alvarez, M. (2019). (Digital) media as critical pedagogy. *Media Theory, 3*(1), 73–102.

Andrade, M. S. (2018). A responsive higher education curriculum: Change and disruptive innovation. In D. Parrish & J. Joyce-McCoach (Eds.), *Innovations in higher education: Cases on transforming and advancing practice*. Intech Open. https://www.intechopen.com/chapters/63117.

Azevedo, F., Jost, J. T., Rothmund, T., & Sterling, J. (2019). Neoliberal ideology and the justification of inequality in capitalist societies: Why social and economic dimensions of ideology are intertwined. *Journal of Social Issues, 75*, 49–88.

Ball, S. J. (2016). Neoliberal education? Confronting the slouching beast. *Policy Futures in Education, 14*(8), 1046–1059.

Blanchard, L., & Nix, M. (2019). Creating spaces for radical pedagogy in higher education. *Human Rights Education Review, 2*(2), 64–83.

Boustani, K., & Taylor, K. (2020). Navigating LGBTQ+ discrimination in academia: Where do we go from here? *Biochem, 42*(3), 16–20.

Boyd, D. (2016). What would Paulo Freire think of Blackboard: Critical pedagogy in an age of online learning. *International Journal of Critical Pedagogy, 7*(1), 165–185.

Bradshaw, A. C. (2017). Critical pedagogy and educational technology. In A. D. Benson, R. Joseph, & J. L. Moore (Eds.), *Culture, learning, and technology: Research and practice* (pp. 8–27). Routledge.

Broucker, B., De Wit, K., & Mampaey, J. (2020). Brand communication of higher education institutions: A call for multichannel communication analysis in higher education branding research. *Higher Education Policy, 34*(9), 928–948.

Brown, R., & Carasso, H. (2013). *Everything for sale: The marketization of UK higher education*. Routledge.

Chun, C. W. (2018). Critical pedagogy and language learning in the age of social media? *Revista brasileira de linguística aplicada, 18*(2), 281–300.

Dhawan, S. (2020). Online learning: A panacea in the time of COVID-19 crisis. *Journal of Educational Technology Systems, 49*(1), 5–22.

Fain, P. (2019, January 10). Takedown of online education. *Inside Higher Ed.* https://www.insidehighered.com/digital-learning/article/2019/01/16/online -learning-fails-deliver-finds-report-aimed-discouraging.

Farrell, O., & Brunton, J. (2020). A balancing act: A window into online student engagement experiences. *International Journal of Educational Technology in Higher Education, 17,* 25.

Fidalgo, P., Thormann, J., Kulyk, O., & Lencastre, J. (2020). Students' perceptions on distance education: A multinational study. *International Journal of Educational Technology in Higher Education, 17,* 18.

Freire, P. (2017). *Pedagogy of the oppressed.* Penguin Books.

Giroux, H. A. (2011). *On critical pedagogy.* Bloomsbury Academic.

Green, K. R., & Chewning, H. L. (2020). The fault in our systems: LMS as a vehicle for critical pedagogy. *TechTrends, 64,* 423–431.

Harrison, L. M., & Risler, L. (2015). The role consumerism plays in student learning. *Active Learning in Higher Education, 16*(1), 67–76.

Herman, P. (2020, June 10). Online learning is not the future. *Inside Higher Ed.* https://www.insidehighered.com/digital-learning/views/2020/06/10/online -learning-not-future-higher-education-opinion.

Kebritchi, M., Lipschuetz, A., & Santiague, L. (2017). Issues and challenges for teaching successful online courses in higher education: A literature review. *Journal of Educational Technology Systems, 46,* 4–29.

Kentnor, H. (2015). Distance education and the evolution of online learning in the United States. *Curriculum and Teaching Dialogue, 17*(1–2), 21–34.

Kumi-Yeboah, A., Dogbey, J., Yuan, G., & Amponsah, S. (2019). Cultural diversity in online learning: Perceptions of minority graduate students. In L. Kyei-Blankson, J. Blankson, & E. Ntuli (Eds.), *Care and culturally responsive pedagogy in online settings* (pp. 230–251). IGI Global.

Lederman, D. (2018, November 7). Online education ascends. *Inside Higher Ed.* https://www.insidehighered.com/digital-learning/article/2018/11/07/new -data-online-enrollments-grow-and-share-overall-enrollment.

Malik, K. (2017, February 19). Are SOAS students right to "decolonise" their minds from Western philosophers? *The Guardian.* https://www.theguardian .com/education/2017/feb/19/soas-philosopy-decolonise-our-minds -enlightenment-white-european-kenan-malik.

Manhaus, P. S. (2012). Role of online education in building brand image of educational institutions. *Journal of Economics, Finance and Administrative Science*, 75–85.

Mapotse, T. (2014). An emancipation paradigm through critical theory in technology education: An action learning paradigm. *Mediterranean Journal of Social Sciences, 17*(32), 5.

McKenzie, L. (2020, April 3). "Zoombies" take over online classrooms. *Inside Higher Ed*. https://www.insidehighered.com/news/2020/04/03/zoombombing-isn%E2%80%99t-going-away-and-it-could-get-worse.

McLaren, P. (2020). The future of critical pedagogy. *Educational Philosophy and Theory, 52*(12), 1243–1248.

Mishra, L., Gupta, T., & Shree, A. (2020). Online teaching-learning in higher education during lockdown period of COVID-19 pandemic. *International Journal of Educational Research Open, 1*.

Mizan, A. S., & Ishtiaque Ahmed, S. (2018). Silencing the minority through domination in social media platform: Impact on the pluralistic Bangladeshi society. In *ELCOP yearbook of human rights*. https://ssrn.com/abstract=3326478.

Moore, S. D. M., Jayme, B. D., & Black, J. (2021). Disaster capitalism, rampant edtech opportunism, and the advancement of online learning in the era of COVID19. *Critical Education, 12*(2), 1–21.

Munro, M. (2018). The complicity of digital technologies in the marketisation of UK higher education: Exploring the implications of a critical discourse analysis of thirteen national digital teaching and learning strategies. *International Journal of Educational Technology in Higher Education, 15*(11), 1–20.

Muthuprasad, T., Aiswarya, S., Aditya, K. S., & Jha, G. K. (2021). Students' perception and preference for online education in India during COVID-19 pandemic. *Social Sciences & Humanities Open, 3*(1).

Neubauer, B. E., Witkop, C. T., & Varpio, L. (2019). How phenomenology can help us learn from the experiences of others. *Perspectives on Medical Education, 8*, 90–97.

Nichols, S., & Stahl, G. (2019). Intersectionality in higher education research: A systematic literature review. *Higher Education Research & Development, 38*(6), 1255–1268.

Olivares, M., & Wetzel, H. (2014). Competing in the higher education market: Empirical evidence for economies of scale and scope in German higher education institutions. *CESifo Economic Studies, 60*(4), 653–680.

Pandit, R. K., & Rahaman, V. (2019). Critical pedagogy in digital era: Understanding the importance of arts & humanities for sustainable IT development. In *Proceedings of International Conference on Digital Pedagogies (ICDP) 2019*.

Patterson Lorenzetti, J. (2015, November 12). Supporting the mental health needs of online students. *Faculty Focus*. https://www.facultyfocus.com/articles/online-education/supporting-the-mental-health-needs-of-online-students/.

Perera Rodríguez, H., & Moriña, A. (2019). Technological challenges and students with disabilities in higher education. *Exceptionality, 27*, 65–76.

Pizarro Milian, R. (2017). What's for sale at Canadian universities? A mixed-methods analysis of promotional strategies. *Higher Education Quarterly, 71*(1), 53–74.

Pizarro Milian, R., & Quirke, L. (2017). Alternative pathways to legitimacy: Promotional practices in the Ontario for-profit college sector. *Journal of Marketing for Higher Education, 27*(1), 77–98.

Sandi-Urena, S. (2018). Phenomenological approaches to study learning in the tertiary level chemistry laboratory. *Química nova, 41*(2), 236–242.

Silverio, S. A., Wilkinson, C., & Wilkinson, S. (2021). The powerful student consumer and the commodified academic: A depiction of the marketised UK higher education system through a textual analysis of the ITV drama cheat. *Sociological Research Online, 26*(1), 147–165. https://doi.org/10.1177/1360780420970202.

Tien, J. (2019). Teaching identity vs. positionality: Dilemmas in social justice education. *Curriculum Inquiry, 49*(5), 526–550.

Tight, M. (2019). The neoliberal turn in higher education. *Higher Education Quarterly, 73*, 273–284.

Toma, J. D. (2012). Institutional strategy: Positioning for prestige. In M. N. Bastedo (Ed.), *The organization of higher education: Managing colleges for a new era* (pp. 118–159). Johns-Hopkins University Press.

Tomlinson, M. (2017). Student perceptions of themselves as "consumers" of higher education. *British Journal of Sociology of Education, 38*(4), 450–467.

Toufaily, E., Zalan, T., & Lee, D. (2018). What do learners value in online education? An emerging market perspective. *E-Journal of Business Education and Scholarship of Teaching, 12*(2), 24–39.

Troiani, I., & Dutson, C. (2021). The neoliberal university as a space to learn/think/work in higher education. *Architecture and Culture, 9*(1), 5–23.

Van Vught, F., & Huisman, J. (2013). Institutional profiles: Some strategic tools. *Tuning Journal for Higher Education, 1*(1), 21–36.

Vidal-Ortiz, S. (2017, November 10). Dismantling whiteness in academe. *Inside Higher Ed*. https://www.insidehighered.com/advice/2017/11/10/how-whiteness-structuring-interactions-higher-education-essay.

Villanueva, C., & O'Sullivan, C. (2019). Analyzing the degree of consensus in current academic literature on critical pedagogy. *Scenario, 13*(2), 70–91.

Webb, A. S., & Welsh, A. J. (2019). Phenomenology as a methodology for scholarship of teaching and learning research. *Teaching & Learning Inquiry, 7*(1), 168–81.

Williamson, B., Eynon, R., & Potter, J. (2020). Pandemic politics, pedagogies and practices: Digital technologies and distance education during the coronavirus emergency. *Learning, Media and Technology, 45*(2), 107–114.

Witze, A. (2020, June 1). Universities will never be the same after the coronavirus crisis. *Nature*. https://www.nature.com/articles/d41586-020-01518-y.

Wong, B. (2020). Universities are failing their students during the coronavirus outbreak. *Times Higher Education*. https://www.timeshighereducation.com/blog/universities-are-failing-their-students-during-coronavirus-outbreak.

Young, J. (2019, June 14). What is critical digital pedagogy, and why does higher ed need it? *EdSurge*. https://www.edsurge.com/news/2019-06-04-what-is-critical-digital-pedagogy-and-why-does-higher-ed-need-it.

Zhu, X., & Liu, J. (2020). Education in and after COVID-19: Immediate responses and long-term visions. *Postdigital Science and Education, 2*(3), 695–699.

Digital Redlining, Minimal Computing, and Equity

Lee Skallerup Bessette

When institutions of higher education moved to emergency distance delivery because of COVID-19 in the spring of 2020, the harsh realities of the economic divide that still exists in the United States were laid bare; students returned home to face a wide variety of stresses, such as food and housing insecurity, inadequate working spaces, caring for family members (sick or otherwise), and having to work in essential services jobs to support their families. Pandemic conditions also made it impossible to ignore the unequal access to technology that students face in the United States; they could no longer rely on places such as libraries or local Starbucks or McDonald's, as inadequate as they might have been under normal circumstances. Many international students were beholden to the systemic limitations of their countries' infrastructure and to the possible censorship of their governments. Under quarantine, students were bound at home and thus unable to access local services, on top of being cut off from the services offered by their institutions. Instead, faculty members and higher education writ large were forced to confront the realities born from various forms of digital redlining—"tech policies, practices, pedagogy, and investment decisions that reinforce class and race boundaries" (Stachowiak & Gilliard, 2019)—and its unequal impact on students, particularly those already at risk. Digital redlining is not limited to those living in the

United States—systemic digital discrimination exists in different forms and formats around the world.

In the following discussion, I will apply key concepts of minimal computing to online/distance learning as a response to digital redlining. Minimal computing invites critical engagement with the following questions.

- What do students need?
- What are the cultural and material contexts of students' remote learning environments?
- How can education be made safer, more accessible, and more equitable?
- Which forms of engagement can be implemented that take these questions into consideration?

These questions and concerns directly intersect with the questions and concerns of critical digital pedagogy: student agency, access, inclusivity, and social justice.[1]

Digital Redlining

Digital redlining takes its name from the historical practice in housing and real estate in the United States of redlining, meaning that primarily black residents would be denied loans, insurance policies, and other resources in their neighbourhoods, leading to depreciating values of their homes, blight, and eventually eviction, leaving the area ripe for gentrification and development. This is a distinctly American phenomenon that started during the Jim Crow era (the late 1800s to the 1960s) but by no means was limited to the South and in fact was more acutely felt in urban areas.[2]

Digital redlining, then, is the systematic denial or the provision of low levels of service, such as providing lower broadband speeds, charging more for the same services offered at lower prices to wealthier, whiter areas, and offering little high-quality mobile coverage (Cornish, 2015; Flahive, 2020; Jackson, 2017; Tveten, 2016). As Gilliard and Culik (2016) put it, digital redlining is not a renaming of the digital divide. It is a different thing, a set of education policies, investment decisions, and IT practices that actively create and maintain class boundaries through structures that discriminate against specific groups. The digital divide is a noun; it is the consequence of many forces. In contrast, digital redlining is a verb, the "doing" of difference, a "doing" whose consequences reinforce existing class structures. In one era, redlining created differences in physical access to schools, libraries, and home ownership. Now, the task is to recognize how digital redlining is integrated into [educational technology] to produce the same kinds of discriminatory results. Armed with the history of redlining, and understanding its digital resurrection, we glimpse the use of technologies to reinforce the boundaries of race, class, ethnicity, and gender. Our experience is that this problem is seldom recognized as an urgent educational issue. (para. 13)

In other words, in the same way that blacks who could afford a loan to buy a home but were denied the opportunity to do so because of redlining, those subjected to digital redlining are denied services or can only access restricted services based upon the confluence of identity and geography.

This kind of restricted and unequal access disproportionately affects communities of learners already labelled the least likely to succeed in the United States: urban community college students, rural students, tribal college students, and so on. For example, when the pandemic necessitated the shutdown of tribal colleges and universities, the impact of digital redlining was felt acutely, with tribal colleges and universities facing aging infrastructure, little experience with online learning, and students widely dispersed with little to no access: "Internet providers are working with local communities like Standing Rock to expand access, but in Indian Country the starting line is far behind the rest of the country. Moreover, there's little to no profit motive for improving connectivity on reservations that are situated in some of the poorest counties in the nation" (Shreve, 2020, para. 20).

Although students might have access to the necessary hardware (desktop, laptop, tablet, smartphone), nonetheless they are less likely to have adequate access to the underlying digital infrastructure necessary to participate fully in online or hybrid classes. A study of the success rates of online versus face-to-face courses at community and technical colleges shows that "at-risk" students do demonstrably worse in online courses, but the study barely notes that the digital divide and digital redlining might have affected students' success rates (Xu & Jaggars, 2014, p. 636). So a student returning to her home on an Indian reservation would have limited access to the digital infrastructure necessary to participate fully in online courses.

Access to technology is not the only consideration for creating truly equitable and inclusive learning.[3] Even if students do have reliable access to the internet, their experience of it is often different (see Noble, 2018). As put by Gilliard (2017, para. 7),

> we might think about digital redlining as the process by which different schools get differential journal access. If one of the problems of the web as we know it now is access to quality information, digital redlining is the process by which so much of that quality information is locked by paywalls that prevent students (and learners of all kinds) from accessing that information. We might think about digital redlining as the level of surveillance (in the form of analytics that predict grades or programs that suggest majors to students). We also might think about digital redlining to the degree that students who perform Google searches get certain information based on the type of machine they are using or get served ads for high-interest loans based on their digital profile (a practice Google now bans). It is essential to note that the personalized nature of the web often dictates what kind of information students get both inside and outside the classroom.

Our policies and practices in higher education have thus reinforced racial and socio-economic stratification: we are practising digital redlining whether we mean to or not. In the following section, I outline how digital redlining is embedded in the systems in which and with which we teach.

The Technologies with Which We Teach

Institutions of higher education in the United States have invested in certain kinds of technologies over the past decade for online learning: large, complicated learning management systems, high-quality video creation and streaming platforms, invasive proctoring and other monitoring solutions, as well as agreements with data-hungry companies such as Google, Blackboard, and Panopto. For a student who lives in an area where digital redlining is prevalent, these tools do not, in fact, improve the learning experience, instead impeding it and thus engaging in digital redlining. Many of these tools share a need for bandwidth and lots of computing power. This is compounded by other circumstances that inform teachers' decisions about how to make course materials available. For example, worries about intellectual property can mean that they turn off students' ability to download a lecture video, meaning that some students then have to watch the lecture video in a place where they have a good signal on their phones, rather than being able to download it and then watch it at home. This has become a health and safety issue under COVID-19 since students have been forced to spend extended amounts of time outside their homes in order to participate in or access the learning materials (see, e.g., Salinas, 2020).

Another example is the sudden ubiquitous use of the video-conferencing platform Zoom for distance education in many higher education institutions in the United States. Privacy and security issues aside (but certainly not unimportant), as well as the pedagogical value of just delivering a lecture via video synchronously rather than in a classroom, students with older computers with inadequate processing capabilities have found themselves unable to select a virtual background during a class meeting and thus might have been put in revealing situations in which they are not comfortable. Recently, a black middle-school student was suspended for having what was clearly a toy gun in the background of his room while participating in virtual learning (Low, 2020). Although this was a case in the K–12 system, it highlights the danger of surveillance that racialized learners face at all levels, leaving them vulnerable to and uncomfortable with the potential policing of their surroundings. In other cases, professors require that students have their cameras on the entire time that they are meeting synchronously, so students with lower bandwidth experience constant delays and other issues during the course, significantly altering their learning experience compared with that of classmates with access to adequate hardware and bandwidth.

Students in authoritarian countries are also at risk on video-conferencing platforms such as Zoom. Recent events involving Chinese dissidents and Hong Kong residents (Soo, 2020) put in stark relief the level of surveillance and risk that Chinese students might be under and fearful of, forcing them to participate in discussions that might be interpreted as "public dissent" or creating a digital trail for documentation that can be intercepted by government officials and used against the students and their families. Although access to information is limited by the government, the students also have to worry about their and their families' physical safety when engaging in course materials and discussions. Also, a student who returns home to China is likely to experience digital redlining because of the government's censorship of part of the internet regularly used and assigned to students in the United States (Li & Lahiri, 2020).

These examples show how our approach to online education more generally, and our shift to distance delivery during COVID-19 more specifically, are in fact *digital redlining in practice*. Faculty members and administrators are reinforcing, through collective, institutional decisions, as well as individual decisions (shaped by the available technologies and the policies that institutions have put in place), the inequities that they claim to be working to overcome.

Who Else Is Being Watched?

Digital redlining also encompasses issues, as seen above, of *surveillance*: "Digital redlining arises out of policies that regulate *and track* students' engagement with information technology" (Gilliard & Culik, 2016, para. 10; emphasis added). Communities subjected to digital redlining are also subjected to higher levels of surveillance generally through the increased presence of cameras, more police officers, racial profiling, and other forms of invasion of privacy. Most recently, for example, it has been revealed that the drugstore chain Rite Aid secretly installed facial recognition cameras and software in its stores, which primarily serve black and Latino populations (Gurshgorn, 2020).

Through our choices of ed tech tools, our universities and colleges further reinforce this mass surveillance culture in the name of accountability, disparately affecting marginalized and vulnerable populations by subjecting them to scrutiny and ingesting them into systems that lack transparency about what is done with their personal information. In his provocatively titled "Against Cop Shit," Moro (2020) outlines all of the ways that ed tech polices students' behaviour, ed tech that institutions and individuals have chosen to use, ed tech that students are forced to engage with, ed tech that monitors and reports their every virtual move. As Watters (2020, para. 7) puts it, "we need to dismantle the surveillance ed-tech that already permeates our schools." COVID-19 has accelerated the adoption of enterprise solutions that specialize in monitoring students, or the use of already-present but little-known surveillance features, such as proctoring software or usage metrics (for more on this, see Chapter 3 of this volume).

Another form of digital redlining in the news because of COVID-19 is grading assigned by algorithms according to socio-economic factors as well as past performances on assessments based upon historical results of people with the same socio-economic profile. Cases in the United Kingdom, where students from underperforming schools had their A-levels downgraded (A-levels, 2020), the United States, and elsewhere when International Baccalaureate (IB) scores were determined by an algorithm that disproportionately affected low-income students negatively (Asher-Shapiro, 2020) show how algorithms are not neutral and can affect students' future access to higher learning. It is outside the scope of this chapter to argue against high stakes testing of any form (see Hagopian, 2014), but this new form of algorithmic oppression is a clear threat that will affect students moving forward.

Another example of algorithmic surveillance and its impact on students is a student heading back home, because of remote studies, in a low socio-economic area who would receive different Google search results because of the zip code and how the student accesses the internet. The

Google algorithm makes certain assumptions about the student because of those factors, which then affect the search results. Without the support of the physical library or zip code of their physical campus, such students are at risk of using less relevant resources for projects and assignments. Even while using a private or incognito window for browsing, without the use of an expensive VPN (virtual private network) (again, this assumes that the students and their families understand what these tools are and why they are important as well as how to use them), a student using public wi-fi would be subjected to greater surveillance, less privacy, and a different internet experience based upon the location and wi-fi access.

Critical digital pedagogy demands that these factors be considered when designing courses. But beyond raising questions and providing flexibility for individual students, there has been little effort to think *systematically* about how to address digital redlining. This is where critical digital pedagogy is confronted with the reality of the systems in which we work: the framework discourages this kind of discourse, trapped in thinking about accessibility through the lens of big ed tech. Proposed here is a completely different approach that critical digital pedagogues can take to address the issues of digital redlining.

Minimal Computing

The concept of *minimal computing* can be helpful in rethinking the reliance on bandwidth and computationally demanding, as well as invasive, enterprise solutions for online learning. Minimal computing (see Gil, 2015) is a movement that grows out of digital humanities, concerned with the environmental impact of large-scale computational initiatives as well as the accessibility, inclusivity, maintenance, and long-term viability of certain large digital humanities projects. How do those who do not have ready access to stable broadband and computational power access digital humanities work done with their intellectual property, history, and archives if that work is locked behind a paywall or on a platform that requires high levels of computing power and bandwidth? Such questions are focused primarily on making research accessible, but often the products can be powerful educational resources if they are more accessible.

Sayers (2016a, para. 4) takes it a step further and asks that we consider minimal design when thinking about minimal computing:

> Following the Unix philosophy of DOTADIW ("Do One Thing and Do It Well"), minimal design applauds and even fetishizes simplicity; it boils practice down to necessities. The Jekyll site generator is an obvious example: "No more databases, comment moderation, or pesky updates to install—just your content." From a technical perspective, this design strategy entails responsiveness across devices, optimization, few dependencies, and an investment in plain text, unembellished layouts, and basic templates. Changes to the style and structure of a project should be few and far between. Both conceptually and practically, design should be in the background; it should not be pronounced or assertive. Sites and software should not be feature-rich, either. While a given project may require some programming (e.g., in Ruby), technical details and configurations are rendered less significant than the message or substance of composition: "just your content."

Sayers goes on to explain how minimal computing and design can accrue net gains on multiple fronts: maximum access, maximum accessibility, maximum justice, minimal connectivity, minimal surveillance, minimal externals, among others (see Sayers, 2016b).[4]

Minimal computing runs completely contrary to how institutions typically have approached online learning. There is nothing minimal about video-conferencing tools, proctoring software, a learning management system (LMS), or lectures streamed as videos. One of the most powerful aspects of a minimal computing approach is asking both creators and users (and in this case faculty members and students) to break open the black box of the software and have a better understanding of how it works as well as how to adapt, adopt, and, most importantly, become creative. Faculty members and students gain a deeper and more meaningful understanding of the tools used, embracing the learning opportunities that this approach presents and reflecting critically on our tech use and reliance, the unseen infrastructure to which some are lucky enough not to have to pay attention. Minimal computing is also minimally invasive because, when asking about what faculty members and students need, the answer is not increased violations of students' privacy.

Why haven't concepts of minimal computing had an impact on online learning? Unfortunately, digital humanities and online learning are rarely in conversation with one another, the two movements developing in parallel to one another but rarely intersecting. An early critique of digital humanities was that it was part of the neo-liberal turn in higher education (Allington et al., 2016) and conflated with MOOCs (massive open online courses) (Svensson, 2016). These projects were also developed in different university silos, centres of digital humanities, and offices of online learning. Digital humanists, instructional designers, and IT staff attend attended different conferences, published and read different journals, and developed independent social and professional networks. COVID-19 has provided a space in which to confront these issues critically and put them in conversation with each other and with a larger audience.

Minimal Computing and Online Learning

The old-school approach to distance online learning (using the postal service, telephones, etc.) shares a couple of important similarities with our current approach to online education: the careful building of the course ahead of time and the importance of the design. However, both approaches still disconnect the student from the *making* of learning, from the messiness of the process. Part of the selling points of many ed tech solutions is that they are *seamless* and *efficient*, the same promises of the slickly designed textbook. One cannot and should not ignore altogether the presence of technology, but minimal computing seeks to make the technology *visible* and *legible*. It seeks to break open the black boxes of technology; even though print is still ubiquitous, most people don't understand the process and production of the printed work, much like an LMS elides the process and production of the course.

What is most interesting about taking a minimal computing approach to online learning is that *the process and production are transparent and clear*. How do faculty members make the technology more visible and accessible and, through that process, make the learning more engaging and purposeful? What do students really need? They need learning materials, engagement, and a form of assessment. How might this be done in a minimal computing environment that makes more visible the process of learning? This is another area of intersection with critical digital pedagogy in which students and faculty members have an opportunity to engage with both the *how* and the *why* of the education in which they are participating.

Although engagement with the process of learning might be easier while taking a minimal computing approach, minimal computing presents a challenge to rethink other forms of engagement: student to student, student to content, and student to faculty. How do faculty members engage with students, the materials, and each other? Taking a community-based approach can provide a balanced way for students to engage based upon their own material situations and make the material relevant and accessible through their culture and community. Have them share their stories with their classmates through letters, for example. Students become active partners in their learning by stripping down the materials to their bare essentials *within their communal and cultural contexts*. Minimal computing takes the end user into consideration, and in the case of education the "end user" is the community where the student lives.

This is where traditional distance education fell short: it did not take a minimal computing approach to engagement, instead focusing almost exclusively on content delivery and assessment pieces, nor did it work to make the mechanics of learning more visible. Certainly, instructors designed activities for students to engage with the materials but did not offer many opportunities for the social-emotional elements of learning that are so important. Conversely, our current efforts in distance and online learning sink billions of dollars into expensive, bloated, enterprise solutions that only simulate engagement in many cases and create barriers for some to be able to participate at all.

Using the principles of minimal computing allows students to take more control of their privacy, minimizing surveillance by the institution to monitor and in fact dictate their engagement, allowing students to decide for themselves the safest ways to engage with their communities and contexts, within the larger culture of mass surveillance of black and brown bodies. By removing the curtain, students can engage more meaningfully and evade other forms of surveillance to which they are subjected.

Taking the minimal computing approach to online learning also forces instructors to rethink their courses and pedagogical practices; one reason that many ed tech solutions are so complex and bandwidth hungry is that faculty members simply want to recreate online what they do in the classroom. *What do you really need?* Instead of thinking that online learning is just a transfer, they have to adapt their practices, their pedagogies, their expectations, and, for some, their egos. No longer the sole arbiters of engagement, faculty members must take a step back and enable their students to be their own arbiters of engagement. It would also require faculty to re-evaluate the perceived need to monitor their students via technology. Even as a thought experiment for faculty members, to ask *if you had minimal digital tools, what would your course look like?* can be a meaningful and powerful way to get them to think about online course design differently.

One important criticism of this approach is how do faculty members ensure academic integrity? That is, how do we know that our students are actually doing the work? Swauger (2019, para. 21) addresses this reliance on the surveillance, as well as the criminalization, of our students, particularly those who are victims of digital redlining. His recommendation is to "design assessments, online or in person, that draw from personal experience or require students to apply concepts in unique contexts." Lang (2013) examines cognitive theory and concludes that, to dissuade students from cheating, faculty members should design activities and assessments that foster intrinsic motivation, aim for mastery, are lower stakes, and instill self-efficacy. As described, taking a minimal computing approach does all of these things and does them well. Although cheating and academic dishonesty might never be completely eliminated, this argument is a red herring for dismissing a minimal computing approach.

There have been a number of interesting innovations when it comes to taking such an approach during COVID-19, specifically in courses that have labs or other hands-on components. Anecdotally, I have seen and heard of instructors asking students to purchase inexpensive science kits to perform experiments at home or engaging students by asking them to perform experiments with materials that they have at their disposal at home or in their environment. Cordell (2020) took this approach with his course that was supposed to take place in a letterpress studio at Northeastern University, but instead he had students use materials that they had on hand as well as the minimal computing program Twine to create interactive publications on the web. These courses distilled their learning goals and activities using the question *what do you really need?* and had students use their own agency and ability to achieve the learning goals.

Other Benefits of Minimal Computing

Examples of a minimal computing approach intersecting with disability and accessibility to online learning are outlined by Friedner et al. (2020). They were inspired to write about their experiences because they "each had profound online teaching and learning experiences in the past eight weeks via text alone" (para. 3). Taking a minimal computing approach, they explore "the possibilities offered through 'platforming down,' or paring down the technology we use for online classes" (para. 2). The platform for one of the courses? A listserv (an email sent and received by a group of people who sign up for it). The authors emphasize that "the presumption that speech is inherently superior to other modes of communication and interaction has directly led (and often still does) to the dehumanization of disabled and neurodiverse people" (para. 27). How much of our approach to online learning, which has been facilitated by bloated ed tech platforms, actually has been informed by our internalized ableism? A minimal computing approach can also help us to understand better pedagogical biases for the benefit of all of our learners.

What would this mean to students, particularly those subjected to digital redlining? They could focus on the course materials and learning outcomes rather than on their own safety and whether or not they can engage and participate effectively in the course. If the technological barriers caused by digital redlining are removed, then students are more likely to engage in an equitable and safe educational experience.

What Would Minimal Computing Mean Institutionally?

As Gil (2015) points out, just because something is minimal for one person does not make it minimal for all people. Good-faith efforts by individual instructors to take digital accessibility into consideration through the practice of minimal computing or other approaches are nonetheless hamstrung by the infrastructure and support structures in place in our institutions. The institutions buy the high-bandwidth enterprise solutions and then provide support staff who have the expertise to support faculty members in using those solutions. Our institutions are set up to resist and discourage a minimal computing approach.

Imagine that, instead of paying millions for enterprise solutions and the people to support them, the institution invests in *more* and *different* people who are experts in learning design and minimal computing to assist faculty members in building their distance courses differently. Instructors are already struggling with the technology provided, largely because it is bloated, complex, and unintuitive, so why not embrace a more inclusive and environmentally friendly approach and support a minimal computing approach? What if institutions did not have to pay not only for the software programs but also for the server space to run them effectively, instead relying on lower-bandwidth and less complex digital and technical solutions? What if most faculty members did not require the most up-to-date and powerful computers to run their online courses (understanding that there would be those doing research and teaching courses that require more processing power) because their minimal computing courses would be accessible even with basic software programs and processors? And what if we invested in more staff who would support instructors pedagogically?

Taking this approach would mean that instructors would have to shift their thinking fundamentally about course design and that institutions would have to rethink radically how they provide hardware, software, and support. Issues of invisible labour, sustainability, and other kinds of work that go into maintaining these enterprise solutions would also be addressed. Which kinds of courses could be created and which levels of creativity could be achieved by redirecting money into hiring, supporting, and paying our faculty and staff members to do this work with the money freed up from not having to pay for access to tech that in fact is inaccessible and even dangerously invasive? Or from the money earned through tuition from students persisting and thriving in this kind of environment, in which access and privacy are not afterthoughts but at the forefront of any decision about teaching and learning?

An institution that takes a minimal computing approach to online course offerings, of course, will probably never happen.[5] Our institutions and our culture are too entrenched in the narrative that more tech ultimately will save us, too heavily invested both literally and figuratively in the solutionism that technology promises us as well as the false promise and security of mass surveillance. What minimal computing teaches us, however, is that equity can be at the core of what we do as online educators, and it does not involve more and more expensive technology. It is not a solution to digital redlining but a response that acknowledges the reality that many of our students face while trying to access education, making their cultural and material contexts central to our design of remote learning environments. Thinking through a minimal computing approach to online learning can help us all to think differently about our institutions and our approaches to teaching and learning.

To repeat: taking a minimal computing approach to online learning invites us to consider closely what we need and, most importantly, what *our students* need. These are (or should be) central questions for any critical digital pedagogue. When designing course assignments or deciding which technologies to use, keep that central question in mind: what, pedagogically, do our students need, and how can we meet that need with minimal computational infrastructure? But we also have to start thinking more about the ed tech and digital infrastructures that we support through our institutions and institutional policies. There is space to be able to make positive change toward a more minimal computing approach, but first we have to understand the inner workings of the technology and our institutions. Because a handful of well-meaning instructors can make a difference in the lives of some of our students, if we can make institutional changes, then we will have exponentially more impact.

Key Takeaways

- We need to understand the impact of digital redlining on our students, especially during COVID-19.
- We should understand the concept of minimal computing.
- We need to apply the key concepts of minimal computing to online/distance learning as a response to digital redlining.

Notes

1   Critical digital pedagogy must take a holistic approach to students' learning and well-being; although this chapter covers access to technology, it is not the only consideration in creating truly equitable and inclusive learning.

2   This is a brief introduction to the long and complex history of redlining in the United States. See Richardson (2020) for a more in-depth history as well as how the impact of redlining is still felt today.

3   For a real-time glimpse of what students are facing, follow #RealCollege on Twitter.

4   For the purposes of this chapter, I am limiting myself to citing Sayers (2016a, 2016b) and Gil (2015), but I realize that this gives the impression that minimal computing is a male-dominated subfield, which could not be further from the truth. I invite readers to go to http://go-dh.github.io/mincomp/thoughts/ to get a more diverse and robust understanding and practice of minimal computing.

5   I was going to write "will probably never happen barring a cataclysmic event that wipes out much of our technology and infrastructure," but I don't want to give 2022 any ideas on how it can "top" 2021 or 2020.

References

A-levels and GCSEs: How did the exam algorithm work? (2020, August 20). *BBC*. https://www.bbc.com/news/explainers-53807730.

Allington, D., Brouillette, S., & Golumbia, D. (2016, May 1). Neoliberal tools (and archives): A political history of digital humanities. *LA Review of Books*. https://lareviewofbooks.org/article/neoliberal-tools-archives-political-history-digital-humanities/.

Asher-Shapiro, A. (2020, July 21). Global exam grading algorithm under fire for suspected bias. *Thomas Reuters Foundation News*. https://news.trust.org/item/20200721145229-gm15u.

Cordell, R. (2020, July 27). Building a (better) book student project demos. https://ryancordell.org/teaching/bbb-student-book-demos/.

Cornish, D. (2015, February 5). Is digital redlining causing internet caste system? *Afro: The Black Media Authority*. https://web.archive.org/web/20200107182626/https://www.afro.com/is-digital-redlining-causing-internet-caste-system/.

Flahive, P. (2020, February 25). Who gets 5G—and who gets left behind—has some worried about digital inequality. *NPR*. https://www.npr.org/2020/02/25/809012775/who-gets-5g-and-who-gets-left-behind-has-some-worried-about-digital-inequality.

Friedner, M., Sanchez, R., & Mills, M. (2020, August 2). How to teach with text: Platforming down as disability pedagogy. *Avidly: A Channel of the Los Angeles Review of Books*. http://avidly.lareviewofbooks.org/2020/08/02/how-to-teach-with-text-platforming-down-as-disability-pedagogy/.

Gil, A. (2015, May 21). The user, the learner and the machines we make. *Minimal Computing*. http://go-dh.github.io/mincomp/thoughts/2015/05/21/user-vs-learner/.

Gilliard, C. (2017, July 13). Pedagogy and the logic of platforms. *Educause Review*. https://er.educause.edu/articles/2017/7/pedagogy-and-the-logic-of-platforms.

Gilliard, C., & Culik, H. (2016, May 24). Digital redlining, access, and privacy. *Common Sense*. https://www.commonsense.org/education/articles/digital-redlining-access-and-privacy.

Gurshgorn, D. (2020, July 31). Rite Aid's secret facial recognition system is the tip of the iceberg. *OneZero*. https://onezero.medium.com/rite-aids-secret-facial-recognition-system-is-the-tip-of-the-iceberg-f5839beeb0ab.

Hagopian, J. (Ed.). (2014). *More than a score: The new uprising against high-stakes testing*. Haymarket Books.

Jackson, D. (2017, April 6). Digital redlining: How major American communication companies are controlling who gets broadband access or not. *Atlanta Black Star*. https://atlantablackstar.com/2017/04/06/digital-redlining-major-american-communication-companies-controlling-gets-broadband-access-not/.

Lang, J. (2013). *Cheating lessons: Learning from academic dishonesty*. Harvard University Press.

Li, J., & Lahiri, T. (2020, August 23). Universities teaching Chinese students remotely need to scale the great firewall. *Quartz*. https://qz.com/1888595/chinese-censorship-is-challenging-us-universities-online-classes/.

Low, R. (2020, September 3). 12-year-old suspended over toy gun seen in virtual class. *KDVR*. https://kdvr.com/news/problem-solvers/12-year-old-suspended-over-toy-gun-seen-in-virtual-class/.

Moro, J. (2020, February 13). Against cop shit. https://jeffreymoro.com/blog/2020-02-13-against-cop-shit/.

Noble, S. U. (2018). *Algorithms of oppression: How search engines reinforce racism*. New York University Press.

Richardson, B. (2020, June 11). Redlining's legacy of inequality: Low homeownership rates, less equity for black households. *Forbes.com*. https://www.forbes.com/sites/brendarichardson/2020/06/11/redlinings-legacy-of-inequality-low-homeownership-rates-less-equity-for-black-households/#3bb4bcda2a7c.

Salinas, M. E. (2020, July 17). Without wi-fi, low-income Latino students resorted to doing homework in parking lots to access public hotspots. *CBS News*. https://www.cbsnews.com/news/low-income-latino-communities-digital-divide-coronavirus-pandemic/.

Sayers, J. (2016a, October 2). Minimal definitions. *Minimal Computing*. http://go-dh.github.io/mincomp/thoughts/2016/10/02/minimal-definitions/.

Sayers, J. (2016b, October 3). Minimal definitions (tl;dr version). *Minimal Computing*. http://go-dh.github.io/mincomp/thoughts/2016/10/03/tldr/.

Shreve, B. (2020, April 14). Coping with the contagion: How tribal colleges are responding to COVID-19, a special report. *Tribal College Journal*. https://tribalcollegejournal.org/coping-with-the-contagion-how-tribal-colleges-are-responding-to-covid-19-a-special-report/.

Soo, Z. (2020, June 11). Zoom caught in China censorship crossfire as meetings foiled. *AP News*. https://apnews.com/article/business-technology-censorship-china-beijing-2ba80f30ecaf5aa37852164c3d149514.

Stachowiak, B., & Gilliard, C. (2019, August 3). Digital redlining and privacy. *Teaching in Higher Ed Podcast*. https://teachinginhighered.com/podcast/digital-redlining-privacy/.

Svensson, P. (2016). *Big digital humanities: Imagining a meeting place for the humanities and the digital*. University of Michigan Press. http://dx.doi.org/10.3998/dh.13607060.0001.001.

Swauger, S. (2019, April 2). Our bodies encoded: Algorithmic test proctoring in higher education. *Hybrid Pedagogy*. https://hybridpedagogy.org/our-bodies-encoded-algorithmic-test-proctoring-in-higher-education/.

Tveten, J. (2016, December 14). Digital redlining: How internet service providers promote poverty. *Truth Out*. https://truthout.org/articles/digital-redlining -how-internet-service-providers-promote-poverty/.

Watters, A. (2020, July 20). Building anti-surveillance ed-tech. *Hack Education*. http://hackeducation.com/2020/07/20/surveillance.

Xu, D., & Jaggars, S. S. (2014). Performance gaps between online and face-to-face courses: Differences across types of students and academic subject areas. *Journal of Higher Education, 85*(5), 633–659. https://doi.org/10.1353/jhe.2014 .0028.

PART III
CHANGE

Our house is on fire. I am here to say, our house is on fire.

Greta Thunberg

Critical Digital Pedagogy and Indigenous Knowledges

Harnessing Technologies for Decoloniality in Higher Education Institutions of the Global South

Jairos Gonye and Nathan Moyo

In this chapter, we rethink critical digital pedagogy as a heuristic for a reimagined liberatory pedagogy that both acknowledges the significance of African Indigenous knowledge systems and disrupts the neo-liberal epistemological hegemony that still pervades the Global South despite the physical departure of the Global North as a colonial "master" (Mitova, 2020). The chapter is largely meditative and reflective as we, the researchers, suggest the notion of digital *hegemony* as a novel yet potentially insightful framework for a nuanced analysis of digital pedagogies (for more on digital hegemony, see Chapters 9 and 10 of this volume). Digital hegemony, an offshoot of critical pedagogy (Freire, 1990; Kincheloe, 2008), as a heuristic of analysis, complicates the often used yet conceptually inadequate descriptor "digital divide," exposing its limitations in conceptualizing the situation among citizens of the Global South and in advancing a transformative critical pedagogy of the "digitally oppressed." Even as educators, we have become aware that "access to digital networks does not necessarily prompt meaningful participation" (Köseoğlu & Bozkurt, 2018, p. 158). In the Global South, generally, there remains the unfortunate popularization of the narrative that higher education institutions simply needed to adopt digital technologies and their online learning platforms. In this way, it is assumed, we can narrow the digital divide. The idea of digital hegemony sensitizes us to the reality that the global architecture of knowledge is skewed in favour of the Global North. For instance, the epistemologies of the Global South (Santos, 2014) extant in Indigenous knowledge systems are conspicuously absent in the dominant narratives that define the world.

Breidlid (2009, p. 141) bemoans the Eurocentric denial of any technological or scientific content and method in Indigenous knowledge systems: "Western knowledge and science have played a hegemonic role in the developmental efforts in the South, whereas indigenous knowledge has been characterized as inefficient, old-fashioned and not scientific, and relegated to the realm of insignificance." In today's digital era, we suggest, digitization of pedagogies tends to replicate, and not recreate, what is known and validated as legitimate scientific/technological knowledge. Mere digitization without a critical literacy that decentres the embeddedness of technological gadgets is likely to perpetuate the exclusionary practices of the knowledges conveyed.

It is against the above backdrop that we seek to unmask the complicity of technological/digital gadgets with the marginalization of African Indigenous knowledge systems in Zimbabwean higher education. We do so by advancing a critical digital literacy that troubles the taken-for-granted neutrality of technology and digitization in knowledge production and learning in the technology-receiving Global South. We draw from our previous works, "forged in the crucible of the anticolonial struggles against Western European imperialism that deployed racism as a tool to oppress Africans" (Gonye & Moyo, 2018, p. 158), to question the hegemonic educational practices fuelled by Euro-American ideologies under the banner of globalization and its concomitant technologization and digitization of knowledge production and learning. As lecturers stationed at a state university located 300 kilometres south of the capital, Harare, and whose mandate is to drive heritage- and culture-based education, we find ourselves appropriately situated to discuss the interplay of digital hegemony and Indigenous knowledge systems. Since at Great Zimbabwe

University we are currently involved in the training of pre-service student teachers and the upgrading of already trained in-service teachers, whose clients are mostly Zimbabwe's outlying rural primary and secondary schools, we consider the interrogation of the digitization of pedagogy and knowledge at the expense of Indigenous knowledges as critical. In this chapter, we extend and deepen our original analysis to focus primarily on how technology and digitization, by virtue of their origins in the Global North, are deeply implicated in the coloniality of power and knowledge (Ndlovu-Gatsheni, 2018), hence the need to deploy a digitally conscious decolonial pedagogy to counteract their effects. To this end, we have argued for an *African critical race theory* (Gonye & Moyo, 2018), an African-stance theory that posits the inclusion of African Indigenous knowledge systems as an epistemic insurrectionary practice for unsettling the dominant grammars of knowledge production and epistemological value from the Global North.

The research question that we address in this chapter is how are African (Zimbabwean) Indigenous knowledge systems marginalized, trivialized, and commercialized through digitization and thus deprived of their cultural and liberatory potential? In answering this question, we explore and suggest critical discursive pedagogies aware of the subtle yet real politics of knowledge construction that permeate technology/gadgets and the digitization of knowledge through online learning platforms. Our argument is that the digital affordances of online learning packages and the gadgets themselves ought to be sensitive to the multiplicity of knowledges, cultures, and histories, and even the languages, of the formerly colonized. It is pertinent to note here that African communities in countries such as Nigeria, Tanzania, Zambia, and Zimbabwe, among others, have demonstrated how Indigenous knowledge systems have facilitated their survival in the past and present in terms of agriculture, health, ecosystem maintenance, food preservation, and traditional education.

Our chapter is organized as follows. The introduction has outlined the research problem that informs this study. The next section establishes our positionalities as critical pedagogues in higher education. Then we explain briefly and justify the concept of critical friendship. Our dialogue as critical friends then ensues as we reflect on our research and practice in order to reposition ourselves continually in the face of incoming digital hegemony. Then we deploy a reimagined critical digital pedagogy to interrogate representations of African Indigenous knowledge systems in YouTube in relation to the disciplines in which we teach. The conclusion sums up the strengths and weaknesses of the implementation of a critical digital pedagogy in higher education.

Authors' Positionality

The critical research approach that we foreground in this chapter recognizes the embodiedness of knowing and is avowedly political (Kress, 2011). This requires that we make explicit our subjectivities and how they are central to the ways in which we research and teach.

> Jairos Gonye: Given my literary studies and theories background, I have been fascinated by postcolonial theorists and writers' act of "appropriating"—be it language, literature, or film—in order to undertake liberatory self-representation. In doing so, I have realized that self-representation does not necessarily bring material empowerment for people of the Global South. As I continue to interrogate the legacies of colonialism as manifested in postcolonial practices, I am even more convinced that there is a need to go beyond the rhetoric—"our African ways were/are also good"—to the act of problematizing how Indigenous knowledge systems are good and sustainable though under threat. Evidence is that digital pedagogy is one of those white normative epistemological promises that needs to be critiqued through African critical digital pedagogy, which interrogates whether these pedagogies can accommodate IKS [Indigenous knowledge systems], be adaptable, or be used sustainably. Thus, my passion is representations of African dance in literature and other media. I have drawn from critics such as bell hooks, Ojeya C. Banks, Brenda D. Gottschild, and Thomas DeFrantz, who reconstruct the denigrated and later commercialized African body as capable of staging its liberation through that body's dance.

Nathan Moyo: I think of myself as both a colonial and a post-colonial subject, having lived through both the colonial and the postcolonial phases of the Zimbabwean nation. My study of African history at university heightened my awareness of injustice and exclusion and the search for social justice and inclusion. Whose story is being told and to whose benefit informed my fascination with critical disciplinary history. In becoming a teacher and later a teacher educator, I encountered the work of Paulo Freire, among other critical theorists, and have embraced his call for an education for liberation as opposed to an education for domestication. Since then, I have become acutely aware of the power-knowledge axis as central in knowledge selection. Hence, I teach undergraduate history education in ways that highlight the problem of representation in a world that remains painfully hegemonic.

Toward a Shared Understanding of Digital Hegemony

In this section, guided by the logic of critical friendship in research (Carlse, 2019; Costa & Kallick, 1993), we recapture our dialogue through which we reflected on Eurocentric hegemonic practices. This dialogue illustrates our continued search for an alternative global architecture of knowledge that affirms and validates the peoples, cultures, resources, and epistemologies of the Global South. Such an alternative had to resonate with a critical media literacy that would be useful in unpacking (mis)representation via digital gadgets and ubiquitous online learning platforms. Through such critical engagement, we sought to "make sense of complex ideas and construct [our] own understanding" (Storey & Wang, 2017, p. 112) of a reimagined critical and emancipatory pedagogy for the digitally oppressed of the Global South. The dialogue unfolded as follows.

Nathan Moyo [NM]: In our previous co-authored work, we appropriated the term "coloniality of power" to show how colonialism attempted an epistemicide of African Indigenous knowledges through denigration and erasure. In particular, African histories and dance practices were targeted. We have argued for an insurrectionary pedagogical practice that recognizes the politics of knowledge in order to include knowledges still marginalized.

Jairos Gonye [JG]: Yes, in this current context of ubiquitous technologies, I watch with interest how the fight between post-2000 Zimbabwe and Britain and the West has been playing out on the techno-digital front following the Zimbabwe Information Ministry's decision to harness popular Zimbabwean anticolonial dances such as *kongonya* through live streaming of all-night musical galas. As you are aware, in 2000 the Zimbabwean government began a program of compulsorily acquiring land that was previously owned by white settlers of mostly British descent, and the program had to be defended digitally. Hence, musicians considered patriotic were/are invited to perform in defiance of the Western European media's representation of that controversial post-2000 land reform program as racial and human and property rights issues. Some of these dance videos are available on the internet (mmeproductions, 2013; Red Fox Wayout Records, 2012).

Again, Nyaradzo Mtizira, the author of *Chimurenga Protocol*, satirizes the West's attempt to control what is disseminated and consumed via digital television through two of his fictional European characters. In the novel, the two characters attempt to control what the viewing public can access on TV by activating the mute mode of the remote control. It is important to recognize that Mtizira recognizes this digital warfare over the airwaves, which, though metaphorical, suggests a self-liberating nation's attempt to free itself from economic exploitation and cultural hegemony and misrepresentation. Yet, when it comes to institutions of higher learning, the government authorities, seemingly aware of the implicatedness of digital technology, encourage wholesale adoption of Western European technologies and the proliferating mass online pedagogies. Worrisome is that the authorities do not bother to encourage research on the neutrality of these innovations prior to their adoption. It is therefore our responsibility as scholars and educators to carry out research that debunks the seeming neutrality of digital pedagogies. Such critical digital pedagogies could promote a return to and harnessing of IKS.

NM: I agree that it is us critical scholars who should be at the fore-front of sensitizing students and the public at large about what you have rightly called the digital hegemony of the West. This reson-ates with the power-knowledge nexus in the Foucauldian sense. Foucault sees knowledge as imbuing the powerful with the means to control and determine narratives that may later on be accepted as neutral in the same way as digital technologies are currently considered as politically disinterested. So, in advancing a notion of criticality that is apposite, the media representations embedded in the technologies seek to promote regimes of "truth" that define what valid knowledge is. These regimes of truth (otherwise false) are by definition exclusionary and hence likely to exclude epistem-ologies of the Global South, including IKS. Therefore, our critique should seek to expose the immanent digital hegemony.

JG: Yes, for me, digital hegemony is a reality that pervades the Global South. Digital hegemony means that the recipients and users of digital technologies and platforms such as WhatsApp, Twitter, and Facebook blithely accept that this is the new, uni-versally efficient way of social communication and learning. It becomes hegemony when these users from the Global South fail to question whether access is fair to them all as well as whether such platforms could accommodate their local ways of solving prob-lems, whether the platforms allow real collaborative and critically informed discussions between lecturers, between researchers, and between students and their lecturers and among themselves.

NM: The examples of latest online digital platforms such as WhatsApp and Twitter that you cite above remind me that even the early anthropologists who came to explore Africa used the techno-logical gadgets available to them then. For example, they had voice recorders, then called tape recorders, as well as black-and-white cameras. These anthropologists used these gadgets—in fact, they manipulated their use to tell particular stories. They chose where and when to photograph the Natives so that this would portray the narrative of Africa consistent with what for [Edward] Said was the *Occident's view of the Orient*. The same would apply to the stories that they chose to record. At bottom, then, technology, as little developed as it was then, was about purging the African Indigenous practices of their usefulness and authenticity in their contextual circumstances and sanitizing them for the consumption of the West.

JG: I find your last illustration above quite apt as it shows that digital technology is capable of freezing, fossilizing, and putting Indigenous practice into some kind of lab where it can be analyzed through received information and communication technology and from the perspective of the digital owner. Such so-called scientific processes often ignore the worthwhile local knowledges of the object of analysis and dismiss their locally framed practices. Therefore, it is in this context that critical digital pedagogy has the potential to give voice to the receiving southerners so that they could handle the non-neutrality dimension of digitalizing an unequal world. Critical digital pedagogy could be stretched by infusing to it an African critical race theory praxis that could generate debate on how to facilitate the emancipation of Africans from a digital hegemony that came wrapped in information and communication technology. With digital pedagogies that draw from African critical race theory and reclaimed IKS, it would become possible to rethink and promote locally generated solutions. That way we might deepen criticality and collaboratively find solutions to the legacies and new hegemonies that impinge on the production and representation of knowledge in higher education as we teach.

NM: Agreed. I see the challenge as being about how we recreate what we have called *transformative uncolonial learning* for transformative practices through a critique that exposes the politics of representation implicit in the technologies and consequent digitization of knowledge. As you have already noted above, YouTube has video recordings that reproduce African Indigenous knowledge systems [AIKS] such as stories and dances that could provide an ideal platform for analysis in our respective modules. It would thus be interesting to re-examine them in the context of both history and dance as repositories of AIKS that the West has sought to sanitize digitally in order to make it non-threatening to the neo-liberal hegemony that pervades the Global South.

JG: Yes, digitization in this view is a continuation of the displacement and/or consignment of Indigenous knowledges to the fringes of knowledge. The coming of digital technology follows the beaten path: that is, from the technologically advanced and skilled to those who lack the technology, skills, and competencies to operate and maintain them. Thus, critical digital pedagogy strengthened by our African critical race theory's emancipatory tenets relevant to the African educator and student would promote critical inquiry. Through collaborative research and discussion, like in our case, many scholars and students could realize that simply accepting digital technologies from the Global North only promotes transfer of knowledge and technology and not generation of locally valid knowledge.

A cursory inspection of how the new digital technologies work convinces me that they have to be appropriated and manipulated first. This should begin with addressing their stubbornness to continually reject or translate the Indigenously informed input that we would have commanded into them (computers), such as our Indigenous mother languages, names, spellings, and syntactic systems. It would also be useful to encourage students to critically analyze how some of the contents and methods that they gain from these internet connectivities illustrate the desire to maintain the Global South as the passive non-negotiating recipient. Thus, critical digital pedagogy and African critical race theory jointly applied might spur the participants to liberate themselves from oppressive and disorienting pedagogies.

Having concluded this dialogue, we agree that critical digital pedagogy could work better if it drew from Indigenous knowledge systems to strengthen the notion of critique in a world where technology has become ubiquitous. Hence, we insist that African critical race theory be the underpinning construct that recognizes the need for technology recipients of the Global South to critique the neutrality of technologies and their embedded digital pedagogies. In the following section, we describe our attempts to enact a critical digital pedagogy in the context of the online representations of AIKS through song as history and then dance representation.

Enacting Critical Digital Pedagogy on Online Representations

The representations that we subject to a digitally conscious critical pedagogy are drawn from YouTube, which most higher education students in the Global South find readily accessible. It is highly likely that some students consume these products in a rather uncritical manner that does not trouble the underlying assumptions of what the representations intend them to think and do. First is an account of the fall of the last Ndebele king, Lobengula, in 1893. King Lobengula's rule sprawled over what today are the Bulawayo, Matabeleland North and South, as well as parts of the Midlands provinces of Zimbabwe. AIKS, through song, records this episodic event in the lives of the Ndebele nation. The song is entitled "Kudala kwakunganje" (translated to mean "Things were not like this in the past"). Through digitization, this song has been recorded and is available on YouTube (Lezulu, 2020). The lyrics of the song in Ndebele are given below:

> Kudala kwakunganje
> Umhlaba uyaphenduka
> Kwakubusa uMambo Lo Mzilikazi, Sawela
> uTshangane saguqa ngamadolo
> Inkos' ULobengula yasinyamala
> Kwasekusini izulu
> Wasenyamalala.

Translated into English, the song goes thus:

> A long time ago, it was not like this
> The world changes
> Mambo and Mzilikazi ruled
> We got to Shangani (river) and knelt down

Then King Lobengula disappeared
It started raining and he disappeared
And he disappeared.

The song recaptures the collapse of the then powerful Matebele kingdom following the British colonization of Zimbabwe. During the battle
in 1893 of the Shangani River, the Ndebele Impis with only their spears
were defeated because of the superior fire power of the invading British
mercenary force. King Lobengula fled and is said to have disappeared.
Vanquished, the Ndebele were left to sing this mournful song in remem-
brance of their fallen kingdom. As such, the song constitutes a specific
and painful historical record, yet representations of the song fail to capture the lamentations of a people who have just lost their kingdom and
independence as well as the defiant warrior spirit of arguably one of the
fiercest precolonial armies. Now, choreographed and sung following
the patterns of Eurocentric joyful choral church music, complete with
flowery attire and a flamboyant conductor, the representations and
cadences of the song are a far cry from the lamentations of a people who
had built their nation through valour and bravery in war. Equally lost
is the symbolism associated with the "kneeling" associated with the rain.
The act of bending the knee could be interpreted as an act of supplica-
tion for divine assistance at a time when all hope was lost, with the enemy
forces in hot pursuit. Thus, the sombre yet dignified posture of appeal to
the divine in readiness to fight to the bitter end is lost. That it then rained
is symbolic in three respects. First, the rain flooded the river, leading to
the massacre of the invading foreign battalion. Second, the rain that falls
after the death of a great man is meant to mark one's departure from the
terrestrial world by erasing the footprints of those who attend the funeral.
Third, the rain is a form of welcome into the celestial world. Such an interpretation would be enhanced by reliance on traditional oral repertoire
extant in AIKS. This suggests that relying on the digital recapturing alone
resembles listening to one side of the story.

For a fuller appreciation, students have to consider critically whether
the recording has captured the sense of both loss of and nostalgia for the
kingdom as well as the defiant, never-die spirit that seeks a reincarnation

of the kingdom. YouTube, like a film, has "a mode of address" (Ellsworth, 1997, p. 7) through which it seeks to position viewers socially. This process makes viewers think in a way that the filmmaker wants them to think. Informed by such modes of address in digital representation, our students tease out how digital reportrayals of historical or cultural events select angles for emphasis in representation. In this case, "the pains of colonialism" (Lunga, 1997, p. 191) are not experienced, thus making the song non-threatening to the neo-liberal epistemological order that prevails.

In developing further our reimagined critical digital pedagogy, we similarly focused on how the function and appreciation of Zimbabwean traditional dances such as *jerusarema* and *mbakumba* could be transformed through representation and consumption via online media such as YouTube. The discussion is housed in the "Theories of Literature and Criticism" module. The module is taken by MEd (English) students at our university. The purpose of the module is to enhance students' appreciation of various literary theories and their application in interpreting cultural/literary representations in which students discuss theoretical concepts such as "framing." Before delving into a discussion of specific literary theories, we ask students to comment on Zimbabwean traditional dances performed for uploading on YouTube.

Students are expected to interrogate how the producer frames the dance in the same manner that they might engage with how literary artists frame their texts. In the discussion in the April–August 2020 semester—conducted online on WhatsApp because of COVID-19—students worked collaboratively and tweeted responses that resonated with how artists used frames that suited their preferred interpretations of the dances as well as influenced the interpretations of viewers. With such an interactive introduction, students were better prepared to appreciate how the application of theory enhanced their understandings of the form, content, and value of a text. For instance, they would understand better the meaning of judgments such as "this is a pagan form of dance" when they applied a theory that focused more on formal textures. Interestingly, through collaborative interaction, students also realized how the West, represented by UNESCO, had framed the Indigenous African dances as suddenly in danger of extinction, hence the need to record them. Students commented, for instance, on how *jerusarema* was declared one of UNESCO's masterpieces of oral and intangible human heritage that needed to be safeguarded, despite the Rhodesian (Rhodesia was the colonial name for Zimbabwe) colonial administrators and missionaries having banned it for being licentious and pagan and promoting idleness (Gonye & Moyo, 2015). This apparently renewed interest has led to uploading on YouTube of performances, even by dancers far removed from the first context of performance, including non-Indigenous dancers and local secular musicians or pupils in modern, out-of-context arenas.

To appreciate the political and cultural import of some traditional dances technologically reclaimed and posted on YouTube, there was a need to reimagine their original performances. That is, in the original lived world, the African/Zimbabwean dancer freely moved her or his body and stamped the ground with energy in sync with prevailing social, political, and cultural functions. It was by defiant performances of the banned dances, particularly *jerusarema*, in their colonized communities that Africans demonstrated their latent desire for liberation. IKS becomes important in appreciating how one way of defying colonial administration and missionary censure was by expressly emphasizing, in their dance, the sexually suggestive gyrations that the authorities had criticized. Although the picture of a small schoolchild performing an African dance suggests the intention to preserve and sustain it, viewers should wonder whether the pupil understands the underlying meanings considering that the curriculum did not emphasize the teaching of dance functions. For secular and non-Indigenous dancers, the appropriation of traditional dance forms through globalizing digital video facilities illustrates the apparent commercialization and commodification of African traditional dance and does not necessarily celebrate what that performance originally meant. There is a need, therefore, for critically conscious video producers to ensure that what appears on YouTube is not, at best, the sexually appealing African body to be gazed at or, at worst, an insipid, non-politically provocative dance form that viewers in the Global North can consume at ease.

Conclusion

In this chapter, we outlined the need for a critical digital pedagogy that would enable the reimagining of an emancipatory pedagogy couched in African Indigenous knowledge systems and, at the same time, interrupt what we, as the researchers, conceive as a digital hegemony stalking the Global South in the wake of global digitization. Being largely meditative and reflective, the chapter presented our ongoing engagement with oppressive epistemologies and negative frames from the Global North that find their way through a non-critical digital pedagogy. We found the term "digital hegemony" to be more useful in describing the condition that the Global South finds itself in rather than the usual term "digital divide."

To tease out the subtle power of digital technologies, we re-examined how digital reportrayals of African historical events and traditional practices demonstrated the salient features of digital hegemony. We found that analyses of both digital recreations of actual African historical moments and traditional dances resonated with the question that Johnson (2014, p. 20) poses: "Who does this film (video) think I am, and am I willing to be that person?" We argued that some YouTube uploads, such as the song "Kudala kwakunganje," are imbued with a framing that privileges certain social positions that disempower viewers in the digitally receiving Global South. This calls for a critical digital pedagogy that exhorts African scholars/educators and students to draw from local theories, such as African critical race theory, as they negotiate new knowledges and pedagogies such as those assumed in new digital and online platforms. Such African-informed critical digital pedagogies, we suggest, can help to address the perennial question of the marginalization of AIKS in Zimbabwean institutions of higher learning, which have shown an increasing appetite for digital technologies and pedagogies. In short, we believe that such all-embracing pedagogies can promote sensitive inclusivity that respects the multiplicity of cultures with multifarious forms of equally valuable Indigenous knowledge systems; at the same time, they emancipate students and scholars from the encroaching digital hegemony.

It is our wish, therefore, that the students whom we teach (both practising in-service and pre-service student teachers) appreciate more the implicated nature of the digitization of pedagogy in African countries such as Zimbabwe. Armed with an African-inspired critical digital pedagogy, our graduating teachers might be able to promote, among their young learners in Zimbabwe's primary and secondary schools, an understanding that there are hidden meanings to what they have been offered/are being offered via seemingly neutral and progressive digital platforms. Drawing from an African critical race theory, our students and readers in general can find ways to integrate digital technologies and their assumed knowledges, and AIKS, to level the epistemic field that for long has been tilted unfavourably against African epistemologies and technologies. It is therefore incumbent on us to empower the young generation of learners, at the mercy of digital hegemony, to reflect critically on the implicatedness of technology. This we do by encouraging them to interrogate dialogically—as they interact with—saliently powerful and ideologically framed technologies from the Global North.

Key Takeaways

- Digital technology/digitization is politically implicated in the production/reproduction of knowledge and learning.
- Critical digital pedagogy can disrupt the subtle hegemonic and oppressive tendencies of technology.
- Representations of Indigenous knowledge systems through online technologies such as YouTube tend to be sanitized and rendered non-disruptive or offensive to persistent neo-liberal hegemony.
- Decolonial pedagogy informed by African critical race theory works to encourage African learners to trust their Indigenous knowledge systems.
- Teachers exposed to critical digital pedagogy might reflect more critically on how they work with technology in their engagements with learners.

References

Breidlid, A. (2009). Culture, Indigenous knowledge systems and sustainable development: A critical view of education in an African context. *International Journal of Educational Development, 29*, 140–148.

Carsle, J. E. (2019). Writing centre consultants as critical friends. *Stellenbosch Papers in Linguistics Plus, 57*, 183–194. https://doi.org/10.5842/57-0-817.

Costa, A., & Kallick, B. (1993). Through the lens of a critical friend. *Educational Leadership, 51*(2), 49–51.

de Sousa Santos, B. (2014). *Epistemologies of the South: Justice against epistemicide.* Paradigm Publishers.

Ellsworth, E. (1997). *Teaching positions: Difference, pedagogy, and the power of address.* Teachers College.

Freire, P. (1990). *Pedagogy of the oppressed.* Continuum.

Gonye, J., & Moyo, N. (2015). Traditional African dance education as curriculum reimagination in Zimbabwe: A rethink of policy and practice of dance education in the primary schools. *Research in Dance Education, 16*(3), 259–275. https://doi.org/10.1080/14647893.2015.1036020.

Gonye, J., & Moyo, N. (2018). African dance as an epistemic insurrection in postcolonial Zimbabwean arts education curriculum. In A. Kraehe, R. Gaztambide-Fernández, & B. Carpenter II (Eds.), *The Palgrave handbook of race and the arts in education* (pp. 157–174). Palgrave Macmillan.

Johnson, T.R. (2014). *The other side of pedagogy: Lacan's four discourses and the development of the student writer.* State University of New York Press.

Kincheloe, J. L. (2008). *Critical pedagogy.* Peter Lang.

Köseoğlu, S., & Bozkurt, A. (2018). #DigPed narratives in education: Critical perspectives on power and pedagogy. *Online Learning, 22*(3), 157–174. https://doi.org/10.24059/olj.v22i3.1370.

Kress, T. M. (2011). Stepping out of the academic brew: Using critical research to break down hierarchies of knowledge production. *International Journal of Qualitative Studies in Education, 24*(3), 267–283.

Lezulu, I. (2020, April 30). Kudala kwakunganje [Video]. *YouTube.* https://www.youtube.com/watch?v=o74QW74Fy8I.

Lunga, V. B. (1997). *An examination of African postcolonial experience of language, culture and identity: Amakhosi Theatre AkoBulawayo, Zimbabwe.* Amakhosi Theatre.

Mitova, V. (2020). Decolonising knowledge here and now. *Philosophical Papers, 49*(2), 191–212. https://doi.org/10.1080/05568641.2020.1779606.

mmeproductions. (2013, October 19). *Sister Constance live @ Zim Dance Gala @33* [Video]. *YouTube.* https://www.youtube.com/watch?v=6gtupRtlIVg.

Ndlovu-Gatsheni, S. J. (2018). *Epistemic freedom in Africa.* Taylor & Francis.

Red Fox Wayout Records. (2012, December 12). *Mic Inity at Unity Gala 2012 Gokwe Centre* [Video]. *YouTube.* https://www.youtube.com/watch?v=MzuK6pXDC2w.

Storey, V., & Wang, V. (2017). Critical friends protocol andragogy and learning in a graduate classroom. *Adult Learning, 28*(3), 107–114.

La Clave
Culturally Relevant Pedagogy in Digital Praxis

9

Maria V. Luna-Thomas and Enilda Romero-Hall

Digital pedagogy, grounded in social justice and anchored by commitment to a democratized educational system, is nascent. For educators thrust into online teaching with little warning or training, fostering inclusive pedagogy might not be a central consideration (Adams et al., 2018). It is in this interstitial moment, caught between traditional classroom teaching and mass migration to online education, that the important work of clos-ing the achievement gap, which persistently affects non-white learners, stands to be forgone. This transatlantic collaboration between two educa-tors with experiential knowledge of how traditional and digital pedagogy misalign with the needs of a diverse body of learners is an effort to attend to the achievement gap in digital praxis. This work is a solution-based endeavour that demonstrates the facility with which a more inclusive and emancipatory digital pedagogy can be espoused. Catalyzed in the theoretical tenets of culturally relevant pedagogy (CRP) (Ladson-Billings 1995a, 1995b), this chapter ventures into under-researched areas in higher education and explores the possibilities of what can be gained from earn-est commitment to asset-based pedagogy, which values students' extant ways of being and knowing, in a digital milieu.

Each year statistical reports of universities in the United Kingdom, where Luna-Thomas resides, yield the same conclusion: the chasm of achievement between BAME (Black, Asian, and minority ethnic) students and white students is unabating. In conversation with Romero-Hall, the persistent cleft between BIPOC (Black, Indigenous, and people of colour) student achievement in the United States compared with their white counterparts was conveyed with equal discontent. Our exchange of observations of why the achievement gap endures led us to question contentious catchall terms such as "BAME" and "BIPOC" that represent non-white students as a monolith forged in homogeneity. Democratic (Giroux, 1986; Ladson-Billings, 2014; Salazar, 2013) and race-critical pedagogy (Ladson-Billings, 1998; Salazar, 2018) would seek to dismantle wholesale approaches to the plurality of student backgrounds that should otherwise be embraced if not at least acknowledged.

We propose that *la clave*, or the key, to closing the achievement gap in higher education is the incorporation of culturally relevant pedagogy and its sister offshoots. Traditional education in the United Kingdom and United States is predicated on deficit-based pedagogy (Ladson-Billings, 1995b), which locates ineptitude in students when they fall short of achieving or adapting to hegemonic ways of being and knowing. This sort of pedagogy is stubbornly imprinted into institutions of higher education and thrives on the circumvention of actionable solutions such as hiring educators who are reflective of the student body or developing teacher training programs that incorporate critical race theory as a framework for reflection (Matias & Grosland, 2016). In response to deficit-based pedagogy, culturally responsive pedagogy sees emancipatory education as predicated on an educator's commitment to critical self-reflection and recognition of teaching as a political act of transferring social values.

More acutely, this work considers how educators can attend to the achievement gap as it stands to replicate itself within the digital sphere. As with in-person classrooms and lecture halls, learning management systems, search engines, social media, and virtual meeting platforms are non-neutral spaces exclusionary by design. We believe that the incorporation of CRP in digital praxis frames technology in critical terms and sets the groundwork for the next evolution of emancipatory education (Emejulu & McGregor, 2016). Engendering democratic, socially just, and inclusive virtual classrooms asks that we embrace our vulnerabilities. CRP in digital praxis will require a distinct set of resources, potentially unfamiliar modes of reflectivity, and a trial-and-error approach (Adams et al., 2018), yet what stands to be gained is a learning experience in which students feel seen, included, valued, and prepared to perpetuate democratic digital citizenship.

The heuristic resources herewith have been forged with allies in mind. We provide exploratory solutions developed for educators who espouse asset-based pedagogies in the classroom and seek ways to foster inclusivity in the virtual lecture hall, those who practise empathy in the seminar group and wish to (re)create safe spaces online, and those who share our experiential knowledge of institutional discrimination and digital hegemony (for more on digital hegemony, see Chapter 8 of this volume).

Context

At the time of writing this chapter, the COVID-19 virus shows no signs of abating, though several vaccines have been developed, and their global dissemination is being strategized. The virus has pummelled global economies, fundamentally changed how we socialize, and for many left lasting impacts on mental health and well-being. In response to the pandemic, higher education has shifted to digital platforms rapidly, en masse, causing significantly destabilizing effects for educators and learners alike (Watermeyer et al., 2020).

As academia is recast in virtual platforms, it becomes imperative to recognize that digital hegemony (Boyd, 2016; Lauzon, 1999) materializes in seemingly race-neutral technologies, affecting BAME/BIPOC students in ways that might not be explicit at first glance. Ruha Benjamin (2019), in her work *Race after Technology: Abolitionist Tools for the New Jim Code*, notes that technological frameworks such as artificial intelligence, digital surveillance, digital marketing, and even automated soap dispensers that fail to recognize black skin are hegemonic instruments that automate and digitize human racism and discrimination.

Further to the point of addressing racism and discrimination, any proper contextualization of this period cannot overlook the global response to the killings of George Floyd and Breonna Taylor. Beginning in the United States, a wave of anger and frustration at systems of oppression challenged structural racism in all of its forms, coalescing in Black Lives Matter protests that ignited across the globe and bolstered existing protests against social injustices. Institutions of higher education are now forced to contend with racist histories, contentious figures reified into statues, and persistent student achievement gaps that negatively affect BAME/BIPOC students in both the United Kingdom and the United States.

The Achievement Gap

United Kingdom

The student achievement gap, or what is known in the United Kingdom as the student *attainment* gap, materializes in statistical reports every year. Data for 2017–2018 show a 13.2% difference in the attainment of top marks, *firsts* or 2:1, between white students and BAME students (Universities UK and National Union of Students, 2019). When the data are examined in greater detail, they reveal that 80.9% of white students obtain top marks compared with black students, who obtain top marks at 57.5%. The chasm in achievement between these racial groups is substantial. Furthermore, statistical data for students in higher education who identify as Hispanic or Latina/o remain invisible since universities do not include Hispanic or Latina/o identifiers in what is likely a reflection of the same omission in the UK census (HM Government, 2011).

Grade attainment is just one way to consider the achievement gap. For any real effort to close the achievement gap in the United Kingdom, universities must consider BAME student retention, the implications for attenuating further education, the growing cost of higher education, the incongruence of white academic staff compared with a growing BAME student population, and curriculums that persistently place whiteness as the normative centre (Universities UK and National Union of Students, 2019).

United States

In the United States, the student achievement gap is palpable. As stated by Samules (2020), "poor students of all races perform worse on tests than more affluent students. And Black students, along with Hispanic and American Indian and Alaska Native students, are more likely than their white and Asian counterparts to be poor." Educational policy helps to enlarge this achievement gap (EdBuild, 2020). The literature on the achievement gap among students in the United States recognizes that societal factors related to structural inequality also play a major role in student achievement (Hung et al., 2020). However, socio-economic issues are only part of the equation. When black and African American youth are asked to reflect on their perceptions of academic achievement, they describe various factors that hinder it: stereotyping and internalizing of negative messages by others, teachers who act as gatekeepers versus supporters of their educational journeys, mixed support from their families and communities, and inequitable distribution of power in terms of cultural considerations that stem from race and ethnicity (St. Mary et al., 2018).

Students Bear the Burden of Closing the Achievement Gap

What remains unclear is how institutions of higher education, particularly those that claim to cater to international and diverse student populations, address the student achievement gap effectively and with evidence of cohesion across disciplines. In attending to factors that contribute to the achievement gap, such as race, language, and culture, McCarty and Lee (2014) add that tribal sovereignty among American Indian and Alaska Native students is a layer of distinction that must also be acknowledged.

Without an actionable blueprint to close the achievement gap, it becomes evident that institutions of higher education locate the problem within the student body. Indeed, the student body continually bears the burden of addressing the achievement gap. Whether marching in anti-black and anti-racist protests, occupying contested spaces, or forging digital counter-publics (Hill, 2018), BAME/BIPOC students have taken up the mantle of reparative action that draws them out of the margins and into the centre (for more on digital counter-publics, see Chapter 10 of this volume). The question that we need to ask ourselves, especially in the midst of this global transition to digital pedagogy, is how can educators actively become allies of BAME/BIPOC students (Adair & Nakamura, 2017)? What can we do to address and ameliorate the student achievement gap the moment that students log into digital classrooms?

What Is Culturally Relevant Pedagogy?

This meditation on emancipatory educational perspectives that seek to radicalize education by creating inclusive and democratic pedagogical practices considers our white allies within the university setting in particular (Adams et al., 2018; Giroux, 1986; Ladson-Billings, 2014). If you are an academic reading this chapter, then chances are you are white, so this shout-out goes out to you. Less than 1% of professors in the United Kingdom identify as black, compared with the 90% who identify as white (Universities UK and National Union of Students, 2019). The same incongruity persists in the United States, where 6% of faculty members identify as black (Davis & Fry, 2019). The data indicate quantifiably that the burden of closing the BAME/BIPOC achievement gap cannot rest solely on black and brown shoulders. The white gaze is reversed here to counter well-intentioned, but socially violent, claims of colour blindness in lecture halls that only work to engender an erasure of students who do not meet hegemonic ways of being and knowing (Howard, 2003; Ladson-Billings, 1998; Matias & Grosland, 2016; Salazar, 2018). We propose that CRP—and a subsequent proliferation of emancipatory and democratic pedagogical frameworks that further this theory—are not the only ways forward but they are viable solutions.

Culturally relevant pedagogy is founded upon the desire to address what Ladson-Billings (1995b) calls "deficit paradigms" of teaching in which students are perceived as inadequate and in need of corrective instruction. It builds upon earlier emancipatory and democratically oriented pedagogies that, at their core, endeavour to foster greater cohesion among culture, home, community, and classroom while validating students' extant ways of being and knowing. CRP is distinct in its insistence that pedagogical application always advances critical consciousness of social and political systems of oppression. Variants of the CRP framework are wide ranging and include vital work such as *culturally responsive pedagogy* (Cazden & Leggett, 1976; Gay 2000), *culturally relevant schooling* (Castagno & Brayboy, 2008), *culturally sustaining pedagogy* (Paris, 2012), and *culturally revitalizing pedagogy* (McCarty & Lee, 2014).

Nearly two decades after Ladson-Billings introduced her momentous and revelatory theory, she offered a retrospective on her research and its theoretical offshoots. *Culturally Relevant Pedagogy 2.0 a.k.a. the Remix* (2014) urges scholars and educators to transition to the more contemporary culturally sustaining pedagogy (Paris, 2012), deeming the framework ideally suited for the burgeoning "multiplicities of identities and cultures" that students embody. Although Paris (2012) lovingly critiqued CRP on the basis that it falls short of centring culture, language, and literacies of systemically marginalized communities represented by multilingual and multi-ethnic peoples, we would argue that these considerations were integrated within the original work of Ladson-Billings (1995a, 1995b). This is particularly evident when she exemplifies linguistic *code switching* between African American vernacular—which conjures Baldwin's *If Black English Isn't a Language, Then Tell Me What Is?* (Baldwin, 1979)—and the dominant, or "standard," English language.

Brown-Jeffy and Cooper (2011) make a compelling observation about CRP in that the framework does not centre race as a site for critical analysis. The proposed solution is an application of CRP employing critical race theory (CRT) as an overlapping framework. Ladson-Billings (1998) lays a foundation in CRT as well. She traces the genealogy of CRT, originally rooted in legal scholarship, to its more recent iterations in education. She defines CRT as the "deconstruction of oppressive structures and discourses, reconstruction of agency, and construction of equitable and socially just relations of power" (p. 9). CRT exposes the current educational system as anchored in white supremacy, which quantifiably benefits white students, teachers, support workers, managers, and administrators (Gomez, 1993; Gomez & Rodriguez, 2011; Johnson, 2002; Ladson-Billings, 1998; Salazar, 2018). As Salazar (2018) notes, education sees whiteness as the "normative" centre, and CRT—which interrogates all aspects of education, including curriculum development, instruction, assessment, funding, and segregation—brings BAME/BIPOC students and academic staff back into the centre (Ladson-Billings, 1998).

As co-conspirators in this discussion on critical digital pedagogy framed by CRP, we pause for a moment to convey our subjectivities since they inform our methodological intentions.

Subjectivity of Maria V. Luna-Thomas

I embody this chapter of my life as an Afro-Latina living in London. Here there are no check boxes for representations of Latinidad. The UK census does not see us. Yet I can hear our voices, our accents—Colombian, Dominican, Chilean—on the streets of London. This data-centric obscurity is reanimated in higher education. My frustration with "colonized curriculums" and the homogeneity of academic and managerial staff motivates my commitment to creating inclusive classrooms in which my students feel seen, heard, and positioned as co-collaborators in the process of expanding our collective knowledge. I engage from the position of a migrant, a Latina who champions her Afro roots, and a feminist who acknowledges her privileges and embraces plurality in ways of being and knowing (Paris, 2012).

Subjectivity of Enilda Romero-Hall

I identify as Latinx, but more precisely I am an Afro-Latinx woman. As part of my upbringing, I completed my K–12 education in Panama. As a young adult, I became an immigrant and a learner in higher education institutions in both Canada and the United States. I do not have a financially privileged background, but because of the importance given to education by my family I have always been motivated to further my studies. My upbringing, educational experiences, and immigrant status have provided a cultural standpoint and disposition toward inclusive, equal, and socially just education.

Affirming the Value of Latino/a Educators

There is value in the deployment of CRP from a subaltern embodiment. Gomez and Rodriguez (2011) comb through studies of Latino/a prospective and practising teachers and highlights their most effective talents: forming family/school connections, leaning toward political consciousness, and developing personal relationships. Our teaching methods, informed by the plurality of our subjectivities, align with these pedagogical modalities. The perception of us as *outsiders* endows us with *insider* knowledge that enables us to practise CRP from a place of empathy whether in-person or online.

Reflection and Culturally Relevant Pedagogy in Digital Praxis

As educators, it is critical to engage in a reflective process that allows us to acknowledge how our life experiences have shaped our positionality and subjectivity as learners in different learning experiences. This reflective process allows us to understand ourselves and to engage in pedagogy that empowers students intellectually, socially, emotionally, and culturally. In a digital environment, there is a tendency to focus more on content and technology use; however, critical digital pedagogy embedded in CRP aims to humanize learning experiences.

Instructors' reflections on humanizing pedagogy entail respecting and incorporating social realities, cultural embodiments, histories, and learner perspectives as integral parts of educational practice (Bartolome, 1994). Reflection as an educator requires you to interrogate your own cultural identity. How would you describe your cultural makeup? Does your place of origin shape your cultural identity? As you prepare to engage your learners, ask yourself just how much you know about their cultural identities, values, and indices. Employ this new knowledge to aid you in designing digital democratic experiences that include all of your learners.

Knowledge Democracy

There are direct connections between CRP and curriculum design. Higher education curriculums tend to discount diverse knowledge systems of the world originating particularly among Indigenous peoples and non-white racial groups. Further erasures are based upon gender, class, and sexuality (Hall & Tandon, 2017). CRP in digital environments lends itself to the decolonization of knowledge by allowing a participatory approach to learning in which knowledge sharing is a social movement that deepens democracy.

Just as we reflect on designing digital democratic experiences, so too we must practise knowledge democracy by acknowledging the existence of multiple epistemological frameworks that include scholars around the world. Curricular sources of knowledge—including books, journal articles, resources, guest speakers, and other instructional materials—should aim to be representative of scholars everywhere whose expertise benefits learners' experiences.

Representation Matters

Romero-Hall et al. (2018) challenge the learning design and technology field by calling attention to our mandate of a "process-based, relational, inclusive, equitable, and transformative community" (p. 27). Yet we continue to oppress and marginalize BAME/BIPOC learners through standard design practice. Too often our learning materials and experiences lack adequate racial and ethnic representation and action. Just as we consider the decor of the physical classroom, which reflects the students who sit in the seats, so too we should consider the "decor" of our digital learning experiences, with images and words that more closely represent online learners. By embracing our BAME/BIPOC students' cultures, we affirm our understanding that cultural distinctions are assets.

Intersectional theory views identities as consisting of multiple social dimensions such as gender, race, sexuality, and/or class. It proposes that the complex interconnections among these dimensions have significant material consequences (Crenshaw, 1989). As instructors and designers, we can showcase the intersectionality of learners by using images that allow them *to feel seen* as part of the learning process. We should aim to use stock photos and illustrations (e.g., Black Illustrations, 2020) featuring people from a range of nationalities, skin tones, and ethnic backgrounds across age, gender, class, sexuality, body type, and physical (dis)ability. Intentionally designed intersectional digital learning materials and experiences with inclusive images acknowledge and benefit BAME/BIPOC learners across all racial groups while also ensuring representation.

Similarly, the representation of a learner's home language matters. It is critical to demystify myths related to language. Mastery of one language or a single variant of it fails to equip learners with the linguistics demanded of the real world (Gay, 2018). CRP in digital learning is truly asset based when home languages are valued and encouraged. Rather than punish learners because of grammatical mistakes, we can be curious about languages and grammatical errors as formative data (Singer, 2018). This can help us to understand what might not transfer from a student's home language and which resources can be provided to support a learner's second-language acquisition. Another way to affirm a home language as an asset is to encourage digital collaboration among learners with fluency in the same language. Encouraging these learners to collaborate or connect facilitates the use of their home language to incorporate prior knowledge, clarify complex concepts, or ask each other questions. Gestures such as embedding multilingual greetings, terms, or expressions in online content, announcements, and synchronous online meetings signal that learners of all backgrounds are valued (Singer, 2018).

Critical Selection of Educational Technology

In teaching and learning, the integration of educational technology provides both opportunities and challenges. One of the main provocations is that educational technology tools are not culturally neutral. Instead, these resources amplify the cultural characteristics of those who develop and promote them, most of whom are members of the dominant culture (Sujo de Montes et al., 2002). As Don Norman stated in *The Design of Everyday Things* (1998), "we tend to project our own rationalization and beliefs onto the actions and beliefs of others" (p. 155). Therefore, as learning designers, we need to internalize the idea that there is no substitute for truly understanding learners, those who engage with the proposed technology.

The critical selection of technology means not turning a blind eye on issues of race, ethnicity, and power dynamics when considering educational technologies to support learning experiences of BAME/BIPOC students. As an example, the adoption of the video-conference platform Zoom by educational institutions across the world during the COVID-19 pandemic left BAME/BIPOC learners and others vulnerable to widespread racist and vitriolic attacks termed "Zoom-bombing" (Ruf, 2020). Such attacks resulted from the lack of privacy features in the video-conferencing tool design and adequate training of instructors before implementation, among other issues. The critical selection of technology also means considering a radical digital citizenship approach. Emejulu and McGregor (2016) explain that this demands the critical analysis of the social, political, economic, and environmental consequences of technologies in everyday life and as a result the consideration of alternatives and emancipatory technologies and technological practices.

Tapping into the Learner's Culture

Knowing your learners is central in CRP. This includes understanding their family lives, histories, and experiences (Gonzalez, 2018). In digital environments, this is even more critical since research shows that interactions in online courses tend to be infrequent and often limited to written texts (Pacansky-Brock et al., 2020). These paradigms can be particularly consequential for students when course work is submitted online. For example, anonymous marking is often engaged as part of the assessment process. However, anonymous marking can inhibit the process of tailoring student feedback. In this circumstance, the incorporation of CRP would facilitate a greater sense of familiarity in the digital classroom, allowing educators to arrive at anonymous marking and recognize students' signature modes of expression.

Tapping into learners' culture can also be nurtured through strategies of social presence (Whiteside et al., 2017). Woodley et al., (2017) specifically suggested validating students' pre-existing knowledge with relevant activities that establish presence, relationship, and rapport. Some of these activities include virtual student introductions in synchronous delivery utilizing directed questions like "Tell me a bit about you," drawing out information about one's hometown, pets or no pets, fun facts, etc., and asynchronous formats (see below sample questions) that encourage learners to share elements of their culture, upbringing, family life, education, and professional experience. As instructors and designers, we can also aim to include activities that aid the development of learning communities within our courses (Bali, 2021). This encompasses digital spaces in which learners feel comfortable sharing with each other in an informal manner such as a *conversation café* with different topics or subgroups (see below for an example of instructions).

Sample Questions

Forum	Description
Tell Us More about You	This is not a graded forum, just a space for you to share about who you are (e.g., family members, friends, hobbies, pets, and so on).
Questions to Classmates	This is not a graded forum. You can create your own forum thread and subscribe to the forum. If you subscribe to it, then you will get an email every time a post is shared.
Interesting Articles	This is not a graded forum. You can create your own forum thread and subscribe to the forum. If you subscribe to it, then you will get an email every time a post is shared.
Wellness and Positivity	This is not a graded forum. You can create your own forum thread and subscribe to the forum. If you subscribe to it, then you will get an email every time a post is shared.

Empathy for and Care of BAME/BIPOC Learners

When embracing CRP, we encourage a learner-centred approach among instructors invested in nurturing the efforts and experiences of BAME/ BIPOC learners (Adeyemi, 2020). Empathy and care are at the core of these nurturing experiences. Caring pedagogues see themselves in a humanizing relationship in which learners' differences are strengths, not shortcomings. This means cultivating an inclusive online course climate that supports cognitive and affective differences. Universal design for learning (UDL) serves a flexible framework that does not assume the "one size fits all" approach; instead, it allows for adjustment to and customization of a learner's needs. As part of UDL, instructors consider digital learning experiences with multiple means of representation, action and expression, and engagement (Pacansky-Brock et al., 2020).

A few examples of UDL that considers empathy for and care of BAME/ BIPOC learners through humanized online teaching include using a liquid syllabus to establish a welcoming tone and effectively support the understanding of content by students from different cultural backgrounds (Pacansky-Brock et al., 2020); using asynchronous discussion boards that allow for multi-modal communication in which learners can compose and share messages using a format (text, audio, or video) in which they feel comfortable (Romero-Hall & Vicentini, 2017); and empowering students through leadership opportunities in the course such as co-designing course activity and/or session facilitation (Woodley et al., 2017).

Netiquette

Ultimately, digital learning experiences that cultivate CRP provide learners and instructors with opportunities to co-create knowledge across cultures, social status, and life experiences. To do so, it is critical to set communication guidelines that acknowledge openness and understanding of difference. A framework that can be used to set these communication guidelines in an online environment is the five *Rs*: respect, relevance, reciprocity, responsibility, and relationships (Tessaro et al., 2018). The five *Rs* have been used successfully to implement online spaces of traditional and non-traditional Indigenous learning in First Nations schools across Canada.

Institutional approaches to digital education often centre on the idea that learners fare best when they adapt learning experiences and institutional values as forms of assimilation. Yet netiquettes that embrace the five *R*s in digital learning environments accommodate and adapt to the learner's needs instead of the other way.[1] The aim of these netiquettes is to ensure that everyone (both faculty members and students) is respectful of others' views and opinions and sensitive to different political and religious beliefs as well as cultural and linguistic backgrounds. Additionally, netiquettes that encompass the five *R*s in digital learning environments can serve as reminders to be respectful of privacy and accurate and factual.

Conclusion

The term "student achievement gap" in education refers to the difference in academic performance among students in subgroups, in which one group of students outperforms another group (Kotok, 2017). Racial achievement gaps are the most studied and discussed because they are significant. Systemic racial inequalities affect educational systems. Therefore, we need policies that protect BAME/BIPOC students from systemic racism in their educational journeys. At the same time, as educators, it is critical to take a stance and truly embrace BAME/BIPOC students. One of the many ways in which we can do so is by valuing distinctions and integrating CRP. There are many declarations and appearances of cultural diversity, but they are more illusionary than real. "The legitimacy and viability of cultural diversity in teaching and learning for ethnically diverse students are far from being commonly accepted among educators" (Gay, 2018, p. 286).

In this chapter, we provided an overview of CRP and stated the need for democratic digital education. We also shared our subjectivity as Afro-Latinx educators and described how it guides our pedagogy. Additionally, we shared actionable practices that aid in the resistance of digital hegemony through the implementation of CRP in digital praxis. These practices include reflection by the instructor on humanizing pedagogy, knowledge democracy by acknowledging multiple epistemological frameworks, design using intersectional visual representations and the use of native languages, critical selection of educational technology, tapping into the learner's culture through the integration of social presence strategies, empathy and care in pedagogy by implementing UDL, and use of netiquette practices that integrate the five *R*s: respect, relevance, reciprocity, responsibility, and relationships.

For educators committed to addressing the attainment gap as it threatens to be replicated online, it is our hope that CRP in digital praxis will aid you in making intentions and objectives manifest. These propositions have also been developed for those who do not know where to begin, those who are faltering in the face of unrelenting change, and those who teach from a place of hope.

Key Takeaways

- Culturally relevant pedagogy and corresponding emancipatory pedagogies address the attainment gap, which disproportionately affects BAME/BIPOC students in the United Kingdom and United States.
- The prevalence of digital learning experiences in all educational levels around the world, further triggered by the COVID-19 pandemic and the expansion of remote learning, engenders greater exposure to digital hegemony.
- Reflective practice is foundational to effective culturally relevant pedagogy online and demands that instructors take a stance in resisting digital hegemony.
- Culturally relevant pedagogy in digital praxis fosters an inclusive environment that embraces multiple ways of being and knowing, promotes democratic learning experiences, validates learners' pre-existing knowledge, is bolstered by empathy and care, and fosters co-creation of knowledge across cultures.

Note

1   The basics of good netiquette:

- Be respectful of others' views and opinions.
- Be sensitive to the fact that online participants represent a wide variety of different political and religious beliefs as well as cultural and linguistic backgrounds.
- Use good taste when composing responses.
- Don't use all capital letters. If you use an acronym, then spell out its meaning first and put the acronym in parentheses, for example frequently asked questions (FAQs).
- Respect the privacy of others.
- Be accurate and factual.

References

Adair, C., & Nakamura, L. (2017). The digital afterlives of this bridge called my back: Woman of color feminism, digital labor, and networked pedagogy. *American Literature, 89*(2), 255–278.

Adams, M., Rodriguez, S., & Zimmer, K. (2018). Studying cultural relevance in online courses: A thematic inquiry. *Online Learning, 22*(4), 361–381.

Adeyemi, S. (2020). *Culturally responsive education in the classroom: An equity framework for pedagogy.* Routledge.

Baldwin, J. (1979, July 29). If Black English isn't a language, then tell me what is? *New York Times.* https://archive.nytimes.com/www.nytimes.com/books/98/03/29/specials/baldwin-english.html?source=post_page.

Bali, M. (2021). Do unto students as they would have done to them. *Times Higher Education.* https://www.timeshighereducation.com/campus/do-unto-students-they-would-have-done-them.

Bartolome, L. (1994). Beyond the methods fetish: Toward a humanizing pedagogy. *Harvard Educational Review, 64*(2), 173–195.

Benjamin, R. (2019). *Race after technology: Abolitionist tools for the new Jim code.* Polity.

Black Illustrations. (2020, November 13). Beautiful illustrations of black people for your next digital project. https://www.blackillustrations.com.

Boyd, D. (2016). What would Paulo Freire think of Blackboard: Critical pedagogy in an age of online learning. *The International Journal of Critical Pedagogy, 7*(1), 165–186. http://libjournal.uncg.edu/ijcp/article/view/1055.

Brown-Jeffy, S., & Cooper, J.E. (2011). Toward a conceptual framework of culturally relevant pedagogy: An overview of the conceptual and theoretical literature. *Teacher Education Quarterly, 38*, 65–84.

Cadzen, C., & Leggett, E. (1976). *Culturally responsive education: A discussion of LAU remedies, II*. Prepared for the US Department of Health, Education, and Welfare. *National Institute of Education*. https://files.eric.ed.gov/fulltext/ED135241.pdf.

Castagno, A., & Brayboy, B. (2008). Culturally responsive schooling for Indigenous youth: A review of the literature. *Review of Educational Research, 78*(4), 941–993.

Crenshaw, K. (1989). Demarginalizing the intersection of race and sex: A black feminist critique of antidiscrimination doctrine, feminist theory and antiracist politics. *University of Chicago Legal Forum*, Vol. 1989. http://chicagounbound.uchicago.edu/uclf/vol1989/iss1/8.

Davis, L., & Fry, R. (2019). College faculty have become more racially and ethnically diverse, but remain far less so than students. *Pew Research Center*. https://www.pewresearch.org/fact-tank/2019/07/31/us-college-faculty-student-diversity/.

EdBuild. (2020, November 13). Nonwhite school districts get $23 billion less than white districts despite serving the same number of students. https://edbuild.org/content/23-billion.

Emejulu, A., & McGregor, C. (2016). Towards a radical digital citizenship in digital education. *Critical Studies in Education, 60*(1), 131–147. https://doi.org/10.1080/17508487.2016.1234494.

Gay, G. (2018). *Culturally responsive teaching: Theory, research, and practice*. Teachers College, Columbia University.

Gay, G. (2000). *Culturally responsive teaching: Theory, research, and practice*. Teachers College Press.

Giroux, H. (1986). Critical theory and the politics of culture and voice: Rethinking the discourse of educational research. *Journal of Thought, 21*(3), 84–105.

Gomez, M. (1993). Prospective teachers' perspectives on teaching diverse children: A review with implications for teacher education and practice. *Journal of Negro Education, 62*(4), 459–474.

Gomez, M., & Rodriguez, T. (2011). Imagining the knowledge, strengths, and skills of a Latina prospective teacher. *Teacher Education Quarterly, 38*(1), 127–146.

Gonzales, V. (2018, August 1). Culturally responsive teaching in today's classrooms. *Diversity Teaching, National Council of Teachers of English*. https://ncte.org/blog/2018/01/culturally-responsive-teaching-todays-classrooms/.

Hall, B. L., & Tandon, R. (2017). Decolonization of knowledge, epistemicide, participatory research and higher education. *Research for All, 1*(1), 6–19. https://doi.org/10.18546/RFA.01.1.02.

Hill, M., & Royal, C. (2018). "Thank you, Black Twitter": State violence, digital counterpublics, and pedagogies of resistance. *Urban Education, 53*(2), 286–302.

HM Government. (2011). Ethnicity facts and figures. https://www.ethnicity-facts -figures.service.gov.uk/style-guide/ethnic-groups.

Howard, T. (2003). Culturally relevant pedagogy: Ingredients for critical teacher reflection. *Theory into Practice, 42*(3), 195–202.

Hung, M., Smith, W. A., Voss, M. W., Franklin, J. D., Gu, Y., & Bounsanga, J. (2020). Exploring student achievement gaps in school districts across the United States. *Education and Urban Society, 52*(2), 175–193. https://doi.org/10 .1177/0013124519833442.

Johnson, L. (2002). "My eyes have been opened": White teachers and racial awareness. *Journal of Teacher Education, 53*(2), 153–167.

Kotok, S. (2017). Unfulfilled potential: High-achieving minority students and the high school achievement gap in math. *The High School Journal, 100*(3), 183–202.

Ladson-Billings, G. (1995a). But that's just good teaching! The case for culturally relevant pedagogy. *Theory into Practice, 34*(3), 159–165.

Ladson-Billings, G. (1995b). Toward a theory of culturally relevant pedagogy. *American Educational Research Journal, 32*(3), 465–491.

Ladson-Billings, G. (1998). Just what is critical race theory and what's it doing in a nice field like education? *International Journal of Qualitative Studies in Education, 11*(1), 7–24.

Ladson-Billings, G. (2014). Culturally relevant pedagogy 2.0: A.k.a. the remix. *Harvard Educational Review, 84*(1), 74–135.

Lauzon, A. (1999). Situating cognition and crossing borders: Resisting the hegemony of mediated education. *British Journal of Educational Technology, 30*(3), 261–276.

Matias, C., & Grosland, T. (2016). Digital storytelling as racial justice: Digital hopes for deconstructing whiteness in teacher education. *Journal of Teacher Education, 67*(2), 152–164.

McCarty, T., & Lee, T. (2014). Critical culturally sustaining/revitalizing pedagogy and Indigenous education sovereignty. *Harvard Educational Review, 84*(1), 101–124.

Norman, D. A. (1998). *The design of everyday things*. MIT Press.

Pacansky-Brock, M., Smedshammer, M., & Vicent-Layton, K. (2020). Humanizing online teaching to equitize higher education. *Current Issues in Education, 21*(2). http://cie.asu.edu/ojs/index.php/cieatasu/article/view/1905.

Paris, D. (2012). Culturally sustaining pedagogy: A needed change in stance, terminology, and practice. *Educational Researcher, 41*(3), 93–97.

Romero-Hall, E. J., Aldemir, T., Colorado-Resa, J., Dickson-Deane, C., Watson, G., & Sadaf, A. (2018). Undisclosed stories of instructional design: Female scholars in academia. *Women's Studies International Forum, 71*, 19–28.

Romero-Hall, E. J., & Vicentini, C. (2017). Multimodal interactive tools for asynchronous online discussions and assessment. In P. Vu, S. Fredrickson, & C. Moore (Eds.), *Handbook of research on innovative pedagogies and technologies for online learning in higher education* (pp. 85–105). IGI Global.

Ruf, J. (2020, April 1). "Spirit-murdering" comes to Zoom: Racist attacks plague online learning. *Diverse Issues in Higher Education.* https://diverseeducation.com/article/171746/.

Salazar, M. C. (2013). A humanizing pedagogy: Reinventing the principles and practice of education as a journey toward liberation. *Review of Research in Education, 37*(1), 121–148.

Salazar, M. C. (2018). Interrogating teacher evaluation: Unveiling whiteness as the normative center and moving the margins. *Journal of Teacher Education, 69*(5), 463–476.

Samules, C. A. (2020). Whose fault is the black-white achievement gap? *Education Week, 39*(17), 6–7.

Singer, T. (2018). *EL excellence every day: The flip-to guide for differentiating academic literacy.* Corwin.

St. Mary, J., Calhoun, M., Tejada, J., & Jenson, J. M. (2018). Perceptions of academic achievement and educational opportunities among black and African American youth. *Child and Adolescent Social Work Journal, 35*, 499–509. https://doi.org/10.1007/s10560-018-0538-4.

Sujo de Montes, L. E., Oran, S. M., & Willis, E. M. (2002). Power, language, and identity: Voices from an online course. *Computers and Composition, 19*, 251–271.

Tessaro, D., Restoule, J., Gaviria, P., Flessa, J., Lindeman, C., & Scully-Steward, C. (2018). The five R's for indigenizing online learning: A case study of the First Nations schools' principals course. *Canadian Journal of Native Education, 40*(1), 125–143.

Universities UK and National Union of Students. (2019). Black, Asian and minority ethnic student attainment at UK universities: #ClosingTheGap. www.universitiesuk.ac.uk/policy-and-analysis/reports/Documents/2019/bame-student-attainment-uk-universities-closing-the-gap.pdf.

Watermeyer, R., Crick, T., Knight, C., & Goodall, J. (2020). COVID-19 and digital disruption in UK universities: Afflictions and affordances of emergency online migration. *Higher Education, 81*, 623–641.

Whiteside, A. L., Garrett Dikkers, A., Swan, K., & Gunawardena, C. N. (Eds.). (2017). *Social presence in online learning: Multiple perspectives on practice and research (higher education)*. Stylus Publishing.

Woodley, X., Hernandez, C., Parra, J., & Negash, B. (2017). Celebrating differences: Best practices in culturally responsive teaching online. *TechTrends, 61*, 470–478. https://doi.org/10.1007/s11528-017-0207-z.

Not Just a Hashtag

Using Black Twitter to Engage in Critical Visual Pedagogy

Mia L. Knowles-Davis and Robert L. Moore

We live in a global society in which we are constantly exposed to new technologies, people, and situations that transform our perceptions and worldviews. As we are exposed to these new experiences, it is increasingly necessary to maintain a critical eye and question what we are seeing. It is not enough for higher education merely to teach material; instructors should also teach the responsibilities and ethics that coincide with it. Encouraging criticality in higher education helps learners to develop a deeper understanding of social justice, inequality, and oppressive systems, and it teaches learners how to combat those issues in their own lives (Chatelier, 2015; Muhammad, 2018). To do so, higher education should seek to adopt a transformative educational lens through which learning is grounded in learners' lived experiences. This can be achieved through the integration of critical pedagogy, which seeks to develop awareness of power structures and one's own position within them, creating the opportunity to implement constructive forms of action (Freire, 2006). Anderson and Keehn (2019) argue that the foundational value of critical pedagogy is the identification and confrontation of power structures that do not support all people. And as Bradshaw (2017) postulates, critical pedagogy necessitates a steadfast and constant review of our daily experiences to ensure that they are responsive to diverse learner needs and experiences.

By aligning educational practices with students' life experiences, teachers can teach more meaningful material.

Digital technologies play an important role in our negotiation of critical pedagogies. Because of our reliance on technology in our daily lives, educators must look for ways to leverage technology in their instructional approaches (Moore & Fodrey, 2018). The pandemic of COVID-19 has demonstrated just how important online learning can be, with instruction pivoting from in-person to virtual settings seemingly overnight in the United States. However, it is critical that the integration of technology into higher education is culturally sensitive and relevant. Inclusive educational technology curriculums are necessary to remove alienating and dehumanizing structures from educational spaces (Bradshaw, 2017). As instructors seek better ways to integrate real-world experiences into their course instruction and delivery (Cho et al., 2015; Lowell & Moore, 2020), they need to ensure that those integrated experiences reflect the lived experiences of students, particularly those from marginalized communities. The challenge can be in identifying and understanding these experiences, particularly when they are outside the lived experience of the instructor. Technology, specifically social media, can provide opportunities to bring those perspectives into the classroom through critical pedagogical practices.

Critical pedagogy involves educating learners to develop a critical consciousness. The critical element requires an ongoing and deep analysis of social stereotypes, hierarchies, and structures in the world, especially those that affect marginalized communities (Bradshaw, 2017). By definition, a marginalized community will not have its perspective or voice integrated into mainstream discussions. Social media platforms such as Twitter present opportunities to give voice to these marginalized communities. In this context, we see Twitter, Black Twitter in particular, as an educational technology tool that can be used to bring marginalized voices and perspectives into the classroom and stimulate critical dialogue. We focus on visual representations in this discussion and use critical visual pedagogy to interrogate power inequalities inherent in media (Shankar, 2014). Next we describe critical visual pedagogy and use Black Twitter as our context for discussing ways to create "counter hegemonic visual presentation[s]" (Shankar, 2014, p. 347).

Critical Visual Pedagogy

Critical visual pedagogy (Shankar, 2014) highlights and investigates the power inequalities reinforced within visual media to pursue counter-hegemonic interpretations and representations (for more on this issue, see Chapter 8 of this volume). This is a method of engaging in visual politics; it has also been utilized to promote the reinvention of radical visual anthropology (Elwood & Hawkins, 2017; Shankar, 2019). Imagery plays a crucial role in creating and reinforcing grand narratives of poverty, suffering, and social status, but critical visual pedagogy promotes the creation of *equitable imagery* (Shankar, 2014; Smiley & Fakunle, 2016). In the context of our discussion, by "grand narrative" we refer to narratives grounded in a Europe-centric interpretation of history used to legitimize oppressive social norms and existing power relations (Linde & Arthur, 2015). The negative stereotypes surrounding natural black hair are an example of a colonial narrative established in the American slave era that has persisted into modern times. This narrative associates natural, protective hairstyles such as braids or dreadlocks with a lack of professionalism and cleanliness (Tharps & Byrd, 2014). Images used in the media perpetuate such oppressive grand narratives. For example, images of India used in anti-poverty agency work and popular US cinematography often depict individuals in a state of struggle and despair but fail to show the diverse lived experiences of the people (Shankar, 2014). To dismantle the power dynamics that use imagery to legitimize oppressive power relations, Shankar (2014) applies some of the key principles of critical pedagogy (e.g., questioning and challenging power structures, using self-reflection, learning through dialogue, and engaging in critical thinking) to interrogate visual media. The objective is to create ethical educational spaces engaged critically and explicitly in the broader social, cultural, political, and economic contexts of education.

Black Twitter as a Site for Critical Visual Pedagogy

An effective way to create ethical educational spaces is by leveraging social media to bring diverse perspectives into the classroom, particularly in less diverse classrooms. Although it was not designed as an educational technology tool, Twitter—a microblogging and social networking tool—provides rich opportunities for critical discourse. When utilizing social media spaces such as Twitter, it is important to consider social media literacy, the understanding of the tasks needed for and the implications of performing those tasks in social media (Livingstone, 2014). Marginalized communities increasingly use Twitter to amplify their calls for social justice and reform (Blevins et al., 2019). Twitter literacy, also known as "Twitteracy," refers to the metaknowledge that users need to interact on the platform, such as sharing tweets or threads and live streaming (Manca et al., 2021). The openness of the platform allows users to take control of the messages and images that they are sharing and gives them the opportunity to broadcast their views to the world. Through the networked connectivity on the Twitter platform, there are opportunities to see how these voices and messages can be shared outside these marginalized communities. Yet millions of tweets are posted on Twitter daily, and navigating through this content can be overwhelming (Moore, 2014).

Filtering tweets using hashtags allows for a focus on specific topics ranging from television shows to subcommunities (Anderson & Keehn, 2019; Moore, 2014). When these hashtags coalesce around a specific theme, they can create a subcommunity within Twitter that can be referred to as a digital counter-public (Hill, 2018): any virtual, online, or otherwise digitally networked community in which members actively resist hegemonic power (on digital hegemony, see Chapters 8 and 9 of this volume), contest majoritarian narratives, engage in critical dialogues, or negotiate oppositional identities created by a dominant culture that alienates individuals to the point that they feel the need to define themselves as juxtaposed to the mainstream instead of defining themselves by who they are (Ogbu & Davis, 2003). One such digital counter-public is Black Twitter—a subcommunity within Twitter specifically interested in issues affecting the black community.

Hill (2018) describes Black Twitter as an online space for rejecting "rigid respectability politics" and organizing resistance to anti-black state violence. Respectability politics is when members of a marginalized group acquiesce to mainstream views to protect themselves from condemnation. But not all discussions within Black Twitter are politically driven. Engagement on Black Twitter can include community discussions of the latest black-themed sitcom or movie—for example works by Tyler Perry—or be a place to highlight, amplify, and bring attention to specific issues affecting the black community. The nature of Twitter allows for a rich discussion with multiple perspectives, and because of the public nature the issues that receive attention within Black Twitter often end up in mainstream media (Knight Foundation, n.d.).

The conversations in Black Twitter regarding social injustices, economic disparities, and other issues affecting the black community globally are invaluable. Within this network, users are empowered to engage in their communities actively and positively and have the agency to partake in these discussions as much or as little as they desire. One example is the Black Lives Matter hashtag (#BlackLivesMatter). It serves several purposes, not only bringing attention to injustices faced by those in the black community but also celebrating the accomplishments of black people and showing solidarity across the Twitter platform. The hashtag was prominently displayed at protests worldwide for the unjust killing of George Floyd Jr., an African American man, on May 25, 2020, by a white police officer who knelt on his neck for 8 minutes and 46 seconds. Indeed, a search for this hashtag will show its broad reach—from a protest in a small US city to a protest in another part of the world. By tagging tweets with this hashtag, anyone can contribute to the conversation. But more importantly, from an educator's perspective, the hashtag is an opportunity to provide real-time insights into the struggles of the black community in the United States and beyond and to bring those experiences into formal learning. Black Twitter is a prime example of how social media literacy can provide opportunities to participate in collaborative spaces that can develop critical thinking skills (Manca et al., 2021).

Tough discussions in the classroom regarding racism and media bias, among other difficult topics, can be facilitated by utilizing discussions on Black Twitter. Anthropology, visual politics, intercultural education, and social justice are a few of the critical pedagogical subjects covered in Black Twitter threads. This is where Black Twitter fills a gap in formal higher education; it identifies areas of concern in a real-time situation and becomes a source for organic instances of critical visual pedagogy. Unfortunately, too often the stories told on Black Twitter remain there and within the black community; we encourage instructors to bring these conversations into classrooms (in-person and online).

Shankar's critical visual pedagogy is a useful approach to make sense of the many narratives on Twitter in ethical ways and to develop aspects of critical pedagogy focusing on the "art-media-technology nexus" (2014, p. 347). The images and narratives shared in Black Twitter tweets are the art, and Twitter itself is both the medium and the technology. Black Twitter, effectively, is a space in which critical visual pedagogy occurs *organically* and provides a platform for practising critical visual pedagogy in a structured way.

The rich conversations on Black Twitter demonstrate that the notion that white scholars are the sole curators of knowledge and the stereotype that young black people are not engaged with the world around them is a serious misconception (Brown & Crutchfield, 2017). Higher education can leverage this wealth of information to identify situations that need attention and design educational experiences for students in a way that can dispel the oppressive grand narrative. Below we provide a few examples that demonstrate why this is important in the US context. This is important for us as black American scholars because grand narratives affect how we, as people, traverse our daily lives. Being a black American means having to be aware constantly of how we perceive our actions, how other members of the community perceive our actions, and how law enforcement perceives our actions. All of these perceptions are affected, influenced, and validated in some way by the images in mainstream media.

Examples from Black Twitter

As we noted, Black Twitter holds a wealth of information, and we think that it is helpful to provide two specific examples along with some broad recommendations for how educators might integrate them into their instruction. Our examples highlight social injustices: how the depiction of crime varies between ethnicities, with black perpetrators typically portrayed in a more negative light than others, advancing an unjust grand narrative of black people as prone to violence and criminality.

Black Twitter often discusses different visual portrayals of criminals along racial lines. Since Black Twitter is an open platform, examples and discussions might not be empirically backed and often integrate the lived experiences of those participating in this discussion. The image attached to Derenic Byrd's (2021) tweet (see https://twitter.com/DerenicByrd/status/1352559036915310594) shows an example of critical visual pedagogy in action. The tweet highlights the varying standards by which black bodies and white bodies are held accountable for their misdeeds. White teenager Riley Williams stole a laptop from Speaker Pelosi's office during the insurrection in Washington, DC, on January 6, 2021, but was released to her mother without incident. In contrast, Kalief Browder allegedly stole a backpack and spent three years at Riker's Island without trial, which resulted in Browder committing suicide. Black teenagers such as Browder are not afforded lenience even when there is no evidence of a crime.

Mainstream media often use labels that vilify black men to shift the blame from the abuse by law enforcement to justify the outcome (Lee, 2017; Smiley & Fakunle, 2016). Black Twitter exposes the double standard in the American justice system that provides an opportunity for redemption, even if it is just in the eyes of the public, for white bodies but not for black bodies. How would you create an activity that helps students to develop critical consciousness of injustices in the American justice system? A visual presentation activity, for example, could challenge students to select a news headline featuring an image that reinforces a grand narrative and then interrogate media through conversations, dialogues, and students working as producers of media. A writing activity could task each student with researching Kalief Browder and Riley Williams and then creating a reflective artifact from the findings. Such artifacts could be created in any medium and shared with others asynchronously or synchronously. In their creation, students would learn about media literacy, design thinking, and critical thinking. It is also important that educators are cognizant of the disadvantages of networked platforms such as Twitter (e.g., echo chambers) and use them as opportunities to discuss important skills such as source checking, digital literacy, and ethics.

As another example, Black Twitter has also noted the frequency with which images of dressed-up white offenders are depicted by the media to show redeemable individuals worthy of a second chance. In a tweet by UrbanTakeOne in 2019 (see https://twitter.com/Urban Take_001/status/1182661482942738433), we see the Walmart El Paso shooter, Patrick Crusius. He is dressed in a suit despite being on trial for the murder of 23 people and the injury of 23 others. In contrast, a black man in a prison uniform, on trial for robbery, is shown with his mouth taped shut by an Ohio judge. Not only is the black man in the prison uniform another example of the representation of a black body being associated with criminality, but also the humiliating implementation of a gag order infringes his dignity. Twitter users argued that there were more humane options such as removing the defendant from the courtroom or fining him instead of gagging him like one might muzzle an animal.

Diminishing black bodies dates back to slave times in which they were treated as products with no say in their own existence (Lee, 2017). Using mugshots of black offenders perpetuates a grand narrative that associates blackness with criminality (Smiley & Fakunle, 2016). Media that feed that narrative to the public deny defendants the innocent-until-proven-guilty standard that the American justice system is intended to uphold. It makes them guilty in the eyes of the public before they have been granted a trial, serving to perpetuate the narrative that black people are inherently criminals. In contrast, displaying white college students in suits and ties contradicts the fact that they are criminals because they are not depicted as such. Since they are presented in a socially acceptable way, they are more likely to receive the benefit of the doubt from the public.

Educators could create a scavenger hunt activity and task students to find other specific examples of images in which a black offender is presented in a more negative light than a white offender. Students could then use online tools of collaboration (e.g., Voicethread or Flipgrid) to share what they have found with their classmates (Lowenthal & Moore,

2020; Oliver et al., 2017). Additional resources for social justice–themed activities can be found using online resources available in the Flipgrid help centre. As the students find examples, they should reflect on their findings. Are they noticing specific sources that tend to portray black offenders more negatively? Are they noticing specific offences that receive more negative portrayals than others? What about communities or socio-economic status, are there any relationships there? In which ways can they see the traces of such grand narratives in content? These critical questions can be extended to other spaces and educational materials. Asking students to examine critically what they see through these types of questions can lead to a deeper understanding of how visual images can be subconsciously advancing grand narratives and how higher education is not immune to such injustices. For example, in a media resource,

- If there are people in a particular image, what are their relationships to each other? Is a hierarchy or social status depicted? How do you come to that conclusion?
- What is the background or setting of the image? Does the setting influence your understanding of the image or the situation?
- What do the textual elements say about the image? How do they align with your interpretation of the image? How do they differ? What does that tell you about the intention of the author/producer?
- How much do you know about the production process? Who designed this image, for whom, and how?
- How would you do things differently? Why?

Asking such questions allows students to critique the content/media creation process and gives them time for critical self-reflection. Would they, consciously or unconsciously, have made the same choices if in the same position? Students need to evaluate critically the impacts of what they design and how their biases and social positions affect their designs. Failure to do so will result in a society that continues to be insensitive to the negative impacts that misrepresentations in imagery and media create for marginalized communities.

Implications

Higher education for some is their first experience interacting with other cultures. Institutions should be responsible, therefore, for ensuring that students obtain critical consciousness of social justice. We recognize that this might be a new experience for faculty members, and we have attempted not only to identify issues but also to provide suggestions for techniques and activities that can be used to integrate these concepts into instruction. Even instructors who are not familiar with critical pedagogy or do not have applicable lived experiences have opportunities to engage their classes in critical discourse. In fact, we encourage those instructors to extend themselves and integrate these conversations about social justice into their instruction. As we have argued here, critical visual pedagogy (Shankar, 2014) can be used as a model to develop instructional activities that foster critical discourse.

In this chapter, we have shown how Black Twitter, and #BlackLivesMatter in particular, serve as a transition from more passive telling of black experiences to showing vividly the grim realities of the black experience in mainstream media. Critical pedagogy encourages individuals to self-reflect and be more sensitive to the realities of others, directly aligning with how #BlackLivesMatter tries to show those outside the black community exactly what it is like within it. Black Twitter makes the movement accessible to others and keeps those following it up to date on every development. Students can learn about the complexities within the black community regarding systemic racism, social justice, and media representation. Individuals outside the black community might not be attuned to the issues or their severity disproportionately affecting that community. The exposure that Black Twitter offers through critical visual pedagogy can broaden students' perspectives not only to increase their awareness of these issues but also to provide them with tactics to identify and address these issues in their own communities. Black Twitter can be used both as a resource to identify incidents and as a source of curation through which instructors and students can engage in critical discussions with individuals in communities different from their own.

As we have highlighted, there are ample opportunities for educators to identify culturally relevant topics and create authentic assignments that foster a deeper level of critical discourse. We also would like to note that we want to see scholars of colour being discussed, integrated, and utilized within curriculums and not simply used as another reading assignment. Although we appreciate hashtags such as #CiteASister that seek to amplify the scholarship of minority scholars of colour, we challenge educators to do more than simply cite these scholars. The negation of grand narratives will require more critical discussion across curriculums and disciplines. The issues affecting social injustice are global and have far-reaching implications.

Conclusion

Globalization has led to more opportunities to experience and interact with other cultures. But along with this shift is the potential to advance grand narratives that warp our perspectives on marginalized groups and countries. We are not always aware when this is happening since it has become so ingrained in our consumption of mainstream media. We have positioned Black Twitter as a digital counter-public that can help instructors to find "blind spots" in their perspectives and experiences. The rich discussions that take place on Black Twitter can present multiple opportunities for instructors looking to identify culturally relevant issues and learn how to integrate these lessons into their instruction. As Black Twitter engages in the critical discussion on the ills of the grand narrative, it also presents resources in terms of both people and scholarship that can be useful for instructors interested in bringing these conversations into their classrooms. Furthermore, Black Twitter plays an important role in integrating critical visual pedagogy into higher education because it provides a starting point for critical discourse. Black Twitter also fosters the voices of people with various lived experiences, whom Bradshaw (2017) recommends seeking input from to engage in more ethical and effective self-reflection and self-interrogation.

To incorporate critical pedagogy into higher education, institutions must establish spaces that foster self-awareness, self-interrogation, and dialogue for individuals to learn from one another. Institutions of higher education that undergo the iterative process of critical digital pedagogy when designing, developing, and implementing learning spaces will foster students better equipped to transform harmful systems. More inclusive and diverse learning spaces that facilitate conversations addressing inequality and cultural bias will create a more just and equitable society. We further challenge higher education to demonstrate that ethical practices within the classroom are not only encouraged by instructors but also essential and directly tied to institutional values and success. We hope that this chapter contributes to the type of transformative change within higher education essential to eradicate grand narratives that further social injustices in society.

Key Takeaways

- It is not enough for higher education merely to teach material; instructors should also teach the responsibilities and ethics that coincide with it.
- Digital counter-publics, such as Black Twitter, can identify our "blind spots" and bring issues involving marginalized people to the mainstream.
- Instructors, even those who are not part of Black Twitter, can use stories in the network to develop critically sensitive instructional experiences for students.
- Institutions of higher education that undergo the iterative process of critical visual pedagogy will foster students better equipped to transform harmful systems.

References

Anderson, M., & Keehn, G. (2019). Tweeting from the tower: Exploring the role of critical educators in the digital age. *Critical Questions in Education, 10*(2), 135–149.

Blevins, J. L., Lee, J. J., McCabe, E. E., & Edgerton, E. (2019). Tweeting for social justice in #Ferguson: Affective discourse in Twitter hashtags. *New Media & Society, 21*(7), 1636–1653. https://doi.org/10.1177/1461444819827030.

Bradshaw, A. C. (2017). Critical pedagogy & educational technology. In A. D. Benson, R. Joseph, & J. L. Moore (Eds.), *Culture, learning, and technology:*

Research and practice (pp. 8–27). Routledge. https://doi.org/10.4324/9781315681689-2.

Brown, A. M., & Crutchfield, J. (2017). Black scholars matter: #BlkTwitterstorians building a digital community. *Black Scholar, 47*(3), 45–55. https://doi.org/10.1080/00064246.2017.1330109.

Byrd, D. [@DerenicByrd]. (2021, January 22). Kalief Browder allegedly stole a backpack at 16, spent 3 yrs at Riker's Island without trial. Riley Williams stole a. [Image attached]. [Tweet]. *Twitter*. https://twitter.com/DerenicByrd/status/1352559036915310594.

Chatelier, S. (2015). Towards a renewed flourishing of humanistic education? *Discourse: Studies in the Cultural Politics of Education, 36*(1), 81–94. https://doi.org/10.1080/01596306.2013.834635.

Cho, Y. H., Caleon, I. S., & Kapur, M. (2015). Authentic problem solving and learning for twenty-first century learners. In Y. H. Cho, I. S. Caleon, & M. Kapur (Eds.), *Authentic problem solving and learning in the 21st century* (pp. 3–16). Springer Singapore. https://doi.org/10.1007/978-981-287-521-1_1.

Elwood, S., & Hawkins, H. (2017). Interdisciplinarity and visual politics. *Annals of the American Association of Geographers, 107*(1), 4–13. https://doi.org/10.1080/24694452.2016.1230413.

Freire, P. (2006). *Pedagogy of the oppressed: 30th anniversary edition*. Continuum International Publishing Group.

Hill, M. L. (2018). "Thank you, Black Twitter": State violence, digital counterpublics, and pedagogies of resistance. *Urban Education, 53*(2), 286–302. https://doi.org/10.1177/0042085917747124.

Knight Foundation. (N.d.). How Black Twitter and other social media communities interact with mainstream news. https://knightfoundation.org/features/twittermedia/.

Lee, L. (2017). Black Twitter: A response to bias in mainstream media. *Social Sciences, 6*(1). https://doi.org/10.3390/socsci6010026.

Linde, R., & Arthur, M. (2015). Teaching progress: A critique of the grand narrative of human rights as pedagogy for marginalized students. *Radical Teacher, 103*, 26–37. https://doi.org/10.5195/rt.2015.227.

Livingstone, S. (2014). Developing social media literacy: How children learn to interpret risky opportunities on social network sites. *Communications, 39*(3), 283–303. https://doi.org/10.1515/commun-2014-0113.

Lowell, V. L., & Moore, R. L. (2020). Developing practical knowledge and skills of online instructional design students through authentic learning and real-world activities. *TechTrends, 64*(4), 581–590. https://doi.org/10.1007/s11528-020-00518-z.

Lowenthal, P. R., & Moore, R. L. (2020). Exploring student perceptions of Flipgrid in online courses. *Online Learning, 24*(4), 28–41. https://doi.org/10.24059/olj.v24i4.2335.

Manca, S., Bocconi, S., & Gleason, B. (2021). "Think globally, act locally": A glocal approach to the development of social media literacy. *Computers & Education, 160.* https://doi.org/10.1016/j.compedu.2020.104025.

Moore, R. L. (2014). Information architecture for social media: A case study on building an event backchannel with Twitter. *International Journal of Social Media and Interactive Learning Environments, 2*(1), 21–36. https://doi.org/10.1504/IJSMILE.2014.059690.

Moore, R. L., & Fodrey, B. P. (2018). Distance education and technology infrastructure: Strategies and opportunities. In A. A. Piña, V. L. Lowell, & B. R. Harris (Eds.), *Leading and managing e-learning* (pp. 87–100). Springer International. https://doi.org/10.1007/978-3-319-61780-0_7.

Muhammad, G. (2018). A plea for identity and criticality: Reframing literacy learning standards through a four-layered equity model. *Journal of Adolescent and Adult Literacy, 62*(2), 137–142. https://doi.org/10.1002/jaal.869.

Ogbu, J., & Davis, A. (2003). *Black American students in an affluent suburb: A study of academic disengagement.* Erlbaum.

Oliver, K. M., Moore, R. L., & Evans, M. A. (2017). Establishing a virtual makerspace for an online graduate course: A design case. *International Journal of Designs for Learning, 8*(1), 112–123. https://doi.org/10.14434/ijdl.v8i1.22573.

Shankar, A. (2014). Towards a critical visual pedagogy: A response to the "end of poverty" narrative. *Visual Communication, 13*(3), 341–356. https://doi.org/10.1177/1470357214530065.

Shankar, A. (2019). Listening to images, participatory pedagogy, and anthropological (re)inventions. *American Anthropologist, 121*(1), 229–242. https://doi.org/10.1111/aman.13205.

Smiley, C., & Fakunle, D. (2016). From "brute" to "thug": The demonization and criminalization of unarmed black male victims in America. *Journal of Human Behavior in the Social Environment, 26*(3–4), 350–366. https://doi.org/10.1080/10911359.2015.1129256.

Tharps, L., & Byrd, A. (2014). *Hair story: Untangling the roots of black hair in America.* St. Martin's.

UrbanTakeOne [@UrbanTake_001]. (2019, October 11). #FridayThoughts #FridayFeeling #justice4all #socialjustice #ElPasoShooting #Blacktwitter #FlashbackFriday #FridayVibes #smh White male kills 22 people in a Walmart and they give. [Tweet]. *Twitter.* https://twitter.com/UrbanTake_001/status/1182661482942738433.

PART IV
HOPE

My hope emerges from those places of struggle where I witness individuals positively transforming their lives and the world around them. Educating is a vocation rooted in hopefulness.

—bell hooks

To Exist Is to Resist

A Reflective Account of Developing a Paradigm Shift in Palestinian Teaching and Learning Practice

Howard Scott and Samah Jarrad

Critical pedagogy is a theoretical position adapted by educators to humanize the learning process. It has a political dimension that seeks, among other things, to dignify and emancipate students by invoking their lifeworlds, critical voices, and outlooks. It also has a pedagogical dimension that sees autonomy, increased choice, and active participation as keys to student empowerment and social participation.

We reflect in this chapter on TEFL-ePal, an Erasmus+-funded project between European staff at the University of Wolverhampton (UK) and Palestinian higher education institutes, where the aim is to innovate local teaching and learning through technologies to "develop flexible curricula, with face-to-face and online courses to be accessible to all learners, with no restrictions" (TEFL-ePal, 2020). Its specific aims are for education to bridge socio-political gaps and give Palestinians a greater voice on the international stage and to develop the use of digital technologies to improve access to and the experience of education. TEFL is Teaching English as a Foreign Language, and the ePal project seeks to enculturate digital tools in Palestinian higher education, but we are mindful that the use of technologies alone is not the way to transform systems.

Our role in the project is to share technological and pedagogical knowledge; however, as we have become immersed in the stories of our partners' lives, it is apparent that transforming traditional methods of teaching is less about practice or teacher knowledge and more about realizing a dignified culture of teaching and learning. As a team rooted in teacher education, we explore in this chapter how digital technologies, aligned with pedagogical strategies, can combine to integrate critical approaches to the professional development of teachers and the dignity of students.

The British partners involved here recognized from the outset the paradoxes and challenges in approaching such a project, and we outline them here.

- We seek not to lead but to learn. In this chapter, we illuminate what we have learned about the context and need for change in Palestinian teaching.
- From the outset, we have understood the potential problems of our presence and have communicated caution to our local colleagues that we do not necessarily hold answers or solutions to complex contexts in which we are outsiders. However, the theme of "outsider" is also imperative to understanding a colonized terrain, and we draw reflections from this theme throughout.
- Furthermore, we understand the cultural limitations involved in transferable concepts and methods as well as the pitfalls in taking an approach that reproduces Global Northern or Western inequalities (e.g., through theoretical reference points or technologies that are monopolistic).
- We acknowledge that technology provides only potential opportunities and affordances.
- We adopt a social constructivist view that this is a multi-voiced project, though its aspirations will be most meaningful where defined by the local partners. However, we believe that participatory dialogue, cooperation, experience, and shared knowledge are keys to multi-stakeholder success.
- We are realistic about what we can achieve but ambitious nonetheless.

We see educational transformation as situated in values that need to be front and centre. In initial sessions with our Palestinian partners, we drew these values out and agreed that focusing education along these lines helps to make a mindset and an ecology possible for critical pedagogy. These shared values favour an educational system that is

- truth seeking;
- forward thinking and nurtures youth as the future and develops leadership capacity;
- implicitly in support of national and local identities while developing a global outlook;
- supportive of an authentic, personalized curriculum that is culturally diverse and open;
- able to utilize flexible, adaptable materials;
- able to foster creative and critical thinking, problem solving, collaboration, employability, and life skills as well as developing character;
- found in an inclusive, safe environment in which student input is (more) active, celebrated, and valued;
- focused on developing mobile and technological capacity in staff members and students in order to support capabilities for autonomous and independent lifelong learning; and
- friendly, facilitating, fair, fun, and firm (plus familiar).

Context

The rationale and the potential for teaching with digital tools to help transform a curriculum that can no longer effectively fit the context are evident when we look at current teaching practice in Palestinian higher education institutions. Educational services are prone to disruption caused by the unique geopolitical context in the region, whether this is the separation wall (which can add up to an hour to a daily commute), checkpoints, and sudden road closures or security restrictions that see institutions close unexpectedly, with timetables, events, and meetings vulnerable to such unpredictability. In extreme circumstances, schools have been demolished or bombed, and soldiers have entered students' family homes at night. Meanwhile, teachers have reported that the regular sight of tanks parked outside schools becomes a common and disturbing distraction (Traxler et al., 2019).

The violence of this external world cannot be left at the threshold of an educational institution for staff members and students. There are frequent gas attacks in Palestinian streets. When students enter classrooms, they commemorate the deaths of peers by leaving their chairs empty but for a photograph: objects become symbols of martyrdom, and the memory is imprinted onto the physical environment and deeper consciousness.

Yet teachers report that "10 minutes a day is wasted talking about the students' stories" (Traxler et al., 2019, p. 10), as if these experiences have no bearing on what takes place within the classroom. This is the power of a critical digital pedagogy—the complex interplay between authentic lived experiences and the affordances of digital tools to communicate such experiences. How can any teaching or learning in such a context as Palestine not confront those realities?

It has long been understood that mobile technologies can bring the outside world inside as well as continue the learning outside the classroom. Technologies can aid a validation of the student's *lebenswelt* (lifeworld), which for Habermas is defined as how our separate realities are shared and communicated in common. In other words, though our social experiences might seem to be private, they are unified through practices and attitudes that inform our perceptions of a shared reality. We are aware as we write that we are toying with the use of *outside* as a signifier of the diminished status that formal education gives to the outside world and the role of outsider—those for whom education does not enable inclusion into the wider world and where the contents of textbooks bear little relevance to it. There is a place within a critical pedagogy framework for realization of the intersubjective through digital activity and its inherently social features—a common convergence of what it is to be outside or peripheral in the world. This has parlance with Palestine's "fragmented existence" (Chomsky & Pappé, 2015, p. 80). At the heart of the occupied Palestinian state is a crisis in sovereignty, which means that a curriculum that promotes self-determination, recognizes national heritage, and preserves Palestinian cultural identity becomes crucial.

Across the TEFL-ePal project, we see the digital as precipitating a dynamic shift in curricular form. This goes beyond the use of tools to access learning to enable a curriculum whose content dignifies its subjects and reifies their world, potentially as co-designed learning in which students and teachers can use participatory tools to "write themselves into being" (boyd, 2008, p. 120) as the authors of their own existence. This is felt particularly in settler-colonialist environments, in which hallmarks of sovereignty such as flags and currencies are oppressed and can vanish at the hands of another. It is perhaps no surprise, but a poignant indictment of the context, that Google Maps has recently removed reference to Palestine from the territory. As a direct challenge, Palestinian educators and students might counter such a move with geotagging themselves, their lives, and their communities onto digital maps so that they enact their existence and integrate themselves into global consciousness. The digital has been said to facilitate a shift toward social constructivist epistemologies (Dede, 2010), for instance through the construction and distribution of knowledge, the blurring of formal and informal learning, and the impact of social network sites to locate identity and to anchor relationships and social activities (Merchant, 2012). As British teacher educators, we want the local partners to talk aloud to the world by connecting and sharing their stories, participating in discourse identities (Gee, 2001), in which communities and individual lives that otherwise would be peripheral are constructed and made visible to the world. This can be enacted in a curriculum that is sovereign and preserves the threatened Palestinian identity.

As stated in our commitments, we recognize from the start that there are limitations to what we can achieve, that there are difficulties in transferring modes from Global Northern and Western contexts, and that the digital only carries the potential for transformation—whether that is practice, curriculum, or both. Traxler at al. (2019, p. 1) argue that a digital literacy curriculum for the Palestinian community is needed, not informed by "dominant conceptions of digital literacy spring[ing] from a largely European context," as we see in traditional practice. In TEFL classroom practice that we observed in Palestinian universities, the native cultures are outside the curriculum. Students studied dilapidated texts from the 1950s, isolating archaic jargon from British literary theory for further discussion in Arabic (rather than the taught language of English). Students sat in a horseshoe layout, which only consolidated the potential for lecturers to direct them, standing front and centre and commanding students' attention from the board to the book and back to themselves, all the while focused on obscure reference points to prosaic English literary texts from the past and checking on memorization with the repetition of pronunciations of words rarely used in modern dialogue. Although it is always unrealistic to generalize, the transformative endeavours of former Minister of Education Dr. Sabri Saidam reveal inherent issues with shifting practice from traditional bases of teaching and learning, in which the learner is the passive recipient of knowledge from an authority to a more progressive perspective.

Attempting to inject modern teaching methodologies into a system reliant on traditional teaching pedagogies, Saidam introduced changes to the schooling system by incorporating technology and making e-school implicit in delivery. E-school is a locally used online portal that gives students access to their grades and what is called qualitative assessment, which usually includes student grades for participation, projects, and presentations. These changes were accompanied by changes in the curriculum to make it more student centred, with portfolios a mandatory part of the assessment of each school subject (up to 30%), thus shifting the assessment paradigm toward alternative, project-based methods.

Unfortunately, the changes were sudden and not well planned and did not take into consideration the different variables that would make an exact transfer of the Western experience unsuitable in the context of Palestine, especially given the huge disparities in class size, availability of supplies, and teacher training. The pilot project proved to be a failure, and the complaints from already overwhelmed teachers and students made it impossible to carry on with it. Therefore, Palestinian TEFL educators have reverted to traditional teaching methodologies, which are still inefficient in helping students reach the expected level of English proficiency that they should have reached for higher education. This situation has led many scholars in the area to research it and address the reasons behind it. It was also reported locally that students were concerned more with buildings being heated properly than with investments in labyrinthine software such as Moodle (a course management system), rarely a decent fit for promoting student-centred learning and too often cast at systemic issues with few nuanced considerations. Moreover, such course management systems are used increasingly by institutions with a surveillance approach, based upon crude learning analytics of how *engaged* students are in top-down teaching methods.

Within higher education, the same mistakes of the Palestinian schooling system recur as teachers replicate the same teaching strategies: rote memorization of vocabulary lists, classic reading texts, prescriptive grammar exercises and exams. Moreover, the testing system functions only to solidify traditional teaching methods since institutions resort to written exams and assign little importance to students' creative and critical thinking skills. There might be occasional in-class presentations, but other than that no modern pedagogical strategies are implemented with technology. Student motivation to learn is low. Once students are in the higher education system, it is extremely hard for university teachers to initiate change since the students have been immersed in a traditional learning environment, and any change is often frowned upon not only by students but also by more traditional instructors, who believe that educators should go with the flow and stop attempting to fix a broken system. It is clear from these reflections that, to transform a traditional system, staff readiness and competence are required to change attitudes toward teaching and learning—to place less significance on what content is acquired and more significance on the process of education. This is the opportunity: to marry pedagogy and technology and to show teachers how technology can be used directly to implement critical pedagogy into cultures of learning.

An increasingly significant dilemma can be added to this binary argument of product and process—that of the *purpose of education.* Along with such didactic and archaic pedagogical constraints are restraints within the geopolitical context of Palestine. Travel, study, and work abroad are inhibited for many Palestinian students, so language learning—though potentially representing a degree of emancipation—can be perceived as contributing to an erosion of national identity and culture that—bound in an environment of geopolitical, economic, and militaristic oppression and isolation—offers little space for agency. This leads us to question reasonably the purpose of an educational system based upon the *banking concept* (Freire, 2014) if its students are unable to be liberated. Such a system, denying emancipation for its participants, can be perceived as offering only the promise to dehumanize them. In critical pedagogy, a rationale can be located—that of empowering students to talk back against outdated and impersonal systems.

Project-Based Learning: A Critical Digital Approach

As British partners on the TEFL-ePal project, we are formally responsible for training local staff by sharing our pedagogical and technological knowledge and skills. Endorsing tools and methods from our own context is problematic, as Traxler (2018, p. 2) observes: "Digital technology that provides challenges and opportunities does however embody language, values, gestures and culture [that] is overwhelmingly Anglophone American and is largely under the control of global corporations and thus alien to many of the world's cultures and communities."

Our approach has been to scale up a project-based learning (PBL), individualized curriculum for two main reasons. First, this approach enables modalities well complemented by digital tools. For instance, portfolios, posters, presentations, videos, or other artifacts can all be designed and disseminated through the use of cameras and free apps on a smartphone. Our approach to PBL enables creativity and collaboration, either curating existing content (via open educational resources) or constructing new material to give much agency and ownership to disenfranchised and potentially passive students. Second, our approach to PBL is personalized and allows students to investigate and represent their own lifeworlds, creating distance between our recommendations and how they are actioned. We ask our partner teachers to engage their students as if they were showcasing their world to an outsider. Through the publication of their world to a wider audience, individuals shape narrative and meaning. Just as Farah

Baker, the Palestinian teenager, managed when tweeting live drones and bomb attacks from her home in Gaza in 2014, so too students can engage in educational acts of resistance where the local population is oppressed (for more on the oppression of Indigenous peoples, see Chapters 1 and 8 of this volume).

The alignment of PBL with critical pedagogy can be drawn from Delpit (2006), who cites Joseph Suina's schematic of three concentric circles of identity associated with different communities: the inner circle is *home/ local community*, the second is *national*, and the third is *global*. PBL is an educational practice that enables an amplification of the local to the outer circles disseminated through digital communication channels—what are described as *codes of linguistic diversity* that enable widespread connections. Using social media, students' stories of local life in peripheral communities can be exchanged globally with other marginalized communities, where acts of resistance to authority have become norms—from Ferguson to Hong Kong via Cairo. Such digital stories have been harnessed widely in citizen journalism that contributed to the Arab Spring or documented abuses that led to Black Lives Matter protests. Although it might be unclear how such literacies are inculcated formally into language learning, a change in what constitutes learning material and educational experience is needed for teachers to conceive that such practices can be applied to learning contexts. It does represent, however, an authentically situated cognition negotiated with and through the real world—a *convergence culture*, as Jenkins (2007) has it, through transmedia storytelling, in which students document their lives across social media. Below is an example of the choices of brief for PBL in the local context to demonstrate how theory is operationalized into activities.

Brief 1: By the end of week 4, you should create a 30-minute "Travel and Tourism" podcast with an accompanying script that describes aspects of local culture for foreign visitors to your home region. The podcast should describe some of the special things that can be found in your locality, from local cuisine to particular music, drama, art, or literature (contemporary or historical). An accompanying Instagram page should be created that links to the podcast and features images and original descriptions of the content featured in the podcast.

Technology required: Instagram, podcast hosting software, Microsoft applications.

Brief 2: By the end of week 4, you should create a YouTube channel with five short (maximum 10-minute) filmed segments included. The contents of the films are your choice but must describe local places and local people, for instance an exploration of a local issue, a report on local social life, an interview with members of the local community (e.g., exploring how life has changed in the area or offering significant stories), or an interesting geographical feature with local historical significance. An accompanying Wikipedia page should also be created that links to the places described in the YouTube videos.

Technology required: green screen, mobile phone, free video editing software (e.g., Splice), Wikipedia.

A personal curriculum is necessary to express and validate the lifeworld of the student in such circumstances—for, as the Palestinians say, "هويتنا كرامتنا" (our identity is our dignity), and to pretend otherwise is emasculating. We perceive how our own pedagogical knowledge can support the values of the project in practice, and they can be borne out with a critical pedagogical lens. In PBL, there is scope for the personal and the cultural, whether by using themes to determine learning content or promoting choice, bricolage in creativity, or exploration of worlds. PBL, alongside other methods of social constructivism (experiential, discovery, problem based) in which interaction, discourse, and mediated meaning drive the process, is an educational paradigm of the possible reified through human agency. Moreover, PBL finds synthesis in digital technologies with socially situated approaches as supporting meaning making, while being highly personalized, as shown by Sung (2007, p. 171) in *glocalized* English as a Second Language classes in South Korea:

> Even though there were designated texts to read, the class moved along with student-chosen topics of inquiry throughout the course.

The topics were important political and sociocultural issues, such as the possibility of [the] reunification of North and South Korea, the popularity of Pokemon characters, the environmental issue of saving the Dong River in the East of Korea, the influence of Japanese media in Korea. . . . [S]tudents were guided to use diverse texts, using multimedia to represent the results of their inquiries. . . . [T]hese students attested that they learned not only English, but also how to use technology in order to construct their understandings of the phenomena.

Reflections on Our Aspirations and Collaboration

Although language learning is the ultimate objective, project-based curriculum sessions are the process vehicle with multi-modal artifacts (e.g., poems, films, discourses, dramas, photographs, stories), an outcome facilitated by a blend of digital tools. In the foreground, critical pedagogy needs to have hope, idealism, and inspiration at its heart—the power of the possible. Dewey's recognition of the power of community to orchestrate cooperation has an implicit place in the modern classroom, and digital tools can facilitate mutual engagement and joint endeavour by methods that encourage "networking practices, information sharing, distributed learning and content creation" (McLoughlin, 2011, p. 850). The nature of digital literacies and the social pedagogies that complement them are inherently collaborative rather than competitive and require assessment that reflects this. At best, student-generated content can reflect an understanding of the world and students' interactions with it—a far cry from examinations that test memorization. To this end, we used the values drawn from our partners at the outset as a kind of philosophical counterweight always to ask in discussions *how does this meet the elements of this framework of values, which are what you and your students expect?* For our part in training and leading elements of the project, this involved

- continually focusing on the Palestinian position in thinking, deciding, and acting;

- making our digital technology workshops cooperative, active, and collaborative (e.g., exploring problem-based learning or colleagues setting a group task using YouTube to upload videos as the site for student-generated artifacts);
- drawing especially from participants' experiences and previous knowledge to inform discussion and activity, particularly by relating every activity to the partners' local contexts (e.g., by asking *how does this work with your students and staff? What are the barriers and constraints? How do you potentially circumvent them?*);
- creating a multi-voiced environment with all views represented, explored, and considered; and
- treating our workshops as social learning opportunities in which we practise what we value (listening, sharing, communicative dialogue, problem solving, respect).

In all of our training sessions, we aimed to inculcate the values outlined by participants in a power-sharing dialogue, seeking to be as inclusive as possible by invoking contributions and reflections rather than presupposing conditions or requirements. We also made an explicit point that this is the way in which we typically teach—with small-group discussions following a task or inquiry, drawing from prior knowledge, building consensus, recognizing different perceptions, and validating those contributions as the basis of a curriculum (though in this instance the *curriculum* became the project's shared philosophical values). Therein, the curriculum is directly representative of the community and its ideas, its values, and contributions help to shape the immediate discourse.

From the initial meeting to launch the project, we recognized some technical constraints and different views. The local partners were keen to invest in computer labs, whereas we perceived this as expensive and unnecessary infrastructure since mobile phones suffice. This is a cultural divergence: whereas smartphones are prevalent in Palestine, coverage is uneven and often unreliable, so hardware becomes a (more) stable resource but diminishes the remote connectivity aspect so valuable to mobile learning practices.

A common need and problem for our partners is finding opportunities to practise spoken language, particularly with native speakers, an issue that might easily be circumvented by technologies that connect remote participants (where available). Digital technology enables the marriage of multi-modal literacies, evoked as a do-it-yourself culture that "incorporates whatever materials and resources are available. . . . [S]poken language, print and other media are integrated; literacy is integrated with other symbolic systems, such as numeracy and visual semiotics. Different topics and activities can occur together, making it hard to identify the boundaries of a single literacy event or practice" (Hamilton, 2002, p. 5).

A partner teacher based in Bethlehem had a unique approach to language teaching, supported by the social network Edmodo. Students prepared short interviews in English about visitors' experiences and perspectives of the environment and city, filmed the interviews, and uploaded them. This was a great example of socially situating mobile learning tools and ideas and the teacher's repurposing of the network as a broadcast channel, utilizing video uploads by students, and providing feedback that became a means of formal assessment.

As partners, we have only minimal influence on such a project, and the needs and desires of local partners are far greater than our powers. As the project progressed, it became clear how much importance the partners placed on the production of course textbooks, the design of which has taken on a traditional and familiar mantle. A textbook can reinforce pre-existing classroom-based power dynamics, a static resource in which information flows one way, an authority figure reading from the front with repetition embedded, content dictating process and assessment. This dependence on textbooks as the main source of learning reflects a lack of synergy with the values that the Palestinian teachers shared from the outset in developing culturally situated pedagogical practices. The Eurocentric learning content, produced by local partners, contained images derived from Western contexts, and cultural activities described in tasks bore little familiarity to Palestinian life or culturally specific notions used for discussion (e.g., in sections that describe how body language carries connotations). The content can be said to signify a level of mimicry of Western norms and potentially dovetails with Suina's schemata of identity, mentioned above, of concentric circles. Such content might have relevance in language textbooks, but it omits notions of social justice and opportunities for students to voice their own realities located in critical theory.

We were interested to note that, as in the United Kingdom, students in Palestine form their own concentric informal learning communities, for example using Whatsapp to practise English, probably accrued in the classroom. This represents an authentic, personalized, social, and repurposed application of classroom-learned content, but informally situating these practices socially among students does nothing to transform the dynamic of the institution as one in which critical pedagogy is manifest in a teacher's mindset, which seeks to challenge the status quo.

Ultimately, we recognize that we have minimal influence on who a teacher is or becomes while training. Available in critical digital pedagogy is the opportunity for teachers to become *change agents*—those who organize situations in which change is possible and active agency can be realized from changes in epistemic perspective and lifeworld ontology. As much as an aesthetic or scientific act, teaching is an inherently political act, wherever it occurs in the world. For disruption to occur, we can either wait for external circumstances to force our reaction or prepare for and enact it.

Key Takeaways

- Digital technologies can operationalize theory that aligns with critical pedagogical principles that enable students to share their lifeworlds.
- Teachers work together to develop a paradigm shift that enables more progressive and active pedagogical practices and an alternative curriculum.
- Integral to this shift is a project-based learning approach, outlined here.
- Working in collaboration with partners on international projects allowed us to identify the values of those partners, based upon their diverse contexts. These values helped to guide our work.

Acknowledgements

With thanks to the Erasmus+ project, which gave birth to the TEFL-ePAL project. Thanks are also due to our partners from Al-Istiqlal University, Palestine Ahliya University, and Al-Quds Open University as well as to our European partners from Chemnitz University of Technology (Germany) and Anadolu University (Turkey), all contributors to the success of this project.

References

boyd, d. (2008). Why youth (heart) social network sites: The role of networked publics in teenage social life. In D. Buckingham (Ed.), *Youth, identity and digital media* (pp. 119–142). MIT Press.

Chomsky, N., & Pappé, I. (2015). *On Palestine*. Haymarket Books.

Dede, C. (2010). Comparing frameworks for 21st century skills. In J. Bellanca& R. Brandt (Eds.), *21st century skills: Rethinking how students learn* (pp. 51–76). Solution Tree Press.

Delpit, L. D. (2006). Other people's children: Cultural conflict in the classroom. The New Press.

Freire, P. (2014). *Pedagogy of the oppressed*. Bloomsbury Academic.

Gee, J. P. (2001). Reading as situated language: A sociocognitive perspective. *Journal of Adolescent and Adult Literacy, 44*(8), 714–725.

Hamilton, M. (2002). Sustainable literacies and the ecology of lifelong learning. *Supporting Lifelong Learning, 1*, 176–187.

Jenkins, H. (2007). Confronting the challenges of participatory culture: Media education for the 21st century (part one). *Nordic Journal of Digital Literacy, 2*(1), 23–33.

McLoughlin, C. (2011, 4 December). Reinventing the 21st century educator: Social media to engage and support the professional learning of teachers. *Proceedings Ascilite*. https://pdfs.semanticscholar.org/3b24/0299c4208dec9e7ab02024b70cb43a8931a1.pdf.

Merchant, G. (2012). Unravelling the social network: Theory and research. *Learning, Media and Technology, 37*(1), 4–19.

Sung, K. (2007). Glocalising critical pedagogy. In P. McLaren & J. Kincheloe (Eds.), *Critical pedagogy: Where are we now?* (pp. 163–181). Peter Lang.

TEFL-ePal. (2020). *What is TEFL-ePal?* https://tefl-epal.ps/what-is-tefl/.

Traxler, J. (2018). Digital literacy: A Palestinian refugee perspective. *Research in Learning Technology, 26*, 1–21.

Traxler, J., Khaif, Z., Nevill, A., Affouneh, S., Salha, S., Zuhd, A., & Trayek, F. (2019). Living under occupation: Palestinian teachers' experiences and their digital responses. *Research in Learning Technology, 27*. https://journal.alt.ac.uk/index.php/rlt/article/view/2263.

Critical Digital Pedagogy
for the Anthropocene

Jonathan Lynch

In this chapter, I suggest ways in which critical digital pedagogy can inform educational responses to concerns about climate change and environmental degradation through learning experiences beyond the classroom. In our current period since the nuclear fallout in 1945, humans have created unprecedented effects on the Earth, with experts suggesting that we have already heralded in a new geological epoch, the "Anthropocene" (Crutzen, 2002). This term denotes that the negative human impact on the planet is so prevalent that it will be identifiable by future generations in the fossil record through the build-up of plastic waste and other markers (Ellis, 2018). As digital educators, how are we to respond to these ecological concerns that can affect our daily lives? For example, recent bush fires in Australia illustrate the possible effects of human-induced climate change (Oldenborgh et al., 2020) and provide a call to response and action. The term "Anthropocene" itself also raises important questions for the human race, such as "what does it mean to be human when this means to be part of a global force that changes everything—even the future of an entire planet? What does nature even mean in an age of human?" (Ellis, 2018, p. 15). As educators in the 21st century, we need to consider how we might harness technology in our educational responses to such questions.

Although educational responses to environmental degradation have existed for some time, they have tended to be pedagogies that privilege a view of the human as separate from nature. If we are to address environmental degradation, then challenging this separation is necessary. Across a subset of disciplines in critical theory and environmental education, there are calls to understand teaching and learning relationally, in which the human and the material worlds are not totally separate (Bonnett, 2004). Such relationality has origins in critical pedagogy, in which education is understood to be shaped by the social, political, and ecological relations within which we find ourselves (Gottesman, 2016). For example, Freire (2013, p. 41) sought to develop a critical consciousness in learners, for "the role of man [sic] was not only to be in the world, but to engage in relations with the world." The attention to relations can provide ways that students might challenge their understanding of power and how they enact their agency.

Establishment of the field of critical digital pedagogy is an important direction for thought and research in education because it challenges the dominance of techno-utopian visions of the future (Facer; 2011; Hannon, 2017). Critical digital pedagogy is a nascent field of theory and practice in which attention to the ecological seems to be missing. For example, Bontly et al. (2017) see "critical digital pedagogy" along citizenship and literacy lines and acknowledge that it is a new term without a clear definition. Yet, writing in sustainability and environmental education, Orr (2017, p. xi) sees both promise and peril in technology and education for the Anthropocene: "I am sceptical about the drift of recent technology, but it is possible that properly used, some of it would enable us to create bonds and actions that amplify our capacities to foster positive changes." In this chapter, I argue that critical digital pedagogy can inform education in the Anthropocene. I start by suggesting how a relational understanding of education that does not privilege the human can help to do this. I then argue that a place-based approach to education in outdoor settings lends itself well to the enactment of critical digital pedagogy. I finish with an example of critical digital pedagogy that I designed and enacted during an outdoor field visit and offer some lessons learned.

Background

Thinking about education relationally encourages us to appreciate our interconnectedness with the Earth. Critical pedagogy has encouraged us to see the importance of relationships with social and cultural systems but has been criticized as a school of thought that privileges the human and human exceptionalism: that is, humans are more important than the more than human (trees, birds, rocks, microbes, etc).[1] For example, some feminist-inspired writing in critical pedagogy has critiqued the notion of the teacher as "intellectual" and argued instead for *standpoint pedagogies* (Noddings, 2012) in which knowledge is seen as situated and embodied. In other words, knowledge is linked to the relations that we find ourselves within and shaped through, not just the actions of an individual educator (Gottesman, 2016).

Although useful responses to climate change need to involve people, imagining solutions from a purely human perspective might not be enough. Theorists across a range of writing in cultural geography (Whatmore, 2006), anthropology (Ingold, 2011, 2013), and feminist materialism (Barad, 2007) are working to address this by contributing to a field of post-humanist thought (Braidotti, 2019; Haraway, 2016). Posthumanism helps us to understand how we might conceptualize and research education in ways that do not privilege the human. In a view of posthumanism inspired by cybernetics, Hayes (1999) challenges Western thinking by rejecting a view of the ontological situation in which we are separated from the world via a subject-object binary. Applying these ideas to educational research, Snaza and Weaver (2015) argue that, as we reconceptualize the human as posthuman, we take a relational view of what were once thought of as discrete entities: human, animal, machine. As a result, within posthumanist thought, agency is not limited to people; it is distributed. Humans are understood, ontologically speaking, not as separate from the environment or the only actants in an educational event (for a more detailed explanation of the distributed agency of posthumanism, see Carranza, 2018).

If we take posthumanist thought into education in outdoor settings, then we find possibilities for reconceptualizing education for the

Anthropocene. Understanding the ontological situation as not being separate from nature means that we are always and already "part of nature." In fact, the term "nature" becomes problematic because it perpetuates dualisms and undoes a relational understanding (Castree, 2000). One approach to this problem is to use the term "more than human," which denotes a non-hierarchical relationship with all that is not human but *includes* the human. The term is important to education for the Anthropocene because it encourages educators to consider a relational or systems view of the environment.

Education in Outdoor Settings

"Education in outdoor settings" is a broad phrase that encompasses experiential education, outdoor education, outdoor learning, environmental education, and education for sustainability. In this chapter, I use the phrase to denote formal education undertaken outside the classroom by tertiary educators. Education outside the classroom can have positive impacts on pro-environmental behaviour, such as instilling a sense of political action for the environment (Chawla & Cushing, 2007) and supporting learners' understanding of global influences on ecological systems (Rickinson et al., 2004). Research has shown that using local places with learners can improve human-environment relations; as a result, there has been much place-based attention to education in outdoor settings (Ardoin, 2006; Mannion & Lynch, 2016; Meichtry & Smith, 2007; Smith & Sobel, 2010).

Although critical digital pedagogy is a nascent field, some of its defined features relate to education in outdoor settings. For example, Morris and Stommel (2018, p. 27) ground their notion of critical digital pedagogy in action; they call on us to focus on the pragmatic in critical digital pedagogy: "So, Critical Digital Pedagogy must also be a method of resistance and humanization. It is not simply work done in the mind, on paper or on screen. It is work that must be done on the ground." To do such work "on the ground," I argue, education in outdoor settings with a place-based approach is one good way to do this.

Education in outdoor settings can improve human-environment relations when it is seen as a pedagogy linked to place. Understanding place through posthumanism can help learners to appreciate their interconnectedness with the more than human and focus education on the relations that we form and sustain with the Earth. The implications of these views are that places can never be just "backdrops" pedagogically. The world is full of abundant relations that can link us to the Earth and the co-implication of any human-environment relation. Snaza et al. (2014) write that, to save the planet and address the environmental crisis, we need to work within a political frame that reduces human dominance. They argue for a politics that puts humans back *into* the web of life, which prevents not only the destruction of animals as a subset of the world but also the destruction of nature for human gain. Next I explain one practical way in which I set out to put humans back into the web of life through an educational activity called *digital wayfaring*.

Digital Wayfaring

In this section, I explain the design of a teaching and learning activity that enacted critical digital pedagogy through education in outdoor settings. In a digital wayfaring activity (see activity briefing sheet on page 209), I encouraged tertiary-level outdoor education students to engage critically with place and human exceptionalism through a video-making task. The students in question were all familiar with making videos on their smartphones but had little prior experience using mobile phones pedagogically outdoors. Although research on digital technologies in education in outdoor settings for improving human-environment relations is scant, Winter and Cotton (2012) did use video-making tasks with students to deconstruct the hidden curriculum of the campus to enhance sustainability literacy. They found that a video-making task enabled students to critique local practices of sustainability and to be creative about sustainability solutions.

The digital wayfaring task was designed using concepts from anthropologist Tim Ingold. His work represents a way of understanding the relationship between our knowledge creation and our perception of the environment that draws from posthumanist thought. Ingold contrasts modern knowledge passed down through cultural, institutional, and state apparatus with local knowledge, such as that linked to places and practices. Local knowledge is "continually generated and regenerated within the contexts of people's skilled, practical involvement with significant components of the environment" (Ingold, 2004, p. 307). With Ingold, then, we can understand learners' knowledge creation as something that develops through a reciprocal relationship with the more than human in places. Learners, then, can be thought of as "wayfarers" (Ingold, 2011, p. 163) who know about the world through their movement through it. This concept of wayfaring is a practical way to understand how we might develop knowledge through practical engagement with the world in ways that do not see us as separate from the Earth.

The design of the video-creation task was influenced by critical pedagogy in the way that it supports authentic problem solving (Kellner & Gooyong, 2010) and encourages learners to enact their agency (Freire, 2013). The use of digital technology was informed by Stommel (2018), who argues that critical digital pedagogy is less about the digital tools and more about creativity with them. Stommel sees digital pedagogy as being about hybridity and working with technology in ways that can extend the role of education in new directions away from notions of standardized tests and siloed curriculums. Informed by these ideas, I designed the task to be transdisciplinary and to encourage students to consider their developing relationships with the more than human through the creation of a video.

A key pedagogical component of the digital wayfaring activity was to challenge learners to think in posthumanist ways and to appreciate their existence as part of the more-than-human world. Ingold's (2011) concept of knowledge creation through wayfaring, involving a skilled and practical engagement with the environment, was integral to this purpose. The activity took place during a day walk in a wild mountainous environment with tertiary-level outdoor education students. During this trek, we encountered stony riverbanks, a dense forest, and steep grassy hillsides.

The digital wayfaring activity started with an introductory discussion on elements of posthumanist thought and the concept of wayfaring. The activity then consisted of two parts: an attunement to place phase and a digital video-making task. First students were asked to walk through the landscape and pay attention to the more-than-human features of place, such as wind, trees, rocks, et cetera. They were then asked to consider that these entities are not separate from us and that we are always tied to them through our relational co-existence. Students were asked to consider these questions:

- How do you understand place? What constitutes place?
- If we take a posthumanist view of place—that we as humans are always co-implicated with places and all living things—then how might we harness place in our pedagogy as educators?

After the walk, the students were encouraged to share how they responded to the human and more-than-human aspects of place that they noticed as a group. For example, they were asked which more-than-human aspects of place did you notice, and how might you harness them in education? Which relations with the more than human did you notice becoming attuned to? Next the students were given a one-hour challenge to create a video with their mobile smartphones.

The digital wayfaring activity briefing sheet

Working in pairs or groups of three, make a short video (minimum 20 seconds and maximum 1 minute) about how places might be pedagogical.

Bring together the concepts of wayfaring and the posthumanist aspects of place that you have noticed.

Your video needs to

(1) involve the views/opinions of everyone;
(2) include the more-than-human features of the place; and
(3) share some aspects of how this place might be harnessed for learning

---

Reflections

Two reflections on the digital wayfaring activity have relevance for how we might understand critical digital pedagogy for the Anthropocene in practice. Across the three groups of students, the task was completed very differently. Some groups created videos that tried to portray the sense of awe and wonder of these places, focusing on birdsong or the sound of walking on gravel riverbanks. Other groups chose to talk to the camera in an interview style, offering thoughts, questions, and ideas about how the places might be pedagogical.

My first reflection is based upon how the technology of videoing produced diversity in the students' responses to place and pedagogy. Like Winter and Cotton (2012), I found that the affordances of videoing seemed to hold potential for creative and varied knowledge construction. As a result, I see that the situated nature of the activity resonates with critical pedagogy in that the students' agency was able to be expressed. Unlike the banking model of education that Freire (2014) critiques, the teacher was not the primary source of knowledge. As a result, we can understand knowledge creation as linked to the relations that we find ourselves within and shaped through, not just the actions of an individual educator (Gottesman, 2016).

Deeper reflections on this activity informed by posthumanism and critical digital pedagogy force me to consider the pedagogical work under way. Taking a posthumanist position in which agency is distributed, we can appreciate how it was more than just the students' agency at play; the more-than-human agencies also played a role in the co-production of knowledge in this wayfaring task. My intention was that the process of the activity itself would encourage the learners to let themselves be attuned to their responses to the more-than-human aspects. Within this attunement and response making through the video creation, the learner works with more-than-human relations in the world. I see that this co-creation of knowledge with the more than human can be understood as critical digital pedagogy for the Anthropocene in action.

I am also left with a concern. The production of digital technologies and the precious metals that they require, as well as the reliance on electricity, do raise questions about the suitability of such tools in education orientated toward care for the environment. That noted, however, using smartphones in education in outdoor settings can help learners to make and sustain relations with the more than human that might not otherwise be possible. For example, videos from this activity could be incorporated into ongoing teaching and learning about the Anthropocene with people who cannot access these places. Additionally, the environmental costs of this technology are starting points for critical education on what relations with the more-than-human world smartphones bring to our awareness. These relations can be destructive through the mining of precious metals or productive in how they help us to see our interconnections with the Earth.

A final word on place. Place is not necessarily just wild land; it can be any location, wild or urban. As a result, I believe that the digital wayfaring activity can be useful in critical digital pedagogy for the Anthropocene in other settings less obviously rich with the more than human. This activity can be enacted in urban environments in which attunement to more-than-human relations or agencies would still have an impact on knowledge co-creation. For example, the digital wayfaring activity might attune learners to plants colonizing a vacant site or unseen microbes in built environments and the relationships between them and the socio-economic and political conditions of living. Posthumanist-inspired theorizations of place-human relationships in cities argue for an appreciation of the distributed agencies of the more than human shaping our lives there. For example, "cities are not simply inhabited but co-inhabited, in ways that are multiple, entangled and disrupt established ethologies and ecologies. Animals, plants, microbes, and the multiple relations within and between these temporary stabilizations, become urban, often in ways that are surprising" (Hinchcliffe & Whatmore, 2006, p. 137).

For learners without access to smartphones, the wayfaring task can still work without digital technology. Learners can capture their responses to the more than human with paper and pen. In summary, regardless of the technology or setting used, the pedagogical vision of seeking to be attuned to more-than-human relations that remind us of our intertwining with all life on the planet is still relevant.

Conclusion

In this chapter, I have shown how places are understood as important sites for knowledge creation and construction: knowledge is situated, embodied, and generated through engagement with the more-than-human world. I have also described how a video-making task, beyond the classroom or lecture hall, can foster creative, independent, and diverse thinking about critical topics such as human exceptionalism.

To conclude, in the Anthropocene, we are never separate from nature. As I have noted, the implications of this view are that places can never be just backdrops pedagogically. The world is full of abundant relations that can link us to the Earth and the co-implications of any human-environment relationship. If our task as educators of critical digital pedagogy in the Anthropocene is to employ and better understand technology to help create new relations between humans and the more than human, then video making is one way to do so. In the process, learners can produce new digital artifacts that portray important human-environment relations. As a result, these artifacts might challenge other audiences to think in critical ways that challenge human exceptionalism.

Key Takeaways

- Places are understood as important sites for knowledge creation; knowledge is situated, embodied, and generated through engagement with the world.
- Critical thinking from a posthumanist perspective can help us to challenge human exceptionalism and appreciate the mutual vulnerability and educational potential of human and more-than-human encounters.
- Digital technologies such as video making offer ways to understand and express critically the relations that we form with places and the more than human.

Note

1   The term "more than human" signifies a way of understanding "nature" that does not set it apart from us or reduce it to something less important than the human (see Abrams, 1996).

References

Abrams, D. (1996). *The spell of the sensuous: Perception and language in a more-than-human world*. Vintage Books.

Ardoin, N. M. (2006). Toward an interdisciplinary understanding of place: Lessons for environmental education. *Canadian Journal of Environmental Education, 11*(1), 112–126. https://cjee.lakeheadu.ca/article/view/508.

Barad, K. (2007). *Meeting the universe halfway: Quantum physics and the entanglement of matter and meaning*. Duke University Press.

Bonnett, M. (2004). *Retrieving nature: Education for a posthuman age*. Blackwell Publishing.

Bontly, S., Khalil, S., Mansour, T. & Parra, J. (2017). Starting the conversation: A working definition of critical digital pedagogy. In P. Resta & S. Smith (Eds.), *Proceedings of Society for Information Technology & Teacher Education International Conference* (pp. 383–388). Austin, TX, United States: Association for the Advancement of Computing in Education (AACE). https://www .learntechlib.org/primary/p/177311/.

Braidotti, R. (2019). *Posthuman knowledge*. Polity Press.

Carranza, N. (2018, November 15). Agency. *Critical Posthumanism*. https:// criticalposthumanism.net/agency/.

Castree, N. (2000). *Nature*. Routledge.

Chawla, J., & Cushing, F. (2007). Education for strategic environmental behaviour. *Environmental Education Research, 13*(4), 437–452. http://dx.doi .org/10.1080/13504620701581539.

Crutzen, P. J. (2002). Geology of mankind. *Nature, 415*(6867), 23. https://www .nature.com/articles/415023a.pdf.

Ellis, E. C. (2018). *Anthropocene: A very short introduction*. Oxford University Press.

Facer, K. (2011). *Learning futures: Education, technology and social change*. Routledge.

Freire, P. (2013). *Freire: Education for critical consciousness*. Bloomsbury Academic.

Freire, P. (2014). *Pedagogy of the oppressed*. Bloomsbury Academic.

Gottesman, I. (2016). *The critical turn in education: From Marxist critique to poststructuralist feminism to critical theories of race*. Routledge.

Hannon, V. (2017). *Thrive: Schools reinvented for the real challenges we face*. Innovation Unit Press.

Haraway, D. J. (2016). *Staying with the trouble: Making kin in the Chthulucene*. Duke University Press.

Hayes, K. (1999). *How we became posthuman: Virtual bodies in cybernetics, literature, and informatics*. University of Chicago Press.

Hinchcliffe, S., & Whatmore, S. (2006). Living cities: Towards a politics of conviviality. *Science as Culture, 15*(2), 123–138.

Ingold, T. (2004). Two reflections on ecological knowledge. In G. Sanga & G. Ortalli (Eds.), *Nature knowledge: Ethnoscience, cognition, and utility* (pp. 301–311). Berghahn Books.

Ingold, T. (2011). *Being alive: Essays on movement knowledge and description*. Routledge.

Ingold, T. (2013). *Making: Anthropology, archaeology, art and architecture*. Routledge.

Kellner, D., & Gooyong, K. (2010). YouTube, critical pedagogy, and media activism. *The Review of Education, Pedagogy, and Cultural Studies, 32*(1), 3–36. https://doi.org/10.1080/10714410903482658.

Mannion, G., & Lynch, J. (2016). The primacy of place in education in outdoor settings. In B. Humberstone, H. Prince, & K. A. Henderson (Eds.), *International handbook of outdoor studies* (pp. 85–94). Routledge. https://doi.org/10.4324/9781315768465.

Meichtry, Y., & Smith, J. (2007). The impact of a place-based professional development program on teachers' confidence, attitudes, and classroom practices. *The Journal of Environmental Education, 38*(2), 15–32.

Morris, S. M., & Stommel, J. (2018). *An urgency of teachers: The work of critical digital pedagogy*. Hybrid Pedagogy. https://urgencyofteachers.com/.

Noddings, N. (2012). *Philosophy of education*. Westview Press.

Oldenborgh, G. J. V., Krikken, F., Lewis, S., Leach, N. J., Lehner, F., Saunders, K. R., ... & Otto, F. (2020). Attribution of the Australian bushfire risk to anthropogenic climate change. *Natural Hazards and Earth System Sciences, 21*, 941–960. https://doi.org/10.5194/nhess-21-941-2021.

Orr, D. (2017). Foreword. In B. Jickling, S. Blenkinsop, N. Timmerman, & M. D. D. Sitka-Sage (Eds.), *Wild pedagogies: Touchstones for re-negotiating education and the environment in the Anthropocene* (pp. vii–xi). Palgrave Macmillan.

Rickinson, M., Dillon, J., Teamey, K., Morris, M., Choi, M. Y., Sanders, D., & Benefield, P. (2004). *A review of research on outdoor learning*. Field Studies Council.

Smith, G. A., & Sobel, D. (2010). *Place- and community-based education in schools.* Routledge.

Stommel, J. (2018). What is hybrid pedagogy? In S. Morris & J. Stommel (Eds.), *An urgency of teachers: The work of critical digital pedagogy* (pp. 174–179). Hybrid Pedagogy. https://urgencyofteachers.com/.

Snaza, N., Appelbaum, P., Bayne, S., Carlson, D., Morris, M., Rotas, N., . . . & Weaver, J. (2014). Toward a posthumanist education. *Journal of Curriculum Theorizing, 30*(2), 39–55.

Snaza, N., & Weaver, J. (2015). *Posthumanism and educational research.* Routledge.

Whatmore, S. (2006). Materialist returns: Practising cultural geography in and for a more-than-human world. *Cultural Geographies, 13*(4), 600–609. https://doi.org/10.1191/1474474006cgj3770a.

Winter, J., & Cotton, D. (2012). Making the hidden curriculum visible: Sustainability literacy in higher education. *Environmental Education Research, 18*(6), 783–796. https://doi.org/10.1080/13504622.2012.670207.

Critical Digital Pedagogy Across Learning Ecologies
Studios as Sites of Partnerships for Strategic Change

Amy Collier and Sarah Lohnes Watulak

Can critical pedagogy provide a framework for enacting strategic change at institutions of higher education? In this chapter, we explore how critical pedagogy informed an approach to strategic change at Middlebury College, led in part by the digital learning organization formed to support Middlebury's strategic framework. We highlight how critical pedagogy helped us to orient our group as a partnership organization, rather than a service organization, to engage students and faculty in critical digital fluency efforts across and throughout learning ecologies—within and outside a formal curriculum. Finally, we share an example of that partnership orientation in practice—the Information Environmentalism Studio's Newspapers on Wikipedia project—and lessons learned from that work.

In 2017, after a 2-year process that engaged faculty, staff, and students in "Envisioning Middlebury," Middlebury College published a new strategic framework that captured the institution's distinctions, strategic directions, and guiding principles for pursuing those directions. Our organization, the newly formed Office of Digital Learning and Inquiry (DLINQ), formulated the mission and goals based upon one of Middlebury's strategic directions, *digital fluency and critical engagement*. Although this strategic direction provided a heading for the new digital learning organization, it presented a challenge as well. How does a digital learning organization, which faculty expect to serve a supporting role on the margins of curricular change, lead curricular change that enacts a strategic direction for digital fluency? Is it possible for groups on the margins of the curriculum to shape how digital fluency is taught and learned at an institution?

As members of this new digital learning organization, our roles were characterized as in service of, not as leaders of, curricular change. Like many digital learning professionals across higher education, we were seen not as educators who could shape what and how students learned but as service providers and supporters of technologies that faculty use. We recognized that a shift in organizational culture was needed to move us from a service to a partnership orientation. The Educause Center for Analysis and Research notes that the work of an IT organization, when seen as a partner, "understands the core business of the institution, provides expertise to integrate across the campus and advance strategic directions, and spends less time focusing on wires and switches and more time building relationships and communicating about how IT can help" (Wetzel & Pomerantz, 2016, p. 18). In the same way that partnership-oriented IT organizations adapt to advance strategy and effect change, we saw *partnership with faculty and students* as the model to lead change effectively at Middlebury. We also recognized that the partnership model made possible new approaches to critical digital fluency. Mercer-Mapstone and Abbot (2020, p. 14) write that "partnership opens up new spaces—spaces in the margin, counter-spaces that challenge; collaborative equitable relationships in teaching and learning. Aspirational, values-based, highlighting the collocations academic selves / student selves, past selves / future selves, we've all been students. Partnership provokes us, destabilizing neat categorizations that abstract us."

Our group recognized the challenge of destabilizing the neat categories of service and support expected of us, and drawing from our educational backgrounds we embraced critical pedagogy as a framework in which to lead curricular change from the margins and into partnership. Critical pedagogy emphasizes attention to the creation and erasure of agency and works toward empowering students typically marginalized by traditional education (Giroux, 2011). We were drawn to how critical pedagogy characterizes institutional change as connected to power, politics, and authority (Tristan, 2013). Mercer-Mapstone and Abbot (2020, p. 13) write that "machinations of higher education are always governed by politics. The -isms are well documented and hard to ignore. Partnership is a political process, questioning taken-for-granted ways, working against the grain." If our goal was partnership to lead change, rather than service to existing approaches, then we needed to develop a framework and language that spoke directly to the issues of power that could impede change.

Critical pedagogy helped us to recognize the messiness and complexity inherent in learning across contexts and within institutions. It encouraged us to push back against the emphasis on formalized curriculum and to recognize the risks of working across pedagogical spaces. We began to understand that, to lead in the area of critical digital fluency, we would not be able to stay in our peripheral areas of work—working on digital projects with interested faculty. We would need to wade into the politics that are part of curricular change. Wading into curricular change is risky, especially for a group considered to be separate from academic affairs. In particular, the risk was that faculty would think that DLINQ was overstepping its role, a role primarily reserved for faculty. Because of the group's location inside the Office of the Provost, and with the support of the provost, we were encouraged to explore models that would allow us to lead co-curricular initiatives that we hoped would seep into and shape broader formal curricular change.

We used the language and framework of critical pedagogy to guide our work with faculty and students as partners in leading efforts toward digital fluency and engagement. As we approached this work, our language included engagement with and reflection on *conscientização*. This word is used by Freire in his seminal critical pedagogy work, *Pedagogy of the Oppressed*, and refers to the development of critical consciousness and engagement with the world (Freire, 2018; hooks, 1994). For marginalized people and communities, *conscientização* involves becoming aware and intolerant of oppressors and oppressive systems and beginning to take action toward their own liberation (Darder, 2020). Freire argued that critical consciousness can be developed only if people are subjects, rather than objects, in liberatory efforts. This notion informed our thinking on the importance of partnership, rather than service, in our work with faculty and students. We envisioned that partnerships would be more likely to create conditions through which faculty and students could engage in critical analysis of "the digital," thus developing *conscientização*. If we are seen as experts, not as service providers who push tools and technologies uncritically, then we are more likely to be able to meet faculty as equal partners.

Student *agency* is a key feature of critical pedagogy (Freire, 2013, 2018). Student agency is not only about giving students choice in decisions related to their education but also about giving them opportunities to transform their world and their knowledge to address social problems, a key feature of *conscientização*. Transformation is the goal of the educational endeavour. Giroux (2007, p. 7) notes that

> critical pedagogy becomes a project that stresses the need for
> teachers and students to actively transform knowledge rather than
> simply consume it. . . . I believe it is crucial for educators not only
> to connect classroom knowledge to the experiences, histories,
> and resources that students bring to the classroom but also to link
> such knowledge to the goal of furthering their capacities to be
> critical agents who are responsive to moral and political problems
> of their time and recognize the importance of organized collective
> struggles.

Student agency involves engaging in what Freire (2013, p. 45) calls "an attitude of creation and re-creation, a self-transformation producing a stance of intervention in one's context." Inspired by this notion, our group set out to centre our critical digital fluency initiatives on developing students' agency in digital spaces.

Gannon (2020, p. 6; emphasis added) writes that "*hope* is the combination of aspiration and agency." hooks (2003, p. xiv) writes that "educating is always a vocation rooted in hopefulness" and that hope is resistance to the cynicism that sustains dominant cultures. Freire (2016,

p. 24) acknowledges the essential nature of hope in critical education: "All liberating practice—which values the exercise of will, of decision, of resistance, of choice, the role of emotions, of feelings, of desires, of limits, the importance of historic awareness, of an ethical human presence in the world, and the understanding of history as possibility and never as determination—is substantively hopeful and, for this reason, produces hope." Engaging with hope is in part a recognition that education is political work that embraces aspirations for a more socially just future. We framed our work as intersecting "criticality and hope"—a recognition that it was both important to question how educational technology and digital learning contribute to marginalization and disenfranchisement and not to accept them as determined and inalterable. Instead, our group was oriented toward hope and the work that we could do in partnership with faculty and students to change the future.

With critical pedagogy informing our approach to our work, and with the goal of partnering with faculty and students to amplify critical digital fluency at Middlebury, we began to structure our work to lead critical digital fluency initiatives. Instructional designers played a key role in our efforts to shift to a partnership model, particularly with faculty, given the direct and relational nature of their work with faculty. In many ways, the shifts were subtle as we worked to destabilize the typical balance of power (faculty member as expert, instructional designer as "mere" technician) by naming the instructional designer's expertise in digital pedagogy and by positioning that designer as a co-expert and co-learner alongside faculty. Whenever possible, we intentionally used the language of partnership in our instructional design processes and documentations; for example, we revised our project charter document to lead with a paragraph about the expectations and assumptions that we brought to the collaboration with faculty. Relationship building was central to our ability both to demonstrate our expertise and to engage in critical conversations with faculty about their pedagogical choices, choices of tool, or considerations regarding student data privacy.

Next we describe the organizational infrastructure that we created (DLINQ Studios) to continue shifting our role toward partnership in formal and informal curricular change, highlighting the Information Environmentalism Studio's Newspapers on Wikipedia project.

Creating Studios through Partnership and Strategic Change

Our critical pedagogy framework laid a foundation for our office, DLINQ, to form partnerships with faculty and students at Middlebury toward critical digital fluency, working within and outside traditional power-informed structures of formal and informal curriculums. A key part of our new organizational partnership-focused infrastructure was DLINQ Studios, a nexus of inquiry and project work on issues related to critical digital fluency. From a pedagogical perspective, the studio approach draws from the metaphor of a learning ecology (Barron, 2004; Jackson, 2013), a framework for looking holistically at the range of opportunities for a student to engage with learning across what Jackson (2013) terms a student's "learning lifespan."

Barron (2004, p. 6) defines a learning ecology as "the accessed set of contexts, comprised of configurations of activities, material resources and relationships, found in co-located physical or virtual spaces that provide opportunities for learning." These contexts and opportunities for learning influence each other as activities, resources, and relationships flow between contexts. Jackson (2013) elaborates four learning ecology scenarios: *traditional/formal*; *enquiry, problem, and project based*; *self-directed but supported*; and *independent self-directed*. These scenarios vary by context and process and by whether they were created by the learner or by others for the learner.

The learning ecologies framework helped us to conceptualize DLINQ Studios—the Information Environmentalism Studio, the Inclusive Design Studio, and the Extended Reality Studio—as situated at the intersection of these scenarios. Modelled on our successful Animation Studio, began via external funding for digital scholarship and later integrated into DLINQ, each studio is led by a DLINQ staff member who can identify and launch projects related to its topic. In addition, students, faculty, staff, and external partners can propose a project to be hosted, coordinated, and/or supported by the studio. For example, students in the

Animation Studio pursue individual or small group animation projects, driven by their own interests. Many of these students use animation as a medium to explore core academic inquiry from a different perspective, and this has been the catalyst for faculty involvement in Animation Studio projects. The studio also produces animated short films, including the award-winning *Estrellita* (see dlinq.middcreate.net), which tells a piercing story about the constant threat of family separation and deportation for undocumented farmworkers in Vermont.

This dynamic of work by a studio and its members, rather than by individual faculty interests, gave DLINQ the opportunity to establish partnerships on projects and ensure that those projects aligned with Middlebury's strategic directions. Launched by Amy Collier, the Information Environmentalism Studio coordinates activities to detoxify digital environments. "Information environmentalism," a term created by Mike Caulfield (2017), signals the need to recognize digital pollution on the web (e.g., mis/disinformation) and take steps to address it. Given our institution's focus on environmentalism, the notion of information environmentalism resonated with faculty and students and created an alignment among multiple strategic institutional foci. Information environmentalism, we argued, fostered critical digital fluency by developing students' ability to engage critically and take action in a digital world dominated by misinformation, toxicity, and extractive data practices of digital platforms.

Led by Collier, the Information Environmentalism Studio launches initiatives that weave together "contexts and interactions that provide [students] with opportunities and resources for learning, development and achievement" (Jackson, 2013, p. 2) and explores what praxis looks like in polluted digital environments that shape students' social, political, and learning/educational contexts. These opportunities sometimes originate in a formal scenario, such as a course; at other times, the learning opportunity arises from an informal, self-directed, but supported workshop. Through studio projects, students are encouraged to critique digital platforms, to examine the role of digital technologies in social and educational spaces, and to experiment with ways of counteracting the deleterious effects of digital technologies on their worlds.

For example, the Information Environmentalism Studio recently joined Newspapers on Wikipedia (NOW), a project founded by Caulfield as part of the Digital Polarization Initiative of the American Association of State Colleges and Universities to combat misinformation and polarization. NOW invited participants to add or improve Wikipedia entries for local newspapers, thus helping professional and citizen fact checkers to find accurate information on Wikipedia about news sources. With more accurate information available via Wikipedia, consumers of news on the web can do lateral reading—the process of verifying a source by reading what others have said about that source on other sites like Wikipedia—and better understand the legitimacy of the news and information that they find. Key to this project is participants' work in the Wikipedia community, authoring and editing articles, to understand Wikipedia's role in the digital information ecology. The DLINQ Information Environmentalism Studio staff lead saw the NOW project as an opportunity for Middlebury students to better understand and combat misinformation online.

For Middlebury's NOW project to succeed, the studio needed to work at intersections between formal and informal learning opportunities. To reach into the formal curriculum, we needed to partner with faculty to bring NOW into their courses. Partnerships with faculty began with building upon existing relationships and then doing outreach to establish new relationships with faculty teaching topics related to NOW. As a result of that outreach, Collier was invited to offer NOW workshops in several undergraduate and graduate classes, including a course on the sociology of big data and a course on news journalism in the digital age. We also helped faculty to develop Wikipedia assignments in their classes that advanced the aims of NOW. For example, we worked with a professor who taught writing and editing courses to create a Wikipedia assignment through which students contributed to the project.

We also provided opportunities for participation as part of an informal curriculum for students. The NOW project offered several paid internships for students to work directly on it, and we invited DLINQ interns, hired to work on a variety of projects, to dedicate weekly work hours to the NOW project.

We hosted two simultaneous NOW edit-a-thons—one on each of our campuses—and invited students, faculty, and staff to join the effort. The edit-a-thons were 3-hour events hosted in active learning classrooms on our two campuses that were connected during the event via Zoom (video-conferencing software used for synchronous communication). Modelled on Art+Feminism Wikipedia edit-a-thons, our NOW edit-a-thons invited students, faculty, and staff to create and improve Wikipedia entries for newspapers in Vermont and California (the states where our two campuses are located). We identified local papers for which there were no existing Wikipedia entries and—coordinating through a shared document—assigned participants to research and write Wikipedia pages for them. To incentivize participation, we invited partnering professors to incorporate edit-a-thon participation as a course assignment; we invited several staff in Library and Information Technology Services to serve as mentors during the event; and we paid DLINQ interns to participate during their shifts. We also offered refreshments, swag, and door prizes. Across both campuses, 30–40 students, faculty, and staff participated in the edit-a-thons.

The results of these efforts were notable. The NOW initiative at Middlebury resulted in the creation of Wikipedia pages for more than 60 local newspapers in Vermont and California; additionally, several students contributed to other NOW initiatives (e.g., helping to research and write articles for a NOW edit-a-thon at the Open Education conference in Niagara Falls that year) (see Students, 2018). Students worked with tools and practices that further developed their critical digital fluency (e.g., editing Wikipedia articles). The experience that students gained through participation in NOW supported their agency by providing a set of tools and practices to go beyond the project and engage in additional information environmentalism work on Wikipedia, on topics of personal interest and concern. For example, several students who participated in the NOW project went on to join the Art+Feminism Wikipedia edit-a-thon to add more feminist content on topics that they were studying, such as equal pay in sports and black feminism in environmentalism.

Lessons Learned

From a learning ecology perspective, our attempt to create learning experiences that intentionally crossed boundaries provided a model for future learning experiences with students and faculty. The Information Environmentalism Studio's location outside the formal curriculum allowed us to create informal, student-centred learning experiences (edit-a-thons) that also intersected with more formal learning spaces (courses). At the same time, even though we worked with students across conceptual spaces in their learning ecologies, during the NOW project, intersections with the formal curriculum emerged from formal partnerships with faculty forged by Collier, as a staff member, in her role as the studio lead. Such relationship building is work—and it is often affective, political, and slow. As brown (2017, p. 42) notes, this work often needs to "move at the speed of trust." Digital learning organizations that want to work across learning ecologies need to provide support and time for staff to pursue trusting relationships with faculty that create opportunities for partnership. Building trust in the context of partnerships involves acknowledging the messiness of the shared space created by the partnership. We recommend that faculty, staff, and students who enter into partnerships have explicit conversations about the partnership itself (Bell et al., 2020)—about their beliefs and values related to partnering, the potential challenges that they might encounter when working in the messy space, and the goals that they hope to achieve together.

More student leadership is needed to increase opportunities for student agency and to weave information environmentalism more fully into the fabric of students' learning experiences. For example, a student might take a project begun in the studio and continue it as part of class work or a senior project. To enable this, institutions and faculty need to foster more supportive structures for students to create their own intersections with the formal curriculum. In our organization, we have increased our focus recently on our student employment program, adjusting DLINQ interns' work to provide more opportunities to explore digital topics across their learning ecologies.

We also suggest that the format of the studio, located at the intersection of formal and informal, provided a space for us to develop and facilitate learning experiences that positioned digital learning organization staff as educators in their own right. Here, outside the existing power structure that dictates who is worthy to teach and what is worthy of being taught, we found an agentive space in which to create meaningful learning experiences for students. Digital learning organizations that want to explore work across learning ecologies must be cheerleaders and advocates for their staff, working continually and intentionally to highlight their expertise as educators and professionals. We should acknowledge, however, that in taking on the role of educators at the intersection of formal and informal learning we became the target of confusion and anger among some faculty. A small number of faculty pushed back against our studios' work by raising budgetary concerns about DLINQ and advocating the elimination of our group entirely. Although they were unsuccessful in garnering support for the elimination of DLINQ, their pushback did shine a spotlight on DLINQ and required us to justify our work, budget, mission, and alignment with Middlebury's strategy.

Conclusion

At the beginning of this chapter, we posed the question *is it possible for groups on the margins of the curriculum to shape how digital fluency is taught and learned at an institution?* Using a critical pedagogy framework to re-envision our organization as partners, we were able to begin a transition in our relationship with faculty, laying the groundwork for the staff of a digital learning organization to be seen as experts and educators in their own right. At the same time, we created a space (studios) outside the formal curriculum in which we could design and facilitate learning opportunities around critical digital fluency that intersected the formal curriculum. The partnership approach was central to our ability to make those connections between informal and formal learning.

The transition to a partnership model is ongoing, and like any context in which power and privilege are at play it has not unfolded in a straight line. For example, the COVID-19 crisis has brought both opportunities and setbacks in terms of our attempts to implement the partnership model. Many more faculty are now aware of, and have interacted with, our organization; however, many of these new interactions occurred when we had to work much more in the support model than the partnership model, as the circumstances required us to help faculty get up to speed with digital tools in order to continue their teaching. Our challenge moving forward will be to reintroduce DLINQ and our partnership approach to these faculty, requiring us to continue to explain and defend our expertise and our field as valid and useful to the academic mission of the institution.

As we look to the future, we anticipate launching more projects through our DLINQ studios, with careful attention to the alignment of those projects with Middlebury's strategic plan and in close partnership with faculty. We also hope to partner with groups like ours at other institutions in order to develop collaborations that increase our digital learning organizations' opportunities to shape students' learning within and across formal and informal ecologies.

Key Takeaways

- As members of a digital learning organization responsible for strategic initiatives on digital fluency, we recognized the need to move from a service orientation to a partnership orientation to effect institutional and curricular change.
- Critical pedagogy helped us to orient our group as a partnership organization by providing a framework and shared language to shape how we work with faculty and students.
- Studios and studio-led initiatives such as the Newspapers on Wikipedia project became successful vehicles for interacting with students and faculty as partners across students' learning ecologies.

References

Barron, B. (2004). Learning ecologies for technological fluency: Gender and experience differences. *Journal of Educational Computing Research, 31*(1), 1–36.
Bell, A., Barahona, S., & Stanway, B. R. (2020). On the edge. In L. Mercer-Mapstone & S. Abbott (Eds.), *The power of partnership: Students, staff, and*

faculty revolutionizing higher education. The Center for Engaged Learning. https://doi.org/10.36284/celelon.0a2.

brown, a. m. (2017). *Emergent strategy: Shaping change, changing worlds.* AK Press.

Caulfield, M. (2017). Info-environmentalism: An introduction. *Educause Review,* November–December, 92–93.

Darder, A. (2020). Conscientização. In S. Macrine (Ed.), *Critical pedagogy in uncertain times: Education, politics and public life* (pp. 45–70). Palgrave Macmillan. https://doi.org/10.1007/978-3-030-39808-8_4.

Freire, P. (2013). *Education for critical consciousness.* Bloomsbury Academic.

Freire, P. (2016). *Pedagogy of indignation.* Routledge.

Freire, P. (2018). *Pedagogy of the oppressed: 50th anniversary edition* (4th ed.). Bloomsbury Publishing.

Gannon, K. (2020). *Radical hope: A teaching manifesto.* West Virginia University Press.

Giroux, H. A. (2007). Utopian thinking in dangerous times: Critical pedagogy and the project of educated hope. In M. Cote, R. J. J. Day, & G. dePeuter (Eds.), *Utopian pedagogy: Radical experiments against neoliberal globalization* (pp. 25–42). University of Toronto Press.

Giroux, H. A. (2011). *On critical pedagogy.* Continuum International Publishing Group.

hooks, b. (1994). *Teaching to transgress.* Routledge.

hooks, b. (2003). *Teaching community: A pedagogy of hope.* Routledge.

Jackson, N. (2013). The concept of learning ecologies. In N. Jackson & B. Cooper (Eds.), *Lifewide learning, education, and personal development* (pp. 1–21). LifeWide Education.

Mercer-Mapstone, L., & Abbot, S. (2020). *The power of partnership: Students, staff, and faculty revolutionizing higher education.* Elon University Center for Engaged Learning.

Students join Wikipedia effort to help verify local news sources. (2018, September 19). *Middlebury Newsroom.* http://www.middlebury.edu/newsroom/archive/2018-news/node/593355.

Tristan, J. M. B. (2013). Henry Giroux: The necessity of critical pedagogy in dark times [Interview]. *Truthout.org.* https://truthout.org/articles/a-critical-interview-with-henry-giroux/.

Wetzel, J., & Pomerantz, K. (2016). *Organizational models for IT service delivery and evolving IT organizations.* Educause Center for Applied Research.

Conclusion

Critical pedagogy can be alienating when it stays in the abstract, when there is no immediate or apparent connection to one's teaching or learning experience. Finding spaces and time in education for authenticity,[1] co-construction, critical dialogue and reflection may be desirable but remain distant for many who are facing the immediacy of their own circumstances, especially in the context of dealing with a global pandemic or the precarious environment that the majority of higher education staff face. Our hope is that the chapters in this collection have provided entry points of relevance and inspiration for critical pedagogical practice. In this conclusion, we look at the chapters holistically and highlight some broad implications for practice through the lens of the four themes that we identified in the introduction: *shared learning and trust, critical consciousness, change,* and *hope.* We hope that a concluding conversation on these themes will help you to engage further with the chapters and find different ways to pursue critical digital pedagogy in your own practice.

Shared Learning and Trust

The chapters in this collection show how important it is to build trust in order to begin engaging with critical pedagogical practices. Trust is the foundation for creating horizontal structures in education, by which we mean democratic, nourishing, and meaningful relationships in teaching and learning. In Chapter 1, Schofield, Johnstone, Kayes, and Thomas argue that "building online relationships . . . must be deliberately interwoven into the learning in an online space" for relational trust. Students need to know other students and their teachers and feel comfortable in their presence. Likewise, teachers need to know their students to be able to relate to them and facilitate educational processes successfully. As Robinson, Al-Freih, Kilgore, and Kilgore write in Chapter 2, "a climate of care in an online learning space—with its focus on community building, relationships, and the learners' expressed needs (versus assumed needs of the instructor, school, or educational system) . . .—can support the development of safe and inclusive spaces that enhance the potential for critical pedagogical practices and aims to emerge and grow." Indeed, how to go about critical pedagogy is not always something that can be known or defined before the actual teaching experience. There is a need for "creating environments that promote discovery, divergent thinking, skepticism, resourcefulness, and creativity," as Acevedo argues in Chapter 3, yet most learning experiences are preplanned, ready to be delivered to imaginary students with imaginary needs. Do we allow spaces for critical pedagogical practices to emerge and grow in our work, whether that is teaching, design, or administration? This is a critical question in teaching with technology in higher education. De Lacey's work in Chapter 4 shows how educators need to have both patience and will to create such spaces in their practices.

The issue of trust (or mistrust) can be extended to the systems, tools, and organizational structures of higher education. Both Acevedo and Collier and Lohnes Watulak (in Chapter 13) show how an academic culture of mistrust often hinders creativity and innovation. Collier and Lohnes Watulak argue that there needs to be structural changes in institutions for the higher education community (including professional services, academic departments, and students) to work together as partners, which calls for transparency and openness to learn from others, as Scott and Jarrad demonstrate in Chapter 11 in their collaborative teacher education work in Palestine. Skallerup Bessette further argues in Chapter 7 that how educational systems and tools work should be "visible and legible" to those who use or are exposed to them. When educators embrace the transparency of educational processes and products as a central value and aim in their work, opportunities for critical digital pedagogical practice emerge. These are opportunities for both educators and students to engage with "the *how* and the *why* of the education in which they are participating."

Critical Consciousness

Critical engagement with educational content, tools, and processes also creates spaces for *critical consciousness*,[2] which can be described as the process of gaining awareness of one's political and social location in society and corresponding responsibilities. Hooks (1994), for example, argued that students and educators should regard "one another as 'whole' human beings, striving not just for knowledge in books, but knowledge about how to live in the world" (p. 15). In online education, there seems to be a need for both educators and students to become aware of and resist the "misleading fantasies of education" (Bayne et al., 2020, p. 13) often perpetuated by neo-liberalism in and out of higher education. As Fovet writes in Chapter 6, "[in a neo-liberal system,] students are often perceived as customers, and courses marketed as commodities, with value for money, convenience, time efficiency, and ease in achieving outcomes seen as key desirable and commercially competitive features." Fovet further notes that "online education—indeed education in every modality—must be examined within a wider neo-liberal context within which it has been reshaped and portrayed": flexible, convenient, cost effective, time efficient, self-driven. Emerging technology solutions in higher education, such as performance tracking, surveillance, or automation (often created in response to arbitrary needs), should also be examined in the context of neo-liberalism. This reflective analysis should be done with students, Fovet argues. In Silver's work in Chapter 5, self- and group reflections and the co-construction of educational content and activities (through co-inquiry, peer-to-peer learning, and interdisciplinary collaborations) help both educators and students to develop their critical consciousness. Teachers see content "in a new light," and students "not only develop academic skills and knowledge but also learn how to become responsible citizens and active participants in their communities" through the digital projects on which they work.

Another example of raising critical consciousness is provided in Chapter 8. Gonye and Moyo engage in critical media analysis through the lens of African critical race theory to show how social media—with their intent, user interaction design, and content—might become tools of cultural hegemony. The authors critique representations of African Indigenous practices and knowledges on YouTube as an example of how one's cultural and historical traditions might be erased—or dismissed—through shared content and user interactions designed around that content (through views, likes, shares, comments, etc.). They describe this as "digital hegemony," a more nuanced understanding of the role of the digital in the Global South compared with the problematic concept of the digital divide.

In Chapter 9 Luna-Thomas and Romero-Hall discuss digital hegemony in a broader context, noting "technological frameworks such as artificial intelligence, digital surveillance, digital marketing, even automated soap dispensers that fail to recognize black skin," as "hegemonic instruments that automate and digitize human racism and discrimination." In other words, such digital tools and systems are expressions of power, whether committed intentionally or unwittingly. In higher education, critical digital pedagogy is decolonial pedagogy when it challenges "power imbalances" (Schofield et al., Chapter 1) brought by colonial education. Critical digital pedagogy, Luna-Thomas and Romero-Hall (Chapter 9) write, "lends itself to decolonization of knowledge by allowing a participatory approach to learning in which knowledge sharing is a social movement that deepens democracy." Again, there is a need to open up spaces in higher education for such approaches, "spaces that foster self-awareness, self-interrogation, and dialogue for individuals to learn from one another," Knowles-Davis and Moore write in Chapter 10. These spaces, they argue, should be "inclusive and diverse" in order to "facilitate conversations addressing inequality and cultural bias."

Change and Hope

We see in the collection how the specific teaching methods used in critical digital pedagogy are diverse and context dependent; critical pedagogy serves as a broad methodological orientation that guides educators in choosing the right tools, approaches, and learning activities for their work. For example, in Collier and Lohnes Watulak's work in Chapter 13, critical pedagogy provides "a framework and shared language" to build critical digital fluency across the institution. Schofield, Johnstone,

Kayes, and Thomas (Chapter 1) use the Pacific cultural model of Talanoa as a pedagogical framework to build horizontal relationships in education. Luna-Thomas and Romero-Hall (Chapter 9) show how educators might complement critical (digital) pedagogy with culturally relevant pedagogy and ethical approaches to learning design to address significant issues in higher education such as closing the BAME/BIPOC attainment gap. Attending to students' cultural and local contexts as content for education also appears as a central theme in de Lacey's work (Chapter 4). Scott and Jarrad (Chapter 11) use project-based learning to help students share their *lifeworlds*[3] and students' digital stories as context for critical digital pedagogy: "Methods of social constructivism (experiential, discovery, problem based) in which interaction, discourse, and mediated meaning drive the process . . . [comprise] an educational paradigm of the possible reified through human agency."

These are the kinds of methods that help educators to connect formal education with life beyond the institution. Silver's interdisciplinary work in Chapter 5 is a good example of this as students from computing and law work together to solve real-life issues in their communities via digital technology. Knowles-Davis and Moore also make a strong argument in Chapter 10 for using social media (i.e., #BlackLivesMatter on Twitter) to "bring marginalized voices and perspectives into the classroom and stimulate critical dialogue."

So far, we have considered the social and social change in digital higher education, which might begin with building relationships, democratic and respectful class activities, and culturally sensitive and ethical approaches to curriculum design, but as Bayne et al. (2020) noted "the social isn't the whole story" (p. 13). Critical digital pedagogy is needed to critique our relations with the environment, the "more than human." Lynch writes in Chapter 12 that "places can never be just a backdrop pedagogically. The world is full of abundant relations that can link us to the Earth and the co-implications of any human-environment relationship." In which ways can we avoid human exceptionalism with the choices that we make and the tools that we use? In which ways can we use digital technologies to build better and meaningful relationships with our environment? How can critical digital pedagogy help us to dignify the non-human world? These are critical questions in the age of the Anthropocene.

A central aim in critical pedagogy is to help educators and students become "critical, self-reflective, knowledgeable, and willing to make moral judgements and act in a socially responsible way" (Giroux, 2020, p. 1). Analyzing a situation through the lens of power and reflecting on it in order to create change might be two habits of mind needed for critical pedagogical practice, but change is a nuanced concept. It might not be visible or impactful right away; it can be slow, small, and intermittent. It might take a lifetime for someone to change ideas or beliefs or how things are done. In some instances, change simply begins as hope, for hope is not only an antecedent to change but also change itself, only perhaps in a less visible and tangible form. To reiterate what Scott and Jarrad wrote in Chapter 11, we believe that "critical pedagogy needs to have hope, idealism, and inspiration at its heart—the power of the possible." We trust that this collection provides some ideas about and some hope for the power of the possible. For an instructor, this might mean creating new opportunities for democratic participation. For a researcher, it might mean directing scholarly efforts toward working with community members to examine and address inequitable educational practices. For an administrator, it might mean viewing institutional policies through a new or different lens, one that includes issues of equity or power. Regardless of your role, we hope that this book offers a glimmer of hope, a glimmer that things can be better, and that you, and us, and our colleagues can and will make something better of the circumstances in which we find ourselves.

Notes

1 Authenticity defined in terms of how knowledge "relates to and develops from the lived experience" of both students and educators (Seal & Smith, 2021, p. 4).
2 Freire (2013, p. 15) writes that "*conscientização* [critical consciousness] represents the *development* of the awakening of critical awareness."
3 Explained by Scott and Jarrad (Chapter 11) as follows: "[A lifeworld] is defined as how our separate realities are shared and communicated in common. In other words, though our social experiences might seem to be private, they are

unified through practices and attitudes that inform our perceptions of a shared reality."

References

Bayne, S., Evans, P., Ewins, R., Knox, J., Lamb, J., Macleod, H., O'Shea, C., Ross, J., Sheail, P., & Sinclair, C. (2020). *The manifesto for teaching online.* MIT Press.

Freire, P. (2013). *Education for critical consciousness.* Bloomsbury Publishing.

Giroux, H. (2020). *On critical pedagogy* (2nd ed.). Bloomsbury Academic.

hooks, b. (1994). *Teaching to transgress: Education as the practice of freedom.* Routledge.

Seal, M., & Smith, A. (2021). *Enabling critical pedagogy in higher education.* Critical Publishing Ltd.

Contributors

Matthew Acevedo is the Executive Director of Learning Innovation and Faculty Engagement and adjunct lecturer in the Department of Teaching and Learning at the University of Miami. He also teaches courses at Florida International University in the Department of Educational Policy Studies and the Honors College. His research interests include educational development, critical pedagogy, and the impacts of neo-liberalism on teaching and learning in higher education. He is on Twitter at @mattacevedo.

Maha Al-Freih holds a PhD in Learning Technologies Design Research from George Mason University and is currently an Assistant Professor of Instructional Design and Technology at the College of Education at Princess Nourah Bint Abdulrahman University (PNU) in Riyadh. She has previously served as the Vice-Dean of Learning and Teaching at the College of Business Administration at PNU and now serves as a senior consultant at the National eLearning Center (NeLC). Her primary research interests include ethics of care in online learning spaces, learners' engagement and persistence in massive open online courses (MOOCs), self-regulated learning (SRL), and design-based research (DBR). She is on Twitter @Maha9313.

Amy Collier is the Associate Provost for Digital Learning at Middlebury College, overseeing the Office of Digital Learning and Inquiry. In this role, she provides strategic vision and leadership for Middlebury to create and sustain a global learning community through the effective use of digital pedagogies and technologies. Her research has been focused on the experiences of teachers and learners in MOOCs, issues of student privacy and surveillance in higher education and K–12, and complexity as a framework for resisting the instrumental role of educational technology in higher education. She blogs occasionally at http://redpincushion.me/.

Alex de Lacey is a Lecturer in Popular Music at Goldsmiths, University of London. His research examines Afrodiasporic music practice in the United Kingdom, with a particular focus on grime, and his teaching is concerned with decolonizing curriculums and foregrounding non-institutional ways of knowing. He is also a journalist and writes for *Complex*, *Red Bull*, and *Songlines*. He is the DJ for grime crew Over the Edge, with a monthly show on Mode FM.

Frederic Fovet is an Assistant Professor in the Faculty of Education and Social Work at Thompson Rivers University in British Columbia. He has in the past held, in turn, faculty positions in the Faculty of Education at University of Prince Edward Island and in the School of Education and Technology at Royal Roads University. His research and practice focus on inclusion, social justice, and critical pedagogy in schools. He has a specific interest in social, emotional, and behaviour difficulties (SEBD). He worked for several years in the field of accessibility, and his scholarship is informed by disability studies.

Jairos Gonye, PhD, MA, BA (Hon), English, (Grad. CE), is an Associate Professor in the Department of Curriculum Studies, Great Zimbabwe University, Zimbabwe, where he teaches English and Business Communication. He is also a Research Fellow in the Department of English of the University of the Free State (UFS), South Africa. His research interests include Afrocentric studies of literature, literary representations of dance, popular culture, and pedagogy. Some of his articles have been published locally and internationally.

Samah Jarrad is a full-time instructor of English as a Second Language at Palestine Technical University—Kadoorie in Tulkarem, Palestine, where she lives and works. She is a PhD candidate in the Department of

Postcolonial Literary Studies at the Universiti Kebangsaan Malaysia and holds an MA in Applied Linguistics and Translation. Her research has been dedicated to understanding the acquisition of English as a Second Language and postcolonial studies from a feminist perspective.

Anna Johnstone is a Postgraduate Director at The Mind Lab, New Zealand, contributing to the Master of Contemporary Education qualification. She is also a Senior Tutor at the University of Canterbury, New Zealand, delivering primary initial teacher education programs. She has had roles in tertiary and primary education as a facilitator, adviser, researcher, and teacher. Her areas of research interest are learner interactions in contemporary environments and the critical moments that influence teacher learning.

Dorcas Kayes is a Postgraduate Director at The Mind Lab, headquartered in Auckland. She currently works as part of the team that delivers the Master of Contemporary Education to in-service educators. Her research has focused on school and community partnerships and pastoral and academic support of postgraduate students.

Thomas Kilgore is a PhD student in Learning Technologies at the University of North Texas and earned a master's degree in Educational Leadership from the University of Texas at Arlington. He has served as a K–12 classroom teacher, instructional coach, and digital learning consultant, and he is a certified school principal in Texas. His research interests include active learning strategies, leveraging educational technologies, and effective use of feedback in improving learning outcomes. He is on Twitter @Tom_Kilgore.

Whitney Kilgore is the co-founder and chief academic officer at iDesign, an instructional design–focused service provider to higher education institutions. She earned a PhD in Learning Technologies at the University of North Texas and has led the development of online and blended learning programs at hundreds of universities around the globe. Her research interests include humanizing online learning, online care theory, and informal learning in networked communities. She is on Twitter @whitneykilgore.

Mia L. Knowles-Davis is a PhD student in Instructional Design and Technology at Old Dominion University and holds a master's degree in Computer Science and Information Technology. Her research focuses on the ethics of educational technology. She can be followed on Twitter at http://www.twitter.com/mialkdavis.

Suzan Köseoğlu is a Lecturer in Higher Education Teaching and Learning at the University of Greenwich (UK). Suzan has been involved in faculty development for more than 10 years in different institutions including the University of Minnesota, Goldsmiths University of London, and University of Greenwich. At Greenwich, Suzan is the university lead for pedagogic research and teaches courses on higher education pedagogy for academic staff and postgraduate students. Suzan is committed to democratic and transparent processes in education. Her research explores the intersection of open online learning and ethical and inclusive approaches to education. She occasionally blogs at https://differentreadings.com/.

Sarah Lohnes Watulak is the Director of Digital Pedagogy and Media in the Office of Digital Learning and Inquiry at Middlebury College, where she works to create digital learning opportunities and environments that support learner agency, equity, and critical engagement with the digital. Her published research focuses on undergraduate technology practices, critical digital literacies, and connected learning. See her website, http://sarahlw.middcreate.net/.

Maria V. Luna-Thomas is an instructional designer who advances digital learning solutions for global entities. She is originally from the United States, and it was there that she cultivated her approach to inclusive pedagogical praxis and grounded her research in Latin American Studies. She then established herself in the United Kingdom, where she joined Goldsmiths, University of London, as an Associate Lecturer in Anthropology. Her journalism repertoire centres on culture, intersectional feminism, and race.

Jonathan Lynch started his career as an outdoor educator across primary, secondary, and tertiary education in the United Kingdom. Moving to Aotearoa New Zealand, he then worked as a Postgraduate Director with The Mind Lab, a future-focused educational company committed to the growth and implementation of contemporary practice in the teaching profession across New Zealand. He has recently taken up a role as Principal Lecturer at Otago Polytechnic (Te Pūkenga). In his research, which is informed by posthumanist and new materialist thinking, he is enthusiastic about education beyond the classroom and improving human-environment relations.

Robert L. Moore is an Assistant Professor of Educational Technology in the School of Teaching and Learning at the University of Florida. He focuses his research on understanding and improving student engagement and learning in distance education settings. He is particularly interested in leveraging learning analytics to study and understand student learning in MOOCs. He can be followed on Twitter at @robmoore3.

Nathan Moyo is a Senior Lecturer in the Department of Curriculum Studies at Great Zimbabwe University, Zimbabwe. He holds a PhD in Curriculum Studies from the University of Johannesburg and teaches Curriculum Theory and History Education. His research interests include curriculum theory, history education, postcolonial theory, and social justice education. He has co-published in these fields in international journals.

Heather Robinson is an online learning consultant and independent researcher residing in Jackson Hole, Wyoming. She earned a PhD in Learning Technologies and teaches courses at the University of North Texas in the Department of Learning Technologies and for Casper College in the College of Business and Industry. Her research interests include care ethics and online care theory, theory and practice of learning communities, and online collaborative learning. She is on Twitter @hrobinson.

Enilda Romero-Hall is a native of Panama. She is an Associate Professor in the Department of Education at the University of Tampa. She is also the Graduate Coordinator of the Instructional Design and Technology program. Most of her research focuses on populations within higher education and industry settings. She is particularly interested in the design and development of interactive multimedia, faculty members' and learners' digital literacy and preparedness, and networked learning in online social communities. See her website, https://www.enildaromero.net.

Chris Rowell is a Senior Digital Learning Coordinator at the University of the Arts, London. Currently, he is a facilitator for the Association for Learning Technologists (ALT) Anti-racism Learning Technology Group and Senior Fellow of the Higher Education Academy (SFHEA). Previously he was a member of the Staff and Educational Development Association's (SEDA) National Executive, ALT's blog editor, and a member of the editorial board for ALT's journal *Research in Learning Technology*. His research engages many aspects of digital education, specifically the use and evaluation of social media by staff and students, sharing good practice and Critical Digital Pedagogy. He writes at https://totallyrewired .wordpress.com/2.

Lynley Schofield was the Program Lead of the Master of Contemporary Education at The Mind Lab. This degree supports the professional development of in-service educators in contemporary educational practice. Her research focused on student interpersonal relationships and pastoral and academic support of postgraduate students.

Howard Scott is part of the Teacher Education team for Post-Compulsory Education at the University of Wolverhampton and teaches research methods through doctorate and master's programs. His research interests involve adult and community learning, innovative pedagogies utilizing digital literacies, and mobile learning, particularly in less formal educational contexts.

Kim Silver is a Senior Lecturer in Law at London South Bank University. Her research interests include the impact of technology on law, legal practice, and legal education, particularly in relation to access to justice.

Lee Skallerup Bessette is a Learning Design Specialist at the Center for New Designs in Learning and Scholarship (CNDLS) and an Affiliate Faculty in the Learning, Design, and Technology master's program. She is interested in the intersections of critical digital pedagogy, affect, design, and technology. Prior to finding alt-ac work in faculty development and instructional design, she taught English primarily at public, regional, state comprehensive institutions that served at-risk populations and where digital redlining was rampant. See samples of her work on her website, www.readywriting.org.

Herbert Thomas is originally from South Africa but now lives in New Zealand, where he is a Postgraduate Director at The Mind Lab, headquartered in Auckland. He currently works as part of the team that delivers the Master of Contemporary Education to in-service educators. His research has focused on the integration of technology into the curriculum from the perspectives of educators, scholars, managers, and leaders.

George Veletsianos is Professor at Royal Roads University, where he holds the Canada Research Chair in Innovative Learning and Technology, and the Commonwealth of Learning Chair in Flexible Learning. He has been designing, developing, and evaluating digital learning environments for nearly 20 years. His research agenda is focused on addressing complex problems related to education and society, such as lack of access to education, and harassment that academics face when they share their scholarship online. In these contexts, he studies learners' and faculty experiences with online learning, flexible education, networked scholarship, and emerging technologies and pedagogical practices. His research has embraced collaboration, interdisciplinarity, and methodological pluralism. He writes at http://www.veletsianos.com.